THE HIGHWAY
OF DESPAIR

New Directions in Critical Theory

NEW DIRECTIONS IN CRITICAL THEORY
Amy Allen, General Editor

New Directions in Critical Theory presents outstanding classic and contemporary texts in the tradition of critical social theory, broadly construed. The series aims to renew and advance the program of critical social theory, with a particular focus on theorizing contemporary struggles around gender, race, sexuality, class, and globalization and their complex interconnections.

THE
HIGHWAY
OF
DESPAIR

CRITICAL THEORY
AFTER HEGEL

Robyn Marasco

Columbia University Press
New York

Columbia University Press
Publishers Since 1893
New York   Chichester, West Sussex
cup.columbia.edu
Copyright © 2015 Columbia University Press
All rights reserved

Library of Congress Cataloging-in-Publication Data

Marasco, Robyn.
The highway of despair : critical theory after Hegel / Robyn Marasco.
pages cm. — (New directions in critical theory)
Includes bibliographical references and index.
ISBN 978-0-231-16866-3 (cloth : alk. paper) —
ISBN 978-0-231-53889-3 (e-book)
1. Criticism (Philosophy)   2. Critical theory.
3. Hegel, Georg Wilhelm Friedrich, 1770–1831.
4. Dialectic.   5. Despair.   I. Title.

B809.3.M364   2015
190—dc23   2014014339

Columbia University Press books are printed on permanent
and durable acid-free paper.
This book is printed on paper with recycled content.
Printed in the United States of America

c 10 9 8 7 6 5 4 3 2 1

Jacket design by Jennifer Heuer

References to websites (URLs) were accurate at the time of writing. Neither the
author nor Columbia University Press is responsible for URLs that may have
expired or changed since the manuscript was prepared.

In loving memory of my father,
Robert F. Marasco

CONTENTS

ACKNOWLEDGMENTS

I have had the privilege to study and teach at great institutions and each has supported my scholarly work beyond measure. I was taught how to do political theory by Wendy Brown and her mentorship allowed me to believe that I might be suited to it. Wendy supervised my work, wrote letters on my behalf, gave essential commentary on several drafts of this work, and responded to every single email. Beyond that, she offered steady encouragement and guidance, patience, and humanity. I am grateful to many other Berkeley faculty—Judith Butler, Martin Jay, Victoria Kahn, and Paul Thomas—for their feedback on my research. Many thanks, also, to the director and fellows at the Townsend Center for the Humanities and to Jean Day, the associate editor at *Representations*.

The intellectual and personal relationships that I formed in my Berkeley years remain my most important and enduring. Sharon Stanley read this manuscript in its entirety and offered astute suggestions for revisions. Jimmy Klausen has been a steady and cherished interlocutor. Beyond that, both Sharon and Jimmy have offered that rare experience of friendship that confirms I am never alone. My thinking has been shaped by many conversations with Yves Winter, George Ciccariello-Maher, Abbey Ciccariello-Maher, Ivan Asher, Simon Stow, Dean Mathiowetz, Bibi Obler, James Martel, Libby Anker, Annika Thiem, Jack Jackson, Julie Cooper, Bob Taylor, Michael

Feola, Ed Fogarty, and Sebastián Etchemendy. I am grateful that Nick Xenos encouraged me to go to Berkeley so many years ago and that he remains a true comrade. Antonio Vazquez-Arroyo deserves special recognition for being my favorite—and most frequent—copanelist.

I spent my first years as an assistant professor at Williams College, where I learned how to teach and why the classroom is an extraordinary place. I profited immensely from discussions with other faculty, especially Michael MacDonald, Darel Paul, Mark Reinhardt, Theo Davis, Keith McPartland, Monique Deveaux, Neil Roberts, Jana Sawicki, and Christian Thorne, as well as several students—José Martínez, Lauren Guilmette, Blake Emerson, Samantha Demby, and Hari Ramesh, among others.

I have been fortunate to expand my intellectual community at conferences and in other academic settings. I want to thank Banu Bargu, Jodi Dean, Patchen Markell, Davide Panagia, John McCormick, Shirin Deylami, Lori Marso, Melissa Matthes, Kennan Ferguson, Tom Dumm, Laurie Naranch, Mort Schoolman, Michaele Ferguson, Jill Locke, Steven Johnston, Paul Apostolidis, Sharon Krause, Andrew Dilts, Corey Robin, Cristina Beltrán, George Shulman, Roger Berkowitz, Jennifer Culbert, Kam Shapiro, Andrew Douglas, Claudia Leeb, Nicholas Tampio, and Michelle Smith for their critical responses to and engagement with my work. And I am especially grateful for an afternoon coffee with Joshua Dienstag and Lisa Ellis at an APSA meeting for the spontaneous and informal "workshop" that resulted in a title for this book. Many thanks to John Lysaker, John Russon, and the other participants in the History of Philosophy Seminar at Emory University, who gave me the opportunity to put Hegel and Adorno into dialogue with the ancients. Chapters from this manuscript were presented to the departments of political science at Yale University and Johns Hopkins University, where I received excellent feedback from faculty and graduate students.

My department at Hunter College has been a vital source of support for my research and teaching. Andy Polsky was department chair when I was hired and a model for how to combine research excellence, quality instruction, and effective administration. Charles Tien has been chair for several years since and a crucial source of encouragement and guidance. My political theory colleagues—John Wallach,

Ros Pechetsky, and Lennie Feldman—are brilliant minds, great mentors, and splendid human beings. And my colleagues in the other subfields have offered generosity and insight, confirming that education is a collective enterprise. I must also thank Jennifer Gaboury, associate director of the Women and Gender Studies Program at Hunter, for her commitment to the college, her tireless engagement with my work, and her invaluable friendship.

Amy Allen is a true inspiration and I am honored to be included in her series. Wendy Lochner has been a terrific editor, offering endless patience and expert guidance. Many thanks, also, to Christine Dunbar, who assisted in the daily tasks of transforming my manuscript into a book. Finally, I am grateful for my anonymous reviewers, who engaged this work with generosity and acuity. They have helped me to produce a book immeasurably better than it would have been otherwise, while granting me the freedom to err in my own fashion.

I am grateful for my parents, Robert and Paula Marasco, who encouraged my scholarly pursuits, and my brother, Stephen, for his political provocations and big brotherly love. Favel Bruno is a beloved friend and confidante. As chance would have it, Luis Alejandro Cruz Hernandez came into my world and permitted me to bring this project to completion. Our life together has become my best argument against all despair. Our daughter, Bianca Bella Cruz Marasco, arrived just as I finished the final draft. She keeps my feet firmly planted in the present, with my heart stretching toward an unknown future. My love for her knows no limits. And I thank God that she was able to meet her grandfather, my father, before his death. This book is for him.

THE HIGHWAY
OF DESPAIR

Introduction

1

This is a book about Hegel and some twentieth-century thinkers who read Hegel for the purposes of radical political thought and social criticism. Though the term "Left Hegelian" is typically reserved for a relatively small group of nineteenth-century Prussian theorists, it might also designate the varied and enduring attempts to bring Hegel's philosophy to bear on radical politics. In this broader sense, then, what follows are close encounters with some twentieth-century Left Hegelians: Theodor W. Adorno, Georges Bataille, and Frantz Fanon, in particular. Each is reckoning with the collapse of revolutionary projects and clarifying the tasks of critique in the context of genocidal racism, capitalist exploitation, totalitarian violence, colonial domination, and the historico-political horizon set by world war. Their readings of Hegel, while of interest to me, are less important than their respective experiments in what the young Marx—still very much under the spell of Hegel—called the "ruthless critique of everything existing." This study is motivated by a question concerning the forms and tonalities such critique assumes when there is no end to or exit from the conditions of existence, and no *rational* hope that a brighter future will repay patient struggle in the present. The thinkers featured in these pages facilitate a recasting of critical theory in which *passion* plays a central part and the pathos of despair frustrates whatever critique has unearthed on the frontiers of human reason.

The "highway of despair" is Hegel's image. It comes from the introduction to the *Phenomenology of Spirit* and indicates the course charted by "natural consciousness"—as I see it, a fitting portrait of the agonies and the ecstasies of ruthless critique in the spirit of Hegel. The first chapters of this book follow this figuration of despair in Hegel's *Phenomenology* and in Kierkegaard's *The Sickness Unto Death*. In these chapters, I depict a distinct pathos in dialectical thinking and draw out some of its vitality and unexpected energy. I read Hegel and Kierkegaard in terms of a dialectic that is driven by the disquietude of despair, even as I concede that both sought to quiet the passions by philosophical science and religion, respectively. Though Kierkegaard's analytic of despair is usually understood as part of his larger critique of Hegel, I see it instead as a significant variation on a minor Hegelian theme. In this respect, and in many others, I follow Gillian Rose in staking out a terrain "not between but *within* the conceptuality of Hegel *and* Kierkegaard."[1] But, unlike Rose, I do not intend to resurrect Hegelian Spirit or Kierkegaardian Faith against the despair that they help us to understand. Instead, both Hegel and Kierkegaard are made to speak to the contours of a condition that survives the ruins of the system.

Theodor W. Adorno, Georges Bataille, and Frantz Fanon are my primary interlocutors in the book's second part, where I consider the different forms that critical theory takes along the highway of despair. They offer models for what philosophical critique looks like when it gives up the urge for rescue from despair and permits itself to the negative, when disquietude becomes a sign of strength. With each of them comes a whole set of collaborations and conversations, reaching across continents. By bringing them together, I hope to expand the range of thinkers and ideas typically included under the banner of critical theory, so that this radical intellectual tradition may continue to surprise us with its richness and value for political thinking. I focus on these thinkers—and not several other obvious candidates—for their deep investments in the dialectic, abiding interest in Hegel's philosophy, and unorthodox political radicalism. Though only one of them explicitly identifies his writings as such,

I present all three in terms of a *negative dialectics*: aporetic, aleatory, and untidy. I am interested in the points of contact between these very different writers—and here I mean political and theoretical connections, though they have certain biographical links as well—and how each of them reads, resists, and refigures a strand of thought in Hegel's *Phenomenology of Spirit*. Beyond that, this study aims at a revaluation of a restless and energetic passion that is too typically thought without political value.

Perhaps despair can only mean intellectual narcissism, the vanities of esotericism, and the arrogant self-satisfaction that comes with what Marx mockingly labeled "critical criticism." Or the politics of despair can only be reaction or resignation from the world, or a perilous withdrawal into abstract aesthetics, as Lukács infamously alleges in the 1962 preface of *The Theory of the Novel*, charging that "a considerable part of the leading German intelligentsia, including Adorno, have taken up residence in the 'Grand Hotel Abyss.'"[2] Some might say, as Lenin did, that despair results from infantile anarchism—"the psychology of the unsettled intellectual or the vagabond and not of the proletarian."[3] Further complicating the class dimension of despair, Slavoj Žižek—leaning on the authority of Hegel this time, not Lenin—links despair to the "rabble" and to the "impotent rage" and "absolute negativity" of frustrated youth reared on the commodity form.[4] Despair of the sort that Žižek says fueled the Tottenham Riots of 2011 portents the pathos of destruction, now manifest as a collective temper tantrum.

This book ventures a different position, one that considers despair not as pathology or paralysis, but in connection with the passions of critique and the energies of everyday life. Hegel's *Phenomenology of Spirit*, as I see it, is a founding document of this despair and a poetics of its persistence. But against the dominant currents in Hegel's speculative system, despair does not find its answer in philosophy or its refuge in World Spirit. Critical theory after Hegel constitutes experiments in thinking and doing in despair, as things come undone and there is no way out suggested by reason or faith. For Adorno, it means the cultivation of a critical comportment and the pursuit of a radical aesthetic. For Bataille, despair is aligned with freedom and the love of chance as a political principle. Fanon sees despair as a sign of deep social disrepair and also as a viable source of revolutionary vitality. Against the imperative that critical theory offer sound reason for hope, these thinkers work at the limits of reason and linger on its border with madness. They abandon any illusions that thinking may be rescued from despair and ask that we treat this necessity as an opportunity for thinking and praxis.

2

Despair is not another word for depression or any related mood disorders treated by psychiatry and medicine. Its humoral cousin, melancholia, is more prominent in the history of medical discourses. Despair, by contrast, is a term connected to religious experience and the most extensive considerations come from theologians, religious philosophers, and poets. As Kierkegaard well understood, despair is not necessarily felt as generalized sadness or grief, nor does it imply any specific emotional experience. For Kierkegaard, the most severe sickness unto death does not manifest in symptoms typically recognized as despair. It often appears, instead, as confidence, audacity, pride, or playful enthusiasm—and despair is thus especially difficult to detect in oneself or others. So, what is typically meant by affect, which involves a certain order of feeling, seems not quite appropriate to capture this condition. Though this study has been enriched by what falls under the "affective turn" in recent scholarship, I do not see despair as an affect precisely; it is closer to a comportment or a posture, but one that invites a range of emotions and is not necessarily tied to any particular private or public feeling.[5]

Certain traditions in modern philosophy treat despair as an epistemological crisis: critical suspicion run amok or universal doubts that result in a complete and incoherent skepticism. Others see it as a dangerous symptom of nihilistic abandon. These arguments seem to me either inadequate or confused. The difference between doubt and despair is not primarily a matter of quantity. This, I will suggest, is one of Hegel's deepest insights. And complete nihilism would spell the end of despair. What is left to despair if only nothingness remains? Does the nihilist despair of anything? Despair might be, in some instances, the surest defense against nihilism.

Diana Coole's *Negativity and Politics*, in which Hegel plays a pivotal part as well, offers a helpful meditation on the difficulty with concepts and their definitions, particularly when it comes to a term like "negativity." The difficulty is not only because negativity means different and incommensurable things to different thinkers, but also because the term itself resists the stable order of classification that definitions offer. As Coole puts it, "to name it would be to destroy it; to render it positive, ideal, and thus to fail at the very moment of success."[6] Yet her study succeeds in retrieving negativity from philosophical obscurantism without settling into the reifying positivity that the term is meant to undo. Negativity remains, for Coole (as it was for Hegel), a *dialectical* concept, never absolute but always born of determinate relations between subjects and objects, never abstract but always concretized in a specific historical order of things.

Despair, linked to negativity in Hegel and especially to the work of determinate negation, poses a somewhat different, though related, conceptual dilemma. Coole is probably right that the negative connotes something profound yet elusive. The problem with despair seems to be that it is at once pervasive and uninteresting, a condition that requires no explanation or definition, not because it is inexplicable or indefinable, but because its meaning and political consequences are supposedly transparent and obvious. To despair is lose hope, to abandon attachments, to give up on projects, to resign.

Yes and no. As I hope to show, despair is a *dialectical passion*. By this I mean that despair is at odds with itself. It militates against itself. It conserves and preserves the possibility of what it also denies. If, in etymological terms, despair indicates the absence of hope, this is no simple absence. Despair can never fully let go of its familiar and estranged other.

Speaking of despair as a "passion" is not unproblematic, and yet it is preferable to "affect," "emotion," "sentiment," or "feeling," for reasons that I hope to make clear in these preliminary pages. Briefly, passion suggests energy, movement, and the extrarational intensities of desire, but also excess, suffering, and sacrifice. It conjures the force of attachment to a particular other or object, as well as the generalized condition of possibility for any and all attachment. But it also anticipates the ordeal of attachments once they are inserted into time and history—how dreams get deferred, projects derailed, and causes lost. And how these deferrals, derailments, and losses always carry with them a new constellation of possibilities and foreclosures. Passion signals some of the torment, too, that has come to be associated with the operations of critique and theorizing more generally. Philosophical writing that falls under the influence of Hegel often expresses this torment on a formal level, as evidenced in the pages that follow. (The pleasurable pain associated with one's first forays into Hegelianese could even seem like a certain induction into the pathos of the system.) But crucially, despair is a historical condition and a social situation; no reasonable or romantic subjectivism, of the sort suggested by the language of passion, brings *this* dimension of despair into view.

The sociohistorical condition of despair is aporetic, in the etymological sense of the term: *a-poros* meaning the absence of a *poros*, "path," "direction," "way." Despair names an aporetic condition in which neither reason nor faith can furnish clear direction, yet the sense of journey and the experience of movement remain. Admittedly, this is not a historical study and the following pages add little to the extensive documentation of historical context for the despair that permeates twentieth-century European critical theory. And this history is profoundly important for detailing the *why* of despair. I am chiefly interested in the *how*—or, the philosophical and poetic forms that ruthless critique assumes under aporetic conditions. Adorno, Bataille, and Fanon write under these terms and draw out themes in Hegel for some guidance. For them, despair does not mean the end of reason or faith; indeed, it very often means intensified attachment to both. Despair does not mean the end of much of anything in the way of thinking or doing; as I argue in the following chapters, everyday life goes on and everything still matters. Despair is not another name for unhappiness, undone by the dialectic. Instead, despair is the name for that undoing that the dialectic endlessly initiates. It is therefore a more complex condition—for philosophical critique, historical consciousness, and political position—than is traditionally assumed. Against a familiar ghost story that warns of the specter of despair haunting radical political vision and the knight of resignation that follows in its path, I will venture an argument that the "negative passions" can enrich the political imagination and enliven political praxis.

This study takes some relief from the normative project in political theory—the articulation of norms, values, rules, and procedures, the construction of political ethics or ontology, the call to civic life, participation, or political action—on the grounds that critique involves what Hegel called the labor of the negative (which is never *simply* negative) and philosophy throws its best light at dusk. Of course, it is precisely this view of critique that leads many away from critical theory, which is increasingly thought to be too theoretical, too morose, too destructive, or too slow in speaking to the urgent political demands of our time. Widespread among both liberals and radicals is the suspicion that critical theory gets caught up and derailed by its own negative procedures, tending toward defeat while the larger project remains deeply structured by what Bernard Yack denounces as "the longing for total revolution."[7] The result is permanent frustration and inaction.

Even—or perhaps especially—those identified with the tradition of Frankfurt School critical theory decry the dangers of aporetic thinking and negative dialectics. The "first generation" of Frankfurt theorists, and Adorno in particular, is said by the second and third to have condemned critical theory to hopeless resignation. Jürgen Habermas criticizes *The Dialectic of Enlightenment* for its "uninhibited scepticism regarding reason."[8] Not only does its "final unmasking" of bourgeois rationality remain ensnared in performative contradiction, but the book "holds out scarcely any prospect for an escape from the myth of purposive rationality that has turned into objective violence."[9] Seyla Benhabib levels a similar charge. "Their relentless pessimism," she alleges of Horkheimer and Adorno, "their expressed sympathy for the 'dark writers of the bourgeoisie'—Hobbes, Machiavelli, and Mandeville—and for its nihilistic critics—Nietzsche and de Sade—cannot be explained by the darkness of human history at that point in time alone."[10] In an ironic twist, this same line of argument is now invoked by third- and fourth-generation critical theorists against Habermas himself. In a book that aims to retrieve a Heideggerian world-disclosing operation for critical theory, Nikolas Kompridis laments that what he calls "normative despair" or "resignation to the contracting space of possibilities, resignation to the thought that our possibilities might be exhausted, that the future may longer be open to us, no longer welcoming," and he implicates an overly rationalist Habermas in this cultural decline.[11] World-disclosure wears a different normative cap, but it too presumes to rescue critical theory from despair.

Jane Bennett, from somewhat different theoretical positioning, puts the matter simply and elegantly: "critical theory (in its generic sense) has devoted too much effort to negative critique and not enough to elaborating an affirmative political response to the moral dangers and political injustices it exposes."[12] And the point is almost persuasive, except where the idea of the affirmative is cover for a more substantial normativity. Bennett underestimates the "affirmative political responses" that come with ruthless critique. What is more, she presumes that it is the task of theory to instruct and guide political life. Critical political theory, from this perspective, must furnish *answers*.

These are familiar positions and will be revisited in later chapters. For now, some questions: What might critique accomplish once released from the expectation that it outline an escape from the conditions it comprehends and laments? Does this expectation betray a frustrated metaphysical urge that no purportedly "postmetaphysical" critical theory can satisfy? What might critical theory become if it is more attuned to the complex of passions that constitute a *critical consciousness*—which is to say, might critique take refreshment from the passions, even negative passions, as a necessary supplement to reason? And could it not be a virtue of theory that it often speaks indirectly and obliquely to politics, not in an instructional voice, but in the form of a constant *questioning*? Fanon concludes *Black Skin, White Masks* with precisely this "prayer" cast in corporeality: "O my body, always make me a man who questions!"[13] Is there no place for this variety of "negative critique" in political theory's arsenal?

"Prayer" is no accidental term in this context, and it is worth emphasizing again that the most extensive treatments of despair in the Western tradition appear not in medicine, but in religious discourses.[14] In Christian meditations on sin, for example, despair indicates a denial, active or passive, of divine grace. To be without hope, when God is the source and confirmation of all hope, is among the most serious of offenses—not simply sickness, but sin. Patristic theologians defined it as one of several cardinal sins. Aquinas called it the "irascible passion" and Martin Luther identified it as the most serious and unforgivable evil.[15] For many Christian thinkers, despair brought the subject into *potential* relation with God and, therefore, to the promise of salvation. Luther stakes out a strong version of this position when he writes: "It is certain that a man must completely despair of himself to become fit to obtain the grace of Christ."[16] But the persistence of despair—and despair is, above all else, a passion that *persists*—is the most powerful obstacle to the receipt of God's grace. It blocks the subject's progression toward salvation and reunion with the divine. Despair, in this tradition, turns on the subject's misrelationship with God, which was thought to result in various maladies of the soul. Even staunchly secular political theory that promises escape from despair may be said, in this context, to participate in a most basic religiosity.

Fanon's supplication, which will resound as a militant's prayer for a people presiding over a dying colonialism, is not quite religion by other means. Like the refracted traces of the Absolute in Adorno's negative dialectics and Bataille's atheology, Fanon's militancy represents a far-reaching and radical effort at working through the political, ethical, aesthetic, somatic, and psychic effects of our concrete and worldly misrelations. The questions are all too human—questions concerning how to be human and what being human requires from and for the other. At stake is not quite a secular translation of a theological concept of despair, but political and theoretical analyses of the sicknesses of spirit in late modernity, attempts to discern what is inhuman in our present condition and how philosophical critique ineluctably participates in the inhumanity it opposes. Salvation stories play no part in these analyses. What Habermas calls "the strong concept of theory"— the view that *bios theoretikos* could secure, through philosophical reflection, the salvation promised by world religion—is surely untenable. And Habermas is right to identify Hegel's speculative system as the apex of this strong conception of theory. All of the thinkers presented in the following pages are post-Hegelian in this respect. With the collapse of a strong concept of theory comes not a defense of its weaker substitutes (as in "weak ontology"[17] or "weak messianism"[18]), but a vindication of the unyielding force of the negative.

To use Habermasian terms, this book aims to recenter passion in the so-called philosophical discourse of modernity. If this discourse has been said to turn on reason and its relation to power, on the forms of rationality that structure modern social life, then I propose to consider that which circulates in excess of reason—not quite in direct opposition to reason, but in discord with its demands—by which the "unfinished project of modernity" has also been constituted. Against the main currents in critical theory today, I do not believe critique suffers a deficit of hope, nor do I think it needs rescue from despair. Indeed, it might be that hope and despair are not quite opposed and that the "principle of hope" (to borrow Ernst Bloch's formulation) is in fact nourished and enlivened by the condition that seems most inhospitable to it. It might also be that the urge to rescue philosophical critique from despair reproduces the very condition it abhors.

Above all, I resist a prevailing assumption that critique today must attend to its reservoir of rational faith. This assumption receives its most elaborate and sophisticated defense in the work of Jürgen Habermas. If I refuse Habermas's confidence in communicative reason, for its rationalization of faith and deification of reason, this is not for the buoyancy of affirmative irrationalism. Nothing of the sort can be found in thinkers considered in the following pages. They are very different, to be sure, and would no doubt rebel against the company in which I have placed them. Yet each helps us to reckon with the shapes of historical life forged along a highway of despair and to maintain felt contact with those forms of hope that survive against all hopes. To this extent they assist us in charting new directions for critical theory.

3

Scholarly work on the politics of despair mostly underscores the conservative and reactionary impulses of cultural despair.[19] But the nostalgic romanticism of conservative cultural criticism is quite different from the tonalities tracked in these pages. What Hegel in the *Phenomenology* describes as "the seriousness, the suffering, the patience, and the labor of the negative" does not mean nostalgia, though despair may be structured by loss, memory, and ruptures in time.[20] Consciousness in despair is not necessarily morose or "unhappy" (in the conventional sense or in Hegel's particular sense of that term), but it is disoriented and uncertain: no one walks sure-footed along this highway.

Several developments in contemporary criticism are germane to this study, yet at some distance from its central concerns and claims. The critical theoretical discourse on melancholia and its political effects, trauma studies in historiography, and the eruption of affect theory in the humanities and social sciences all speak in important ways to the themes considered here. In each of these areas of research, psychoanalytic theory plays a major role, as it does for the thinkers considered in the second part of this book. So why do I resist the language of melancholia and employ that of despair? Are they the same? Is despair another name for trauma, individual or collective, and its effects? Why emphasize despair in particular? Is it not one of many negative affects in circulation as the contemporary politics of feeling? And what distinguishes despair from pessimism, cynicism, or related conditions?

Social and political interpretations of melancholia in recent scholarship are of some assistance in mapping a dialectical concept of despair. Melancholy is an ancient term, appearing in Greek philosophy and medicine to designate the depression believed to be caused by the excess of black fluids in the human body (*Melankholia*, literally *melas*, "black" + *khole*, "bile"). Hippocrates was the first to articulate a science of the human body as comprising four humors: phlegm, blood, black bile, and yellow bile. Normal variation in the distribution of these humors explained variation in human temperament and disposition. According to the Greeks, the excess of any single humor produced mental and physical disorder: melancholia—symptoms of which include prolonged sadness, fear, paranoia, distrust, and delusion—signaled the excess of black bile in the body. Aristotle further developed this humoral theory of melancholia, positing a connection between the abundance of black bile and creative genius.[21] In the discourses of Greek physiology, medicine, and science, melancholia was the diagnosis for a primarily somatic sickness with deep mental symptoms.[22] This ancient humoral-somatic view of melancholia was eventually replaced by a modern medical account that turns on how we interiorize external experience. As Dana Luciano has pointed out, "from the classical period through the nineteenth century, the primary cause of melancholia was believed to be not external loss but physiological predisposition."[23] Psychoanalysis, in particular, represents a decisive shift in the genealogy of melancholy, centering on the psychological impact and management of objective conditions. If melancholy was once thought to be "without cause" (a subjective experience of body and mind largely independent of external pressures), psychoanalysis ventures an altogether different position. It moves from the interpretation of melancholia's effects to a preoccupation with its source beyond the self. Just as the clamp tightens around a clinical concept of depression, the idea of melancholia opens up to social criticism.

The psychoanalytic account of melancholia begins with Freud's publication of "Mourning and Melancholia," the textual starting point for a whole range of subsequent inquiry into individual and collective loss. In this essay, Freud considers the alternative responses to the death of loved ones, developing a distinction indicated by the title and now quite familiar, between mourning and melancholia. Mourning, or what Freud calls the "normal" reaction to the death or disappearance of a loved object, involves the withdrawal of the libido from the lost object and the relocation of libidinal attachment onto a new object. Because libidinal investment always carries with it a degree of ambivalence, mourning provides an occasion for the healthy recognition of such ambivalence and the slight loosening of the ties between the subject and his or her object choice. Melancholia, by contrast, resists this release from the bondage of libidinal attachment, instead preserving the lost object—or, at least, *the attachment to it*—by means of incorporation and identification. In melancholia, the subject incorporates the lost object into the self and identifies the ego with what has been lost, thus preserving attachment to the object as attachment to one's ego. This process is devastating to the psyche: as "the shadow of the object [falls] upon the ego," the subject proceeds as though its own ego were the abandoned object.[24] Object-loss in melancholia is transformed into ego-loss, producing symptoms of self-hatred and self-reproach in the patient. If mourning is a form of reconciled anguish, in which the lost object is grieved as a genuine loss while new attachments are formed, melancholia is a pathology in which the lost object is never really lost, but preserved within the subject as a steady reminder of abandonment.

Contemporary thinkers have drawn from this psychoanalytic concept of melancholia to investigate forms of racial and gender subjection, "wounded attachments" to lost objects and ideals, and identities constituted through the inability to mourn what has passed.[25] What is so exciting about this work is its demonstration of the social character and political effects of our seemingly private and subjective struggles. But I intend to think despair apart from mourning and melancholy—which is to say, to think despair apart from the question of loss that underwrites both. Despair is not quite "aberrated mourning," or the mourning that fails to return to the fullness of life in the present and becomes, as a result, melancholic, as Gillian Rose argues.[26] Despair is not quite Left-wing melancholy, the refusal to let go of lost causes in our political thinking and practice, as Wendy Brown says.[27] If melancholia is a pathology pertaining to the loss of attachment, Lauren Berlant's concept of cruel optimism considers attachments from the perspective of their unfortunate persistence. Berlant writes: "Cruel optimism is the condition of maintaining an attachment to a problematic object *in advance of its loss*."[28] But "cruel optimism" remains ensnared in the melancholic drama of loss, now as a certain future as opposed to an unreconciled past.

Each of these theorists tells us something significant about the pitfalls of our political attachments, and one hesitates to add more terminology to an already crowded field, but despair names something different from these disordered affects. It is a crisis in movement and direction, not chiefly a response to loss. Frustrated or disappointed desires—what Berlant aptly describes as "clusters of promises"—may be occasions for crises, but they are also set off by the unexpected and the unforeseen. Despair is a misrelation to a present that concretely is, more than a past that never was or a future that ought to be. Even when it bears witness to a critical "cessation of happening" (to use Walter Benjamin's phrase) and comes to a standstill, negative dialectics also admits the inability to assemble what is manifestly happening into a viable project or a just purpose. Consider Kierkegaard's account of despair at its heights: "to be unwilling to hope in the possibility that an earthly need, a temporal cross, can come to an end." Despair is the refutation of the end of history: It is that dynamic and restless passion that keeps things moving as earthly projects and

purposes fall into disrepair. Rather than lament or regret this condition, I wonder if something might be mined from it—and, contrary to
every expectation about the politics of despair, something that links it
to a concrete experience of freedom.

Sara Ahmed's vindication of unhappiness, like Berlant's critique
of optimism, resonates with aspects of the argument developed in
these pages.[29] For Ahmed, the imperative to "be happy" is a disciplinary technique that rewards social conformity and political passivity.
Unhappiness, by contrast, is a measure of cultural resistance. Exemplary of affect theory more generally, Ahmed's project maps the public
import of our private feelings. She retrieves figures of unhappiness—
the feminist killjoy, the angry black woman, the unhappy queer—for
their diverse struggles against social oppression and the false promise of happiness. Like the imperative to be happy, the imperative to
be hopeful can be a disciplinary technique and a political trap. But
despair is not unhappy. And though she remarks on the ambivalence of affects, Ahmed treats feelings as discrete and unequivocal.
Put differently, against the happiness regime, Ahmed installs the
unhappiness project. The freedom to be unhappy—or what Ahmed
even calls the *right* to be unhappy—is no less problematic as a cultural and political ideal than happiness, for this is a "freedom" that so
many experience as an unfortunate necessity.[30] What is more, Ahmed
assumes that public feelings are a direct and transparent expression
of individual experience and accepts them as the real measure of our
political virtue. Ahmed insists that "it is important that we not produce a heroic model of the unhappy revolutionary whose suffering is
a gift to the world," that one "can be unhappy as a way of doing nothing," particularly when it involves being unhappy about anything and
everything.[31] The main problem, as I see it, is not that the unhappy
revolutionary will appear as a hero, or that all forms of unhappiness
will seem revolutionary. The problem is that ordinary unhappiness
will be measured according to its willingness to "do something" and
nonetheless the politicization of unhappiness will remain an entirely
subjective affair. In a word: heroic.

Trauma studies, which has also flourished in certain quarters of
the humanities and interpretive social sciences in recent decades,
addresses some of the themes I will explore in the following chapters.

The meaning of violence, the uses (and abuses) of memory, the aims of critical historiography—these are central questions for the thinkers treated in the following pages and for specialists in trauma theory, especially those seeking a sociopolitical perspective on trauma. Dominick LaCapra describes trauma as follows:

> Trauma is itself a shattering experience that disrupts or even threatens to destroy experience in the sense of an integrated or at least viably articulated life. There is a sense in which trauma is an out-of-context experience that upsets expectations and unsettles one's very understanding of existing contexts. Moreover, the radically disorienting experience of trauma often involves a dissociation between cognition and affect. . . . Here one has an aporetic relation between representation and affect with the possibility of an uncontrolled oscillation between poles of a double bind. Indeed, one might postulate that an aporia marks a trauma that has not been viably worked through, hence inducing compulsive repetition of the aporetic relation.[32]

LaCapra goes on to distinguish between the traumatic event, which is more or less bounded in time, and traumatic experience, which knows no temporal cohesion, but is brought into coherence through some manner of "working through" the impact of an event, often in narrative, storytelling, music, dance, or sacred ritual. The aporetic dimension in traumatic experience, the gap between what is known and what is felt, between what can be said and what eludes representation in discourse, resonates with the thinkers considered here. For Adorno and Fanon, in particular, some manner of "working through" traumatic experience is fundamental to both critical theory and political praxis, though they will differ on what it requires.

Where both Adorno and Fanon are quite different from trauma theory is in the conviction, ironically consoling, that aporia is aligned with the extraordinary (as opposed to integrated into the realm of ordinary experience), that it is out of context (as opposed to embedded in particular contexts), that it is a rupture in historical processes (as opposed to their fulfillment). This study resists LaCapra's odd protectionism toward traumatic experience and, more importantly, rejects his implicit prohibition on aporia, which he associates with anarchic tendencies ("uncontrolled oscillation") and neurotic symptoms ("compulsive repetition"). Further, I place emphasis on the ordinary and quotidian element of despair, both how minor traumas *accumulate without adding up* and how the aporetic conditions of late modern life are not rooted in a single traumatic event—or even an extended trauma—but structured by ordinary experience, the repetition of reinforcing relations of domination, cruelty, and inhumanity.

My thinking about despair also takes some inspiration from Joshua Dienstag's recent work on pessimism, in particular his sustained examination of a "form of life" too often mistaken for an emotional complex.[33] Ultimately, however, I share Gillian Rose's view, articulated with reference to a mistaken reading of Adorno as a pessimist, that negative dialectics "is not a pessimistic science" in that it "rejects any dichotomy such as optimistic/pessimistic for it implies an inherently fixed and static view."[34] Further, while Dienstag calls pessimism "something more than a sensibility, but less than a doctrine," it is also a deeply unhistorical ethic.[35] To be sure, Dienstag makes the powerful argument that the pessimistic tradition relies upon a distinct time-consciousness in modernity. But this tradition also seems curiously separate from historical processes, social life, and political values. Dienstag distinguishes his philosophical presentation of the pessimistic tradition from a cultural account inspired by Raymond Williams, which treats pessimism as a "structure of feeling." Yet if this cultural approach blurs the distinction between theory and emotion so crucial to Dienstag's anatomy of pessimism, it also has the virtue of treating both thoughts and feelings in their historical specificity.[36]

Even the "pessimism of the intellect, optimism of the will," counseled by Antonio Gramsci following Romain Rolland, does not quite capture the condition tracked in the following pages. Despair rebels against the quiet comforts of both optimism and pessimism, as well as the dichotomous separation between thinking and doing. Quite unlike pessimism, despair sees limitations everywhere while also having the tendency to embolden thought and praxis to press against the limits of existing conditions. It registers a revolt at what is given. In this way, despair preserves the possibility of something radically different and conjures the spirit of hope that it also quiets. As Adorno puts it in *Negative Dialectics*: "Grayness could not fill us with us with despair if our minds did not harbor the concept of different colors, scattered traces of which are not absent from the negative whole."[37] Despair appears, in this light, as the negative imprint of hope. In Adorno, it is linked to "that which was or is doomed." In Bataille, the impossible becoming possible. In Fanon, the eve of a real struggle. For all of them, despair is aligned with the absurd, the extrarational, and the excessive, as well as any meaningful practice of justice and freedom. The thinkers of interest in this study stake out opportunities for radical thought and practice under hopeless conditions: hope where there is no hope, hope that is not quite irrational but exceeds the limits of reason alone. And each allows critical theory to take relief from the prohibition on despair.

Bataille and Fanon treat despair differently and less directly, but like Adorno, they appreciate how negative dialectics demands that we deal with it proactively. Bataille links the negative passions to joy, the extreme limit of the possible, nonknowledge, writing, and forms of freedom suggested by chance and accident. Fanon will consider despair a question concerning history (the histories of slavery and colonialism) and embodiment (the violence to which black bodies are routinely subjected, as well as the disfigurations done to oneself when domination is epidermalized). Though he will treat it as symptomatic—"a society that drives its members to despair is a nonviable society, a society to replace"—in sickness there is also a sign of a struggle. And Fanon's entire philosophy of praxis is nourished by signs of struggle.

What Lucien Goldmann in *The Hidden God* calls "world vision" is helpful in this context: "a convenient term for the whole complex of ideas, aspirations, and feelings which links together the members of a social group (a group which, in most cases, assumes the existence of a social class) and which opposes them to members of other social groups."[38] Goldmann appropriates the term from Wilhelm Dilthey and hopes to give it a "scientific" status (in the Hegelian sense), by which he means that a study of world vision must be able to distinguish the essential from the accidental and trace the underlying coherence between particularity and totality. This method yields an extraordinary presentation of a seventeenth-century "tragic vision" in Pascal, Racine, and Kant. But, contra Goldmann, essentiality and coherence are difficult to establish in the realm of ideas, much less in aspirations and feelings. I will be satisfied with an unscientific concept of "world vision," one that is not premised on banishing the accidental and that does not strive chiefly for coherence, but that retains its social and historical shape. Adorno, Bataille, and Fanon—very different thinkers, to be sure—together demonstrate how ruthless critique lands in despair and how it nevertheless draws its force from this very fate.

4

This book might have featured substantive chapters on Walter Benjamin, Max Horkheimer, Herbert Marcuse, Ernst Bloch, or any of the more recent Frankfurt School theorists now most often identified with the term "critical theory." But Benjamin is not really a Hegelian. Horkheimer is more the pessimist, especially in his mature writings. Marcuse is constitutionally averse to a comportment of despair (for which he should to be celebrated and cherished, but in a different book). And Bloch would have directed this study toward the principle of hope, when it is my aim to throw light on the negative. Adorno's collaborations and correspondences bring all of these thinkers into the background of this story, but he is the lead. The dialectical view of despair and the view of the dialectic *as* despair are, to my mind, rooted in a reading of Adorno's critical theory. And it is through Adorno that this book maintains its deepest connection with the radical intellectual tradition born in Frankfurt.

Bataille and Fanon are less obvious or familiar members of critical theory's canon, but they are important interlocutors in the history of Left Hegelianism nevertheless. Reacquaintance with them allows critical theory to venture into different terrain, test untried positions, and pursue new political and theoretical possibilities. Bataille extends our consideration to the other participants in Alexandre Kojève's lectures on Hegel and the Collège de Sociologie, as well as more secretive associations. And his importance for later French thinkers like Michel Foucault and Jacques Derrida suggests there is much to be mined from his texts. But precious little has been said about Bataille as a resource for philosophical critique and political theory. Bataille appears in these pages in terms of an alternative "negative dialectics," an aleatory dialectic that hangs on chance and retains a radical political character. I see his interest in Nietzsche as the continuation of his prior investment in Hegel and Hegelian concepts. And I measure the political purchase of Bataille's philosophical writing in its resolute antifascism and its fidelity to an idea of freedom. Though he does not give explicit attention to the concept of despair, Bataille's "will to chance" is a comportment adjusted to it, to devastating historical conditions and to the complex of passions that keep things moving as oneself and one's surroundings come undone.

With Fanon, the orbit extends to Aimé Césaire, Maurice Merleau-Ponty, Jean-Paul Sartre, and the Algerian FLN. He pushes critical theory out of the university and the library and into the clinic, the countryside, and the streets. Political questions—questions concerning race relations and the effects of racial oppression, histories individual and collective, the legacies of European colonialism, the psychic and somatic effects of domination, the border between reason and madness—come to the fore. And though Fanon is typically put into conversation with Sartre on philosophical questions, his distinctive philosophy in exile bears some surprising affinities with Adorno.

Sartre raises the more general question of French existentialism and its connection to the themes considered in this study. Admittedly, French existentialism represents yet another important episode in the history of Left Hegelianism and, it could be argued, another important statement of despair. Simone de Beauvoir's efforts, in *The Ethics of Ambiguity* and elsewhere, to push existentialism away from Sartrean ontology toward an ethics are especially germane.[39] Beauvoir says her existentialism is "beyond any pessimism, as beyond any optimism," and is fueled by the passions.[40] And her ethical position is inseparable from her political commitment. But ultimately, I think Adorno is right that existentialism "is too optimistic, even as an expression of despair; one cannot conceive of a versatile spontaneity outside of its entwinement with society."[41] This is to reiterate the (Hegelian) dictum that there is no image of freedom unmediated by social structures and relations. The existentialist image of freedom is a distorted image: it feeds on a fantasy of heroic escape from unfreedom, as if the experience of freedom is uncorrupted by prevailing inequality and oppression. What is more, the image of freedom *as versatile spontaneity*—to which Beauvoir herself remains deeply wedded, which poses all sorts of problems for *The Second Sex*—is itself a product of objective conditions. Fanon extends the critique: for him, the existentialist subject never loses possession of itself, never comes undone, never makes real contact with a world of others. Fanon invokes none other than the authority of Hegel in his critique of Sartre's hasty dialectic.

What may be more problematic than any conceptual claim and more difficult than any interpretive position taken on Hegel, Kierkegaard, Adorno, Bataille, Fanon, or any of the minor figures in the story that follows is the implicit claim that frames all of these textual encounters: that Hegel and a radical tradition that comes after Hegel have something to do with critical theory and politics in the present. I return to this claim explicitly in my brief conclusion, but all of these pages turn on the conviction that despair is a political category. By this, I mean that subjective life cannot be considered apart from its objective conditions and ruthless critique today cannot be thought apart from the despair that energizes and frustrates it. What is more, I intend to complicate the conventional wisdom that says that the politics of despair is either reaction or resignation and consider what is learned from the passions. I remain unconvinced that despair is as corrosive of political vision as philosophers and politicians would have us believe—or that hope is as unequivocal a political virtue as their sermons would suggest.

This book proceeds as a collection of close readings and philosophical-political profiles. The first part, which includes chapters on Hegel and Kierkegaard, provides a reconstruction of despair as a dialectical passion. I focus on the *Phenomenology of Spirit* and *The Sickness Unto Death* to show how both Hegel and Kierkegaard see despair as a dynamic force, one that exceeds the boundaries of reason and religion. Hegel and Kierkegaard point to passion as the place where thinking gathers its energy and see despair as an element of the experience of freedom. I read Hegel's concept of despair in distinction from the more familiar condition of unhappy consciousness and focus on the figure of "natural consciousness" in the *Phenomenology*.

More generally, I want to linger on that voice in Hegel that speaks not of certain beginnings or achieved endings, but of an overflow of passion at any given moment. And I see Kierkegaard's analytic of faith as a significant reworking of the problem of despair in Hegel. Indeed, Kierkegaard is the only thinker considered here who really discusses despair, at length and in detail, as a philosophical problem. The result is a more comprehensive conceptual account, but also a more intense urge for some way out.

The second part of the book, which comprises chapters on Adorno, Bataille, and Fanon, tracks experiments in thinking at the heights of despair. These chapters are not *about* despair per se, but studies in what critical theory can do when freed from the demand that it furnish a way out of despair. Each thinker offers important critical interpretations of Hegel, but this is only a small part of my story. The bigger part deals with how they take up the tasks of critique without the edifying assurance that the world may be rescued from negativity. Each models a way of speaking to despair that never, as Adorno insists, gives despair the final word. Not because some other word—hope, love, affirmation—will be last, but because "negative dialectics" admits no finale and because despair always says two things at once: it says all hope is gone, except for the "hope without hope" to which all despair bears witness.

Part I

▼

DIALECTICS AND DESPAIR

1

Hegel, the Wound

One cannot "read" Hegel, except by not reading him. To read, not to read him—to understand, to misunderstand, to reject him—all this falls under the authority of Hegel or doesn't take place at all.

—Maurice Blanchot, *The Writing of the Disaster*

One thing is clear: *we* cannot now begin with "Hegel," nor with the "System." . . . Perhaps we may begin by asking why the tradition sets up—in order to worship and to denigrate—the idol of the "System" and the imperial sovereignty of "Hegel": authority and author.

—Gillian Rose, *The Broken Middle*

1

Hegel did not describe his work as critique.[1] In the *Phenomenology of Spirit*, he portrays his efforts not in terms of critical philosophy, which would have aligned him squarely with Kant, but as an attempt to unite the desire for knowledge with actual knowing.[2] What Hegel had in mind in this union of philosophy and science was not quite critique in the Kantian sense, but rather the *consummation* of the love of knowledge (philosophy) with the historical and phenomenological experience of knowing (science).[3] Hegel aimed to "complete" philosophy, not only by giving it a definitive reality in human history, but also by merging its theoretical and its practical tasks. For Hegel, no edifying discourses on abstract reason or faith could do justice to the phenomenology of human freedom, nor could stargazing substitute for concrete knowledge of all that this freedom entails.[4] Like Marx after him, Hegel scoffed at merely "critical" theories and understood his own project as something rather different, one that demanded a scientific outlook from philosophy.

That Hegel took his distance from the language of critique presents an immediate challenge to the argument developed in the following pages, which turns on a link between Hegel and critical theory, between a pathos in the dialectic and the passionate side of the critical tradition. What could Hegel possibly have to do with critical theory and its passions, if his philosophical science is not properly called critical and if it assumes the task of *overcoming* what he took to be the inescapable disappointments and frustrations that inhere in the mere love of philosophy? In what sense can Hegel's philosophy be called critique?

Robert Pippin provides one answer and one approach. He argues that Hegel is best taken as a postcritical philosopher rather than a precritical metaphysician, by which he means that we ought to view Hegel as a sort of Kantian, one who radicalizes the idealist principle of Transcendental Deduction, or the unity of apperception, through which Kant tries to establish the objective validity of the concept and the foundations for a priori knowledge.[5] For Pippin, the question of whether Hegel's speculative system can be called *critical* rests exclusively on its relationship to Kant, its adherence to the "identity theory" in German Idealism, its redefinition of concepts and intuitions, and its response to the specific points of failure in Kantian critical philosophy. And Pippin calls "revisionist" the various encounters with Hegel that draw selectively and partially from his writings, most often the *Phenomenology of Spirit* and the later work on politics and history, to clarify and advance the tasks of critical theory.

But it is in *these* various strands of thought, from Marxism to existentialism, from phenomenology to anticolonial theory, from the Frankfurt School to the Collège de Sociologie, all of which converge on the primacy of critique and Hegel as one of its great practioners, where we discover another sense in which Hegel's philosophy is unmistakably critical. For the variety of thinkers and traditions now collected under the big tent of "critical theory," the "restlessness of the negative" has been a steady source of inspiration, if not edification.[6] If Hegel can be called critical because he builds upon the Kantian project before him, he can also be called critical in light of his supreme importance for a whole range of radical thinkers that came after him. If critique, for Kant, involves reflection on the limits (and possibilities) of reason, Hegelian critique involves reflections on the possibilities (and limits) of a philosophy that aims to do justice to reason as it actually appears in the world.

In a different context, this time an essay on Nietzsche and the melancholic moods into which modern philosophy has fallen, Pippin fires another shot at "critical theory":

> We do though need some explanation for why the dominant academic and high culture trajectory for so many years has been so self-critical, self-exposing, ruthlessly suspicious and morbidly fixated on failure, pretension, negativity and the like; why have we been "doing this to ourselves," as it were, why we have taken such an interest in our own failure, hypocrisy and self-delusion, why the dominant theory has been "critical theory."[7]

Pippin does not provide this explanation, but only suggests that we need it. And his reading of Nietzsche, which reconsiders the well-known announcement of the death of God that comes in section 125 of *The Gay Science*, does not aim at a diagnosis of the present intellectual disorder. Rather, it offers an important reminder that Nietzsche did not partake of the melancholy of late modernity and indeed provides a touchstone for thinking against it. Pippen hopes to exonerate Nietzsche from guilt by association, to restore the gaiety of *The Gay Science*, and to reclaim "philosophy with a hammer" from the self-indulgent and narcissistic negativity of the present.

Pippin is a gifted reader of Hegel and Nietzsche, and perhaps right to suggest that the past century of critical theorists have engaged both thinkers for political and philosophical purposes that were not their own. Though I do not share Pippin's misgivings about critical theory, I concede that various signs of the "negative"—loss, lack, failure, abjection, melancholia—circulate in contemporary intellectual discourse and that this tells us something about the "spirit of the age" and the direction of cultural criticism. What I seek to do in the following pages is offer some explanation—not the exclusive and certainly not an exhaustive one—for the situation Pippin describes. Where I depart from Pippin most decisively is in my suggestion that critical features of Hegel's *Phenomenology* constitute the necessary starting points for an answer to the question of why we have been "doing this to ourselves"—or, better, why in so doing we could be said to follow in *a spirit of Hegel*.

The argument I develop turns on a figure in Hegel's *Phenomenology of Spirit*, that of "natural consciousness" (*natürliche Bewußtsein*), and the despair this figure is said to suffer. Getting at the meaning of despair in Hegel's sense is my primary task, for this can assist us in discerning a distinctive—and enduring—feature of the dialectic that survives the ruins of the speculative system. The German word Hegel uses is *Verzweiflung* and "despair" is, as we will see, a somewhat imprecise and inadequate translation. It risks obscuring the distinction between the state of despair as Hegel portrays it at the onset and the more familiar condition of "unhappy consciousness" (*unglückliches Bewußtsein*) as it is described later in the *Phenomenology*. Despair in Hegel has to do not just with a split or a tear in consciousness, as the root *zwei* suggests. It involves a more radical fragmentation, an "utter dismemberment" that shatters the split vision of skeptical and unhappy consciousness. And despair is a vital passion, by which I mean that it is the site of a struggle that propels the subject forward. My argument is not simply that despair persists beyond the resolution of unhappy consciousness—itself a reappearing figure in the *Phenomenology*—but that despair is the condition of possibility for *any* resolution to be found in the text.

To be sure, Hegel presents natural consciousness as a limited and inadequate form, as "only the Notion of knowledge" as opposed to "real knowledge," and this inadequacy calls forth the scientific standpoint that corrects it.[8] And it is undeniable that the entirety of the *Phenomenology* is an exercise in clarifying and completing the view from natural consciousness with a science of Spirit. Nevertheless, though it is an "unreal" form, it is also certain that natural consciousness cannot be thought apart from or in simple opposition to a scientific standpoint. Indeed, both are achievements, results, or effects of a journey "free and self-moving in its own peculiar shape," and each holds a mirror to the other.[9] When cut off from consciousness,

cognition, and concrete life, the methodism of science is no less limited and limiting, no less "unreal." The *Phenomenology* insists emphatically on the interpenetration of science and consciousness, scientific
modes of study and "natural" modes of knowing and acting.

My argument echoes Jean-Luc Nancy's suggestion that "Hegel is
the inaugural thinker of the contemporary world" and this because
he revealed the "constitutive unhappiness" (here again, I would suggest a different terminology) of the modern subject in its ecstatic relation to objects and others.[10] I want return to the terms of that inauguration address and track how the subject is brought to life in the
Phenomenology of Spirit and how Hegel aims to give meaning—what
Gillian Rose has provocatively described as Hegelian comedy—to
the *ordeal* of consciousness. Is there a formula for despair, which is
not quite coterminous with unhappy consciousness or tragic vision,
that the dialectic requires and reproduces? Might this suggest that the
Phenomenology is best read not as a roadmap to reconciliation or the
detailed history of consciousness in advance of the satisfactions of the
Absolute, but as a philosophical staging of despair and its persistence?
Does this despair circulate within the boundaries of reason, as Kant
suggested of religious faith and the principle of hope, or does it point
instead to the passions that give life to the system and the affective
forces upon which Hegel's science depends? If we must dispense with
the conceit of going beyond Hegel—a procedure that Kierkegaard
well understood as distinctly Hegelian—and instead ought to take
measure of the Hegelian debt that underwrites contemporary critical
theory, then I am proposing to take account of a pathos that inheres
in the dialectic.

To be sure, this revaluation of despair in Hegel works against the
triumphalist tones with which the system is so often made to speak to
politics and world history, by its champions and its opponents alike. I
would not deny this element of Hegel's authorship, nor confine it the
later writings on the state and world history.[11] But this is not the whole
of it. Critical theory, for the most part and for most of its history, has
found its footing elsewhere in Hegel's vast terrain.

Patchen Markell, in his study of the politics of recognition, notes
two distinct voices in Hegel's writing, the most familiar being the
"'reconciliatory' voice . . . the voice of the system—the voice that

promises us that at the end of this journey there lies the prospect of homecoming, of finally arriving at a state in which contradiction, division, suffering, and other manifestations of negativity have been not necessarily eliminated, but at least redeemed as moments of an intelligible, internally articulated, encompassing whole."[12] (I would add that this is the voice in which Hegel undertakes to make a science of philosophy, to transform the complex passions at play in the love of knowledge into the wounded satisfactions, if not the imperial sovereignty, of actualized knowledge.) Markell retrieves a different voice in Hegel, one he calls the "diagnostic voice" and identifies primarily with the method of inquiry developed in the *Phenomenology of Spirit*: "It is the voice of Hegel the phenomenologist, whose great skill lies in the ability to notice and represent, often dramatically, the ways in which determinate theoretical perspectives, forms of knowledge, modes of action, and social orders fall into contradiction on their own terms."[13] In this voice, most audible in the struggle for recognition and the master-slave dialectic, Hegel reveals how particular modes of relating to others not only fail to secure human freedom, but actually consolidate dependence and reinforce the bonds of servitude. That Hegel could show the error in particular ways of knowing, organizing, and acting in the world and also disclose how they fall into error by their own lights—this, for Markell, is the diagnostic lesson of the *Phenomenology*. He shows, convincingly, how "Hegel's diagnostic voice cuts against his reconciliatory voice" and suggests that this demands a rethinking of the politics of recognition as "*part of the problem rather than part of the solution*."[14] Markell heeds what he calls the "the ontological lessons" in Hegel, and the diagnostic critique of recognition finds its supplement and solution in the ontology of acknowledgment.

I wonder: Does the proliferation of voices in Hegel's authorship, which do not quite cohere into a scientific univocality, press against the very idea of a closed system and caution against the search for solutions *of any sort* from the *Phenomenology*? Could we also say that the two voices in Hegel seem to call forth for each other, and at times reinforce each other, so that freedom might take the shape of a path, a journey, "the cold march of necessity" and the subject might appear the portal and the carrier of Spirit?[15] Perhaps both the diagnostic and the reconciliatory voices reinforce this view of the phenomenology of the subject (and the history of the world) as a road or a pathway, a view that permits movement forward and backward and even allows for retrenchments and reversals, but prohibits a leap sideways or into the abyss of chance.[16] Might there be yet another voice in the *Phenomenology*, a *revelatory* voice, a voice that relays the movements by which consciousness "presses forward" as passion play and the play of passions, as the dramatic enactment of the Absolute in the trials of natural consciousness? Is this the voice in Hegel that assures us that despair finds its answer not in the hope that reason may be mined from the ruins of the past or the faith that there is some meaning or purpose to be found in historical suffering, but in the real freedom gained as the "life of Spirit . . . in utter dismemberment . . . finds itself"?[17]

Much recent work in critical theory is premised on the implicit or explicit claim that knowledge and praxis worthy of an emancipatory tradition mustn't give way to despair. Yet I suspect that the most radical idea in the *Phenomenology*, a text with no shortage of them, turns on the scandal that critique—or reason's self-reflection in the thoughts and deeds of human beings—*is* the work of despair. This is a variety of despair that bears no resemblance to simple resignation or retreat. Indeed, despair *is* the restlessness of the negative, or the energetic force with which consciousness keeps moving.

Recall Hegel's claim that philosophy's fear of making errors about knowledge, which results in a general suspicion of all knowledge claims, is *itself* the error. I am concerned that the felt need to find rescue from despair—in intersubjective communicative reason, weak ontology, minimalist theology, political liberalism, or democratic faith—is precisely what cements its hold on critical political consciousness. If contemporary critical theory has struggled to find its political bearings without reliance on a teleological-progressive concept of history or a civilizational ideal of *Bildung*, perhaps this is because many of its finest practitioners have also presumed that critique today must renew its reserves of rational hope. What if, instead, we took some cues from the elusive figure of natural consciousness along the highway of despair, "induced by it knows not what to walk on its head"—which is also to say, *think on its feet*.[18] In this figure, the aporetic condition of thinking and acting, marked by the absence of passage from concrete experience to philosophical knowledge, by the nonidentity between objective and subjective spirit, yields spontaneous immersion in a world of others and objects. This is a form of life that is propelled into the future not by rational necessity or a science of the concept, but by chance and desire, by accident and passion, by forces and circumstances that reason cannot quite catch, much less capture. That Hegel sought to transcend the view from natural consciousness with the determinations of absolute knowledge does not require that readers of the *Phenomenology* follow his lead, nor does it diminish the significance of this "natural" and all-too-human life in the drama of Spirit.

This is all still too abstract and sketchy; in the sections that follow, I develop an interpretive argument through close reading, focusing first on Hegel's portrait of despair in the introduction to the *Phenomenology*. Here I hope to detail an approach to the *Phenomenology* that turns on the figure of natural consciousness, but also to show how this approach draws and departs from other ways of reading Hegel. Then I examine key episodes in the *Phenomenology*, focusing in particular on the descent into unhappy consciousness and some of the reappearances of unhappiness later in the text. These textual encounters are to distinguish despair from the more familiar condition of unhappy consciousness in Hegel and to underscore the primacy of passion in the drama of Spirit. There is a reason that despair—as opposed to unhappiness—does not appear in the *Phenomenology* except a couple of times in the body of the text. I will suggest this is because despair is not a moment within the dialectic of Spirit, but its very condition of possibility. Despair is precisely *not* the condition that consciousness transcends; it is not unhappiness. It is elemental to knowledge. In this way, I hope to set apart despair as the enduring *energeia* of the dialectic.

What I have found in the authorship of Hegel—that unflinching champion of reason as a historical and phenomenological reality, as substance and subject—is the rather surprising opportunity to revalue the passionate side of what Habermas has termed "the philosophical discourse of modernity." For Habermas, this discourse turns solely on the protected status of reason and the a priori view of modernity as (unfinished) project. Here, the genealogy of modern critique appears in a different light. In recasting critical theory by the din of reason's constitutive others—passion, violence, force, revelation—I hope to take relief from the (deeply Hegelian) approach to freedom as a project and the (also Hegelian) urge to rescue knowing and acting from a state of despair.

2

My adventures in the *Phenomenology* begin with a curious passage from its introduction, where Hegel provides a striking account of the sorrows of consciousness:

> Natural consciousness will show itself to be only the Notion of knowledge, or in other words, not to be real knowledge. But since it directly takes itself to be real knowledge, this path has a negative meaning for it, and what is in fact the realization of the Concept, counts for it rather as the loss of its own self. The road can be regarded as the pathway of doubt, or more precisely as the highway of despair.[19]

This excerpt comes in the context of Hegel's elaborations on how philosophy ought to deal with ordinary ways of knowing and their purported distance from truth and scientific certainty. My main argument is that this figure, natural consciousness, is crucial to the drama of the *Phenomenology* and the despair of natural consciousness is so integral to the dialectic that Hegel's philosophy might be said to fail at the very moment it succeeds in overcoming despair. Or, conversely, Hegel succeeds at those moments that the system fails to overcome despair.

Admittedly, natural consciousness is not *real* knowledge. But it is knowledge that takes itself to be real. Its gains are counted as losses. What are, for Hegel, positive developments have a negative significance for natural consciousness. But its road is the itinerary of Spirit and so the movements of natural consciousness are vital to the project that Hegel sets out for a philosophical science. Making sense of this figure and the highway that it travels requires making sense of what is going on in the introduction to the book, as well as how the introduction relates to the rest of the work and to the preface that precedes it.

First, the preface. As is well known, Hegel wrote the famed preface, with which the *Phenomenology* opens, *after* the book's completion. Its aims are at some remove from the rest of the work, including the introduction, as Hegel takes stock of his efforts, establishes their place within the speculative system, and relates them to other recent developments in philosophy. Rhetorically, it is a strange text, and not only for the way that Hegel repeatedly distances himself from the preface he has written and invites readers into the book by questioning their seriousness in reading it. Its tone is retrospective, as one would expect given the history of its composition, but oddly so, for it is neither a preliminary report on what's to come nor a conclusive statement of the book's findings. Above all, the document testifies explicitly to the challenge of beginnings in philosophy, both the difficulty in launching a philosophical inquiry and the impossibility of identifying, a priori, fixed points for starting and stopping. Hegel spends much of its first few pages explaining why it will not do what prefatory remarks typically do, namely, offer a "statement of the main drift and point of view, the general content and results, a string of random assertions and assurances about truth."[20] This is because, for Hegel, knowledge is a *process* as well as a product, "the result together with the process through which it came about."[21] As product alone, presented in the form of preliminary statements of this or that truth or principle, philosophy is lifeless abstraction, "the corpse which has left the guiding tendency behind it."[22]

Any philosophy worthy of the name, any *live* thinking, does not merely differentiate and distinguish among viewpoints as if they constituted "simple disagreements," pass judgment on others, and assert itself as truth. To judge a thing is not necessarily to know it, and knowledge of a thing may even require the suspension of judgment to get at what's critical about it.[23] Simply cataloguing and classifying knowledge, distinguishing right from wrong and true from false, passing judgment on others—the traditional elements of critique, we might say—appear as modes of *evading* the very things we presume to know. "For instead of getting involved in the real issue [*die Sache selbst*]," Hegel notes, "this kind of activity is always beyond it; instead of tarrying with it, and losing itself in it, this kind of knowing is forever grasping at something *new*; it remains essentially preoccupied with itself instead of being preoccupied with the real issue and surrendering to it."[24] The real issue? Hegel does not specify, nor will he devote attention to those unnamed thinkers who create only "the impression of hard work and serious commitment while actually sparing themselves both."[25] To do so would be to indulge the narcissism of philosophy and to violate the first principle of the *Phenomenology*, that knowing *is* doing, that knowledge inheres in actually doing, *and* that doing manifests and expresses ways of knowing.

Hegel devotes its final pages to repeated insistence that his preface will not satisfy casual or superficial readers, or those who seek to place the *Phenomenology* within a given field of philosophical possibilities and make its author speak on behalf of a fixed position.[26] Those who look to philosophy as a prop for their own egos, who reduce philosophical inquiry to abstract thought experimentation or cocktail party conversation pieces, or who "in order to keep up with the times and with advances in philosophy . . . read reviews of philosophical works, and perhaps even read their prefaces and first paragraphs," will be especially disappointed.[27] What these readers will find is a prose style and form too esoteric for quick consumption and a preface too circuitous for simple summation. Though most commentators acknowledge that Hegel's language is inseparable from his thinking, that the cryptic form and structure of the *Phenomenology* is an expression of its content, it is nevertheless commonplace to take Hegel's esotericism as exemplary of philosophy's vanity and its exaggerated sense of profundity. The preface seems to say something different though, and presses against familiar conceits about the politics of philosophical language. For Hegel, the esoteric is a *defense* against the peacocking that passes for philosophy *and* its formal critique. And while many have noted the sarcastic tone in the preface—a tone that has put off even his most sympathetic readers—few have had much to say about how Hegel's sarcasm relates to the seriousness of the system or how his esotericism takes aim at the self-satisfactions of knowledge.

The preface concludes with Hegel's demand that "philosophizing should again be made serious business," and here he invokes the example of the ancients (Hegel's interlocutors and influences go, for the most part, unnamed in the preface, which makes the closing nod to Plato and Aristotle all the more striking) to clarify the *labor* that philosophy entails.[28] This is how he puts it in a rare moment of frankness and lucidity:

> In the case of all other sciences, arts, skills, and crafts, everyone is convinced that a complex and laborious programme of learning and practice is necessary for competence. Yet when it comes to philosophy, there seems to be a currently prevailing prejudice to that, although not everyone who has eyes and fingers, and is given leather and last, is *at once* in a position to make shoes, the everyone nevertheless *immediately* understands how to philosophize, and how to evaluate philosophy, since he possesses the criterion for doing so in his natural reason—as if he did not likewise possess the measure for a shoe in his foot.[29]

Jacques Rancière underscores the pivotal role played by the shoemaker in Plato's *Republic* and in the social division of labor that Platonic justice demands.[30] Given Hegel's subsequent praise, just a few paragraphs later, for Plato's *Parmenides* ("surely," he remarks, "the greatest artistic achievement of the ancient dialectic"), the inspiration here is unmistakable. Philosophy is a distinctive kind of labor activity and, like all others, requires study and training, the development of certain skills, and the cultivation of specialized knowledge. But if Plato's philosopher-king stands opposed to and above the shoemaker as "a specialist in non-specialization" (while the shoemaker must, alas, specialize in a single thing, namely, making shoes) and this rule is secured by the noble lie that all must assume their appropriate place— gold, silver, or bronze—in the social hierarchy, then the philosopher-sage is comparatively egalitarian.[31] Hegel's point is not the classically elitist claim that some are innately equipped to do philosophy and some are not, that the mental faculties are more acutely developed in some than others, that the gift of genius is available only to a select class of men. Rather, it is that the gift of natural reason, genius or not, is no reliable compass for navigating the complex terrain that philosophy inhabits. Though what masquerades as philosophy "strides along in the robes of a high priest, on a road that is from the start no road . . . the genius of profound original ideas and lofty flashes of inspiration," a genuinely critical inquiry takes its bearings from the road itself, from "the long process of culture [*Bildung*]" of which philosophical discourse is but a part.[32]

In an important way, then, what Jean Hyppolite calls Hegel's "voyage of discovery" results not in the declaration of its novelty or its originality (remember, the preface is written after the book's completion), but in a preliminary insistence that any philosophy that drapes itself in novelty or originality, that heralds a new world or a new order of things, is the burnt offering from "dead men when they bury their dead."[33] If Hegel indeed "makes himself hermetic to the tomorrow," as Ortega y Gasset argues, this is not for the system's ban on a contingent futurity, but for his critique of a fetishized relationship to the new by which the modern has been constituted—*and his refreshing receptivity to the today.*[34] In endless pursuit of something new, says Hegel, modern philosophy has taken either to dismiss our "ordinary way of looking at things" or to impose upon our flawed or incomplete cognition "the intimation it gives us of something better to come."[35] Both strategies take flight from the real: this is philosophy as stargazing. Bringing philosophy down to earth, for Hegel, means taking seriously the concrete shape that knowledge and action assume under certain conditions and at particular moments. What this procedure reveals is no theater of human happiness. Against its urge to be edifying, Hegel demands that philosophy neither condemn these historical shapes as "mere appearances" nor incorporate them into a metaphysical ideal of what's to come. Neither would do justice to a painful reality—or to the radical potentiality that the concept of futurity promises. In Hegel, philosophy is *worldly revelation*: it discerns and deciphers the shapes and patterns of freedom—and its failures—as they actually appear in the world.

Hegel reserves his prospective gestures for the introduction to the *Phenomenology*, which was written contemporaneously with the rest of the book. It is much shorter and considerably more modest in scope and tone than the protracted and somewhat digressive preface.[36] It is in the introduction where Hegel spells out precisely how philosophical knowledge intersects with ordinary ways of knowing— or, put differently, how he intends to rescue the familiar from philosophy's neglect. And it is also here where Hegel first introduces the figure of natural consciousness and the concept of despair.

Jean Hyppolite writes of the introduction to the *Phenomenology*:

> More so than the preface, it allows us to determine both the mean-
> ing of the work that Hegel wished to write and what the technique
> of phenomenological development was for him. The preface is an *hor
> d'oeuvre*; it contains general information on the goal Hegel set for
> himself and on the relation between his work and other philosophi-
> cal treatises on the same subject. The introduction, on the contrary, is
> an integral part of the book: it poses and locates the problem, and it
> determines the means to resolve it.[37]

What is this problem? And what are the means determined to resolve
it? Robert Solomon, among Hegel's leading English-language commentators, has argued that the introduction "is concerned with a single, distinctive, and familiar problem—the tendency of modern philosophy, beginning with Descartes and Locke in particular, to end up
in skepticism, which Hegel considered an utterly absurd position."[38]
And Solomon interprets the figure of natural consciousness as a half-
hearted "tribute to Descartes," through which Hegel demonstrates
how doubt as philosophical method lands ineluctably in despair.[39] He
notes the implicit reference to Descartes's "resolution" in his *Discourse
on Method* and the first of the *Meditations* in Hegel's description of
"the *resolve*, in Science, not to give oneself over to the thoughts of
others, upon mere authority, but to examine everything for oneself
and follow only one's own conviction, or better still, to produce everything oneself, and accept only one's own deed as true."[40] On this reading, natural consciousness is the figuration of modern European philosophy, beginning with Descartes and Locke and extending through
Hume and Kant; it is the consciousness of a preliminary doubt that
really means despair. While Solomon insists emphatically that "Hegel
is part of the tradition he attacks even if he tampers with and ultimately destroys its basic machinery," he takes the *Phenomenology* to
demonstrate how radicalized doubt, the reductio ad absurdum of
modern epistemology, can only yield despair.[41]

Though it captures some of what is going on in the introduction, Solomon's reading also obscures the important distinction
Hegel draws between Cartesian resolve and the highway of despair,

as well as the tacit opposition between modern skepticism and an ancient skeptical technique preserved in the figure of natural consciousness. Indeed, Hegel explicitly differentiates the "thoroughgoing skepticism" of natural consciousness from the resolutions of modern philosophy. Consider the following elaborations on the passages of natural consciousness:

> The series of configurations which consciousness goes through along this road is, in reality, the detailed history of the education of consciousness itself to the standpoint of Science. That zealous resolve represents this education simplistically as something directly over and done with in the making of the resolution; but the way of the Soul is the actual fulfillment of the resolution, in contrast to the untruth of that view.[42]

Here Hegel indicates that natural consciousness is involved in the business of *actually doing*, through the repetition and reoccurrence of self-loss, what philosophy merely posits as its starting point. Natural consciousness lacks the zealotry of personal conviction, not for any indifference to truth, but because the road traveled "brings about a state of despair [*Verzweiflung*] about all of the so-called natural ideas, thoughts, and opinions, regardless of whether they are one's own or someone else's."[43] This despair leaves consciousness "for the first time competent to examine what the truth is" precisely insofar as no given order of truth is held intact; *everything* is subject to critique, not by the philosopher who resolves to doubt, but by the consciousness that follows the highway of despair as its own itinerary. Put another way, Hegel's point is not to criticize the tendency in modern philosophy to land in despair; it is to revalue despair as the condition for real knowledge and the forms of freedom that come with it.

The term *Verzweiflung* will appear just a few more times in the *Phenomenology*, specifically in Hegel's discussion of sense-certainty. What the introduction suggests, however, is the overall significance of despair for the structure of the work as a whole and the project Hegel undertakes. The German word hangs on "two" (*zwei*), as in a splitting, a tearing, a doubling, a duplication of consciousness, and so bears on its surface a complexity lost in the English translation.[44] But beyond doubt (*Zweifel*), despair is intensification and augmentation (*Ver-*) of a division—a shattering even, so that what was once divided is now disassembled. And so, yes, despair pertains in an important way to doubt and to the legacy of Descartes, Locke, Kant, and the range of philosophical positions that begin from a modern skeptical outlook. But despair is also a negation of doubt, a negation of the simple negation that is doubt—in a word, dialectics.

These excerpts also suggest the importance of despair in the project of knowing and doing, for it is the "negative meaning" (*negative Bedeutung*) that consciousness will give to its accumulated knowledge and its initiation into rites of "real knowledge" (*reales Wissen*)—or, knowledge as it actually develops in and though one's doings. As Hyppolite argues, the *Phenomenology* "insists on the need to place oneself at the point of view of natural consciousness and to lead it gradually to philosophic knowledge: one cannot begin with absolute knowledge."[45] What this means is that Hegel's introduction to the *Phenomenology*, so crucial for its explication of philosophical method, determinate negation, the dialectic of experience, and the formative education of consciousness, also aims to retrieve the ordinary—ordinary experiences and ordinary ways of knowing—from philosophy's scorn and neglect. This is not to say that there is no error in the everyday, or that cognition supplies reliable information about itself and its objects, but it is to insist upon the truth-content contained in the apparent "untruth" of phenomenal knowledge. (Adorno, as we shall see, seizes upon this point, and the result is a variety of critical theory quite distinct from the mandarin elitism with which he is typically aligned. Even his most acerbic remarks on the Culture Industry and mass entertainment express the conviction that critical theory must become philosophically literate in the culture forms of everyday life—Donald Duck, Betty Boop, astrology, Beethoven, jazz, radio, film, existentialism—for the refracted light it casts on the historical shape of knowledge.) "Quite generally, the familiar, just because it is familiar, is not cognitively understood"—by which Hegel means not only that too many of our cherished values "are uncritically taken for granted as familiar, established as valid, and made into fixed points for starting and stopping," but also that those everyday experiences we take for granted remain, paradoxically, opaque to our understanding.[46]

And it is here, in Hegel's revaluation of concrete knowledge, that despair "comes on the scene" and leaves its indelible marks on critical theory. In the *Phenomenology*, despair designates that condition of "natural consciousness which presses forward to true knowledge; or as the way of the Soul which journeys through the series of its own configurations as though they were the stations appointed for it by its own nature."[47] I will return to Hegel's adaptation of Christian imagery later in this chapter, as if in the Stations of the Cross there is an intimation of the trials—and suffering—of consciousness. At this point, it is worth noting that despair appears in this context not as a rare affliction reserved for extraordinary individuals in extraordinary circumstances, but as an ordinary passion.

Tracking the movements of natural consciousness ought not to be mistaken for an injection of "common sense" into the speculative system. Though the concept has some significance in German Idealism, most notably in Kant's *Critique of Judgment*, Hegel treated common sense with considerable disdain. "Since the man of common sense makes his appeal to feeling, to an oracle within his breast," Hegel notes, "he is finished and done with anyone who does not agree; he only has to explain that he has nothing more to say to anyone who does not find and feel the same in himself."[48] For Hegel, the idea of common sense is essentially antiphilosophical, a supplicant to the stirrings in one's heart that, by virtue of the interiority of feeling, cannot venture outside of itself, "cannot focus its thought on a single abstract position, still less on a connected chain of them."[49] Far from opening up the particularity of feeling and sensation to a real and concrete humanity, common sense indicates instead "the anti-human, the merely animal," in that it "consists in staying within the sphere of feeling and being able to communicate only at that level."[50] Natural consciousness, by contrast, consists precisely in this movement outside of and beyond itself; "it is something that goes beyond limits, and since these limits are its own, it is something that goes beyond itself." This is a transcending consciousness, and in its own transcending activity it finds confirmation of the inescapability of limits. Natural consciousness, in contrast with the man of common sense, is armed with an impulse to exteriorize, to engage a world of objects and others, even if this engagement is also "absolute dismemberment"—in this way, it is a foot soldier of freedom in Hegel's distinctive sense. The man of common sense is antihuman; natural consciousness is all too human.

Furthermore, natural consciousness mustn't be mistaken for a static or fixed state, against which the innovations of culture ought to be measured, what Hegel will sometimes call life in its immediacy or, again, animal life.[51] Nor does it correspond to the "state of nature" in social contract theory—a timeless and unchanging condition ruled by natural law—in that the "natural" here names the dynamic interface between the subject and substance. Consciousness, in Hegel, is always *on the move*, "by its own nature" propelled forward "so that it may purify itself for the life of the Spirit."[52] "If it wishes to remain in a state of unthinking inertia," Hegel adds, "then thought troubles its thoughtlessness, and its own unrest disturbs its inertia."[53] This point is crucial for appreciating why the condition of despair is not quite that of unhappy consciousness, an issue to which I will return in the next section. For now, suffice it to say that natural consciousness has nothing to do with any contemplative inwardness, detached sentimentality, or even an ironic pragmatism. This is a form of life thoroughly immersed and earnestly engaged, not only in the pursuit of self-knowledge, but in the worldly conditions of its existence. Nancy is right to remind us that the "Hegelian subject is not to be confused with subjectivity as a separate and one-sided agency for synthesizing representations, nor with subjectivity as the exclusive interiority of a personality."[54] This subject is always outside of itself, always at odds with itself, always in active misrelation to a world of others and objects.

If natural consciousness is not quite the skeptical subject of modern philosophy, this is also because it is aligned with the wisdom of the ancients. In the preface Hegel notes that "the manner of study in ancient times differed from that of the modern age in that the former was the proper and complete formation of the natural consciousness," meaning that ancient philosophy strove to infuse every aspect of existence with the universality of thought.[55] "Putting itself to the test at every point of its existence, and philosophizing about everything it came across," the ancients made of sensuous and concrete life the subject and object of philosophy. Spirit, too, is defined by this work of spinning all elements of everyday life through the wheel of conscious self-reflection: "[the] life of Spirit is not the life that shrinks from death and keeps itself untouched by devastation, but rather the life that endures it and maintains itself in it."[56] For the ancients, philosophy meant injecting abstraction into the ordinary and bathing concrete, sensuous experience in the light of pure thinking. For the moderns, by contrast, "the abstract is ready-made" and disconnected from the real. What is needed, says Hegel, is a philosophy bent not on "purging the individual of an immediate, sensuous mode of apprehension . . . but rather [on] just the opposite, [on] freeing determinate thoughts from their fixity so as to give actuality to the universal, and impart to it spiritual life."[57]

Judith Shklar's political interpretation of the *Phenomenology* pays particular attention to Hegel's esteem for the Greeks and presents the work from 1807 as Hegel's philosophical requiem to this lost order of things. Here is Shklar:

> Later Hegel was to ask us simply to forget the lost world and to accept the rules such as they are. The *Phenomenology* was, however, his elegy to that world of freedom. It is the remembrance of the steps which led mankind away from experienced happiness to a vision of truth, from freedom as ethics to freedom as the knowledge of necessity. These two freedoms have nothing in common. The freedom of knowledge is not any sort of happiness and Hegel did not claim that it was.[58]

Shklar's is a wistful and elegant reading of the *Phenomenology* as remembrance, and I think she is right—though this is hardly the prevailing view—that there is no "experienced happiness" in Hegel. For Shklar, the promise of happiness is embedded in either a nostalgic longing for an ancient and irrecoverable Athens or a utopian gesture toward a free polity. Shklar again: "They are the only real examples of a happy consciousness. Their happiness is one that mankind has lost or *maybe* has not yet attained. In either case, it is the 'utopia,' the nowhere, which illuminates what freedom, in contrast to lordship and bondage, would be."[59] What does Shklar mean by freedom in this context? What it so frequently means in Hegel: the absence of a tension—if not an established harmony—between individual and ethical life, between one's particular desires and the general demands of the community, between subjective and objective spirit. I think Shklar is correct that this idea of freedom is a utopian one in the *Phenomenology*, either past or future but nowhere present. But I also think there is another idea of freedom that is an undercurrent of the *Phenomenology*, resolutely presentist, and which at once deepens and complicates "the knowledge of necessity." This is the freedom that draws its strength from the passions. Shklar's reading also suggests that the evolution of Hegel's thought involved trading a youthful romance with the Greeks in Jena for the adult embrace of the fate of modernity in Berlin. (Might this also mean that the *Philosophy of Right* is best read not as the consummation of the endlessly deferred political dream of the *Phenomenology*, but as an elaboration on the political consequences of *amor fati*?) Ultimately, I am suggesting that Shklar is too quick to pass over the figure of natural consciousness, at once ancient and modern, in whom freedom is neither ethics nor knowledge of necessity, but consists in tarrying with the negative.

Natural consciousness is no undifferentiated unity, no archaic wholeness, no original self-sameness; consciousness "begins" in diremption. The highway of despair is steady and patient struggle interrupted by episodes of self-inflicted violence. Here is Hegel again: "When natural consciousness entrusts itself straightway to science, it makes an attempt, induced by it knows not what, to walk on its head too, just this once; the compulsion to assume this unwonted posture, and to go about in it is a violence it is expected to do to itself, all unprepared and seemingly without necessity."[60] Hyppolite has argued for reading this passage as a critique of Schelling, as if consciousness can be made to walk on its head without that long and difficult journey which is also the preparation of consciousness for a scientific standpoint. The paragraph that follows seems to support this reading, in which Hegel insists that this formative education "will not be what is commonly understood by an initiation of the unscientific consciousness into Science" and criticizes "the rapturous enthusiasm which, like a shot from a pistol, begins straight away with absolute knowledge."[61] Later in the preface, in the context of a retrieval of the truth-content contained in falsity, Hegel will again reject an approach to knowledge that begins "straight away" with science.[62] Yet the refusal of enthusiasm and the insistence that philosophy ought not to presume as a point of departure what is, in truth, the result of a process do not wholly resolve the question of violence raised in the passage quoted. Hegel's philosophy, too, bears witness to the movement of consciousness from an "unscientific" to a scientific standpoint, a movement for which consciousness qua consciousness can *never* be fully ready. Self-inflicted violence is everywhere in the *Phenomenology*. Indeed, Hegel's emphasis on the processual quality of knowledge may intensify the problem: since science is not just a product but a process, not a singular achievement but the repetition and consummation of a certain comportment, this is a seemingly unnecessary violence that is also unending. Of course, these self-inflicted wounds of Spirit only *seem* unnecessary; Hegel's point is that they are in fact integral to the process.

This image suggests a somewhat surprising link between science and violence—a necessary violence that consciousness suffers at its own hands no matter its readiness, but violence still. There is, too, some absurdity attached to this figure: it does not know why it does what it does, and it endures its self-imposed suffering as if for no good reason. And this ordeal is corporeal. There is physicality in thinking and bodily conditioning that comes with regular adjustment to the rigors of real knowledge. It is a reminder that Hegel's idealism draws its nourishment from somatic experience and material existence.

Might it be that walking on one's head—and, presumably, thinking on one's feet—is itself a pleasure, a felt compulsion that becomes delight? And might it be that the episodic joys of the dialectic reside right here, in the contortions of the negative, in the place where we will also find despair, where movement is "all unprepared and seemingly without necessity"? In posing these questions, I reveal my hesitation with Hegel's insistence about the Absolute, that "progress toward this goal is also unhalting, and short of it no satisfaction is to be found at any of the stations on the way."[63] This hesitation is, in part, because Hegel here assumes a dialectic that never stands still or veers off course. Further, Hegel is otherwise all too aware of the temporary satisfactions found at *every* station on the way—*and the more lasting pleasures that comes with disquietude.* Despair is not unhappiness, for reasons I will detail in the next section. Katrin Pahl calls it elastic: "Consciousness always bounces back" and, for her, the highway of despair is a rubber road.[64] On my account, despair is the passion with which the subject keeps things moving, not necessarily forward and not at a steady pace, not for good reason or by the guidance of faith, but by the accidental and occasional suspension of routinized activity—or, the "just this once" that might also be called *freedom*.

3

Consider how the approach developed here differs from the one advanced by Kimberly Hutchings in her book *Hegel and Feminist Philosophy*, this notwithstanding my support for her efforts to bring Hegel into conversation with feminist critique. She reads Hegel as "the first philosopher to identify his philosophical project with moving through and beyond the 'way of despair,' in which the inadequacy of thinking in terms of binary oppositions is demonstrated and overcome."[65] Bringing a Hegelian perspective to feminism, says Hutchings, reveals how the social, political, legal, and linguistic forms that produce our gendered order also produce a set of binaries that feminist theorists, despite their best efforts, unwittingly reproduce. While she admits Hegel's own "patriarchal and at times misogynist" attitudes toward women, Hutchings also insists that a renewed Hegelianism promises relief from feminist despair. Hegel's philosophy undoes the antinomies of modern thought and, Hutchings concludes, spells the end of despair. I do not see despair as another word for binary thinking, undone by the dialectic. I see despair, instead, as the name for that undoing that the dialectic initiates.

Hutchings continues in the venerable Hegelian tradition charted by Gillian Rose, for whom the Hegelian procedure is the absolute repudiation of despair—and the repudiation of despair in the Absolute. This procedure is expressed in what Rose would make the epigraph to her remarkable philosophical memoir, repeating Saint Silouan: "Keep your mind in hell, and despair not."[66] Indeed, the virtuosic interpretation of Hegel that Rose develops, first in *Hegel Contra Sociology* and then more systematically in *The Broken Middle* and the posthumously published *Mourning Becomes the Law*, constitutes the most serious and formidable foil to the reading I propose in this chapter. Tracking the mishaps and errors of recognition and the missteps and misadventures of the self on the journey toward the Absolute, Rose cautions against a caricatured view of Hegel that would reduce his thinking—and his writing—to a completed and closed system. "Perhaps we may begin by asking," Rose speculates, "why the tradition sets up—in order to worship and to denigrate—the idol of the 'System,' and the imperial sovereignty of 'Hegel': authority and author."[67] Her study of the *Phenomenology* aims to correct this view of Hegel— a view that reveals more about the "tradition" and its idolatry than it tells us about Hegel—by calling attention to the dramatic play of personae in the text. Here is Rose:

> First, spirit in the *Phenomenology* means the drama of misrecognition which ensues at every stage and transition of the work—a ceaseless comedy, according to which our aims and outcomes constantly mismatch each other, and provoke yet another revised aim, action, and discordant outcome. Secondly, reason, therefore, is comic, full of surprises, of unanticipated happenings, so that comprehension is always provisional and preliminary. . . . Thirdly, the law is no longer that of Greek ethical life; it is no longer tragic.[68]

Comedic in its tone and in its fate, the *Phenomenology*, for Rose, chronicles not the imperial triumph of reason transparent to itself, but the theatrics of selves as they endlessly strive to know their world and one another. To underscore the tonality and temperament of this comedic spirit and distinguish it from any melancholic torpor, Rose references Hegel's depiction of the comical in his *Aesthetics*: "[The] comical as such implies an infinite light-heartedness and confidence felt by someone raised altogether above his own inner contradiction and not bitter or miserable in it at all; this is the bliss and ease of a man who, being sure of himself, can bear the frustrations of his aims and achievements."[69] Against the hyperindividualistic "logophobia" of the postmodern and "all dualistic relations to 'the other,'" Rose attends to the "broken middle" that emerges in Hegelian philosophy, "the third term which arises out of misrecognition of desire, of work, of my and of your self-relation mediated by the self-relation of the other."[70] This "broken middle" constitutes the secret of Hegel's (and Kierkegaard's) philosophy, and Rose deploys it against the antinomies of conventional metaphysics and those inadvertently perpetuated by the more recent attempts at postmetaphysical thought.

The view from the broken middle is distinctly Trinitarian, this notwithstanding Vincent Lloyd's elegant depiction of Rose's project as the renewal of a *secular* faith.[71] To my mind, "secular" seems not quite the right term, for it typically denotes either the separation between religious and political orders or the division between the faithful subject and the "living" law that expresses this faith, however imperfectly. Law, for Rose, militates *against* the separation implied by the idea of secularism. Here is Rose, again, on the law as the "third term" that emerges out of the drama of recognition: "The law, therefore, is not the superior term which suppresses the local and the contingent, nor is it the symbolic which catches every child in the closed circuit of its patriarchal embrace. The law is the falling toward or away from mutual recognition, the triune relationship, the middle, formed and deformed by reciprocal self-relations."[72] The ambiguity in this last sentence is revealing; the law appears as *both* the expression of a relationship of recognition *and* that which establishes and secures that relationship, if not in a "patriarchal" fashion, then at least in a manner *becoming* of the law, befitting the logos of the law. If the law is the historical iteration of the broken middle, it is also that which bears witness to the universality of reason.

"Postmodernism" signifies, for Rose, a "*despairing rationalism without reason*"—a formula for "*aberrated* not *inaugurated*" mourning, a lamentation that "*cannot work*" because it substitutes the "pathos of the concept in place of its logos."[73] In its multiple variants, from deconstruction to ironism to cultural pluralism, postmodernism is the generic pejorative for the various "attempts to quiet and deny the broken middle," where the work of mourning becomes the law.[74] Postmodernism, says Rose, is not simply antinomian; it bears the mark of the unemployed, the unworkable, the laziness of a lament that has neither the will nor the energy to *work* at itself, the idleness of philosophy that becomes idolatry (evidenced, one presumes, by the prevailing wisdom about "Hegel"—the author of the system).[75] In this reconfiguration of the broken middle, Rose locates the real and lasting wisdom of Hegel's thought: its comprehension of *misrecognition* as provocations to persevere in the difficult work of recognition, its elevation of the law as the fragile and fractured site from which recognition succeeds or fails, and its representation of the movement of the Absolute as divine comedy.

For Rose, Hegel is a philosopher not of redemption or even reconciliation, but *revelation*—and in this respect, my approach to the *Phenomenology* draws heavily from her work. At the same time, she betrays her deepest Hegelianism in her language of inauguration and completion. Mourning must *become* the law in order to avoid the lapse into melancholia, and any philosophy worthy of the name cannot but *work*. Moreover, for all her attention to the complexity and open-endedness of the drama of recognition, and notwithstanding efforts to dethrone Hegel as the "authority" presiding over a closed system, Rose has no explanation for why and on what grounds the "tradition" has so poorly (mis)understood him, how it is that "Hegel" has proved such a dependable idol. She so assuredly discards a reading of Hegel in terms of the system and its completion that she neglects those passages in the *Phenomenology* and elsewhere that lend support to this approach. More importantly, what she describes as Hegel's "authorship without authority" seems to verge close to a representation of *this* authorship as authoritative, untouchable, decisive to the point of being nearly indistinguishable from authority.

And what is authorized, exactly? Timothy Bahti poses a number of relevant questions about what we are doing when reading Hegel:

> In "looking upon" . . . the unfolding of its argument, are "we"—can "we" be—doing anything other than reduplicating and re-presenting . . . Hegel's argument about consciousness' knowing itself as knowing of its alteration of the object of knowledge into its knowing or consciousness of the object? Or are "we" knowing not only what consciousness comes to know, but also what it does—or can—not? . . . Do "we" do this through "mere looking upon" the argument, as if a passive seeing were interpretive reading and philosophic understanding? Or does "our" reading somehow perform, participate in, and bring about what the writing—Hegel's text here—only represents or signified, *vorstellt* and *nennt*?[76]

It is not clear why these questions do not apply to any number of writing and reading practices, or what restricts these questions to the study of the *Phenomenology* and to the preface in particular. That said, Bahti is right to emphasize how reading the text is to "somehow perform, participate in, and bring about" what the writing presents. But it is also true that the reader does not initiate this drama, but is rather initiated into it. And just as the reader is asked to perform the movements of consciousness, she is also reminded that she needn't perform them because another figure—neither author nor reader—has endured this lonely highway.

<h1 style="text-align:center">4</h1>

Natural consciousness is a naïve consciousness, and its flawed and narrow truths will be systematically disrupted and its attachments continuously loosened by the acquisition of knowledge, by the encounter with others, and by an objective world that it erroneously sees as separate from its subjectivity. On the other hand, natural consciousness is the most "experienced" of participants in this drama of Spirit, and its experience is the model. This is a resilient figure, more so than most readers who will not get past the preface. And I am suggesting that, in the contortions of natural consciousness, we can catch a glimpse of a hidden undercurrent in the *Phenomenology*, an idea of freedom that is linked not to reconciliation or remembrance, but to the restlessness of the negative. If there is pathos in this experience of freedom, in this invitation to utter dismemberment, there is also pleasure. This is precisely why negativity always threatens to become furious, to be absolute fury.

The privilege of spectatorship, though, also means being spared the suffering that comes with the passages of Spirit.[77] Readers do not endure the repeated loss of self, the recurring assault on conditional truths, the wounds of Spirit precisely because the highway has been traveled before. The work of the negative has been done. In this way, natural consciousness is a sacrificial figure in the dialectic of Spirit, undone at every turn so that the revelatory truth of negativity might be reassimilated into a philosophical retrospective. Many commentators have pointed to the Christological dimensions of the *Phenomenology*, but these analyses have focused for the most part on the Trinitarian structure of the Hegelian system, on the significance of Christian incarnation for the synthesis of particularity and universality in the Absolute, or on Hegel's use of the example of Christ to develop an ethical teaching in a post-Christian world.[78] My point here is at once more particular and more generic: I am concerned with the specific depiction of natural consciousness in the *Phenomenology* as the figuration of a despair, absorbing the violent and destructive fury of negativity in a march toward freedom. In this way, the text reads as a philosophical *passion play*, a staging of the somatic suffering and spiritual torment that natural consciousness suffers so that we—author and readers—may be free. And in this freedom, our attitude toward natural consciousness is ever shifting: we are led, at different points, to admire the tenacity, admonish the naïveté, and imitate the patient suffering. I am not advancing a strong argument for the Christian character of the *Phenomenology*. I am highlighting certain Christological tropes in Hegel's portrait of despair and underscoring the sacrificial scene upon which Hegel's revelation depends.[79] Hegel mobilizes despair as a worldly passion, without dispensing with the theological traces and revelatory powers that a long line of Christian thinkers has believed to be harbored in despair. And the *Phenomenology* might be read as an induction into a dialectical practice of despair.

Despair is not itself a symptom of a "religious consciousness" torn between worldly and divine orders. And I do not see despair as a "stage" in the progression of Spirit, one that indicates and anticipates its overcoming. Despair is not unhappy consciousness. Consider in this context Hyppolite's claim that

> Unhappy consciousness is the fundamental theme of the *Phenomenology*. Consciousness, as such, is in principle always unhappy consciousness, for it has not yet achieved the concrete identity of certainty and truth. The happy consciousness is either a naïve consciousness which is not yet aware of its misfortune or a consciousness that has overcome its duality and discovered a unity beyond separation. For this reason we find the theme of unhappy consciousness present in various forms throughout the *Phenomenology*.[80]

My position is different. Despair, as I see it, is the animating force of the *Phenomenology*. Consciousness, as such, is in principle always in despair, for it is always on the move, always coming undone. Note how Hyppolite's treatment of unhappiness implies the promise of a future reconciliation; the *Phenomenology* chronicles the movements of consciousness into and then out of unhappiness. The negative is central to Hyppolite's interpretation of Hegel, central to his commentaries on both the *Phenomenology* and the *Philosophy of History*. But his interpretation is also guided, at every point, by this promise of a future reconciliation, which Hyppolite likely absorbs from Hegel's ambitions for a philosophical science, but which only sometimes seems the animating force of consciousness itself. Other times, consciousness seems guided not by the promise of a future reconciliation, but by what is revealed—and what practices are made possible—when things come undone in the present.

Considering Hegel in terms of what has come apart in our present, Judith Butler describes the transition from "Lordship and Bondage" to "The Freedom of Self-Consciousness: Stoicism, Skepticism, and Unhappy Consciousness" as "one of the least interrogated of Hegel's philosophical movements."[81] She suggests that this neglect has something to do with the way in which the Left has learned to rely on Hegel:

> Perhaps because the chapter on lordship and bondage secured a liberationist narrative for various progressive political visions, most readers have neglected to pay attention to the resolution of freedom into self-enslavement at the end of the chapter. Insofar as recent theory has called into question both the assumption of a progressive history and the status of the subject, the dystopic resolution of "Lordship and Bondage" has perhaps regained a timely significance.[82]

Unhappy consciousness is the portrait of ourselves after dreams have become dystopia, after liberatory projects have fallen into disrepair, after progress, meaning, and reason in history give way to complexity, contingency, and new forms of subjection and unfreedom. Butler casts the movement from freedom-in-bondage to Stoicism as a "fearful flight from fear"—a formulation that points out not only the importance of the passions in Hegel, but also how the passions are set in

motion against themselves. Following Hyppolite, I would also emphasize the importance of unhappiness as a recurring condition of consciousness in the *Phenomenology*. Against Hyppolite, I see this condition as one for which *despair is the only way out*. Again, despair is not
unhappiness; it is the radical unmooring that allows consciousness to
negate unhappiness.

In Stoicism, this fearful flight is represented as an attachment to
disembodied thought: consciousness renounces the body as that finite
shell that preserves the tremble of death. This consciousness refuses
the fruits of work, for left on them are the imprints of dependence and
servitude. Stoicism means the disavowal of all that is exposed and vul-
nerable in bodily and natural existence. It is a repudiation of "precarious life" by way of the withdrawal into pure thought. Robert Solomon
is right that "Stoicism is a rejection of the master-slave dialectic, for it
realizes that whether as master or as servant, there is no escape from
dependency"—what is so fascinating is how, in the Stoic imagination,
the exposure entailed in embodied existence comes to seem like another
imprisonment.[83] Stoicism is the retreat from the world of objects
and others into the interior life of thought itself. At this stage, self-
consciousness postulates the movement of life as pure thought,
absorbing the world of detail, difference, and density into "the pure
movement of thinking."[84] Things in their specificity lose all significance in themselves and consciousness attends only to the free movements of abstract thinking. However, as Hegel argues, Stoic freedom is
radically incomplete, for it remains the philosophical worldview of an
enslaved subject, bearing the wounds of bondage. Stoic consciousness
takes refuge from slavery in "the pure universality of thought" without
dismantling a structure of dependence.[85] The interior freedom of pure
thought is contradicted by external subjection, by the persistence of
a world over which self-consciousness cannot be free. Therefore, Stoicism remains a fundamentally incoherent position, in which the subject attempts to enact an impossible withdrawal from the world. From
its contradiction emerges Skepticism. If Stoic consciousness withdraws
from the world of determinate things, Skepticism represents the active
negation of the determinate character of life itself. Stoicism involves a
retreat from the world, anchored by a presumption that only thought
itself can capture the reality of existence. Skepticism, by contrast with a

Stoic posture, dispenses with all conceits concerning the reality of the world: if there is a world at all, it remains essentially unknowable and unintelligible. As Charles Taylor puts it, Skepticism "is the polemical consequence of Stoicism."[86] It represents not simply indifference to the objective world, but an active denial of it. And yet, Skeptical consciousness remains mired in precisely the conundrum Stoic consciousness confronts: despite its now active denial of the determinate world, an embodied subject cannot fully liberate oneself from the mutability of embodied existence. Consciousness at this stage remains caught in incoherence: the Skeptic denies the existence of a world using arguments and positions drawn precisely from the world it purports to deny. Here is Hegel: "It affirms the nullity of seeing, hearing, etc. yet is itself seeing, hearing, etc."[87]

As the Skeptic discovers that he cannot simultaneously deny the world and then anchor that denial in considerations gathered from the world, the new form of consciousness emerges, the interiorization of this contradiction. Unhappy consciousness is this inner life of division, turmoil, contradiction, and schizophrenia. On the one hand, the self is dependent upon the contingencies and changes in the life process. On the other hand, the subject longs to be self-identical, unchanging, and immutable. Consciousness becomes unhappy to the extent that it remains at odds with itself, alienated from itself and its freedom. Longing for transcendence and yet mired in the contingency and dynamism of the life process, the self "which reaches its fulfillment in the figure of unhappy consciousness is only the torment of the spirit struggling to rise again to an objective state but failing to reach it."[88] Unhappy consciousness, to manage this inner oscillation and anxious longing, displaces the desire for independence onto a divine realm of freedom, identity, and immutability. At the moment that consciousness might mobilize passion against resignation from the world, unhappy consciousness shrinks into the consoling arms of a wholly remote and mysterious divinity. It is "unhappy" not because of its faith, but because of the resignation implied in its faith.

Unhappy consciousness proceeds through three distinct phases, of which only the last offers the hint of its resolution. The first, which Hegel describes as the "musical state of the soul," describes the immediate encounter with God. At the foot of the cross, the disciple beholds the divine, rejoicing in the possibility of a mutual recognition between God and man. Yet consciousness stands before God as an *embodied* creature, a finite subject of will, passion, desire. Consequently a new master-slave relationship is established, propelling the subject to the second stage in unhappy consciousness, in which the self dutifully engages in practices of thanksgiving for a self and a world that are God's creation. All this thanksgiving serves to reinforce the all-too-human imperfections of the subject before God. It is a posture of *devotion* that mimetically reenacts the unfortunate scene of judgment. Unhappy consciousness deems itself unworthy of God insofar as it stands before the Absolute as corporeal and finite, bearing the wounds of negativity and bondage, moved by desires and passions now internalized as sins to repent. Butler suggests that the pathology of unhappy consciousness is a "negative narcissism, an engaged preoccupation with what is most debased and defiled about it," and she has traced an echo of the Hegelian critique in Nietzsche's attack on the ascetic ideal and Freud's account of instinctual sublimation.[89] Unhappy consciousness renounces the body in all its particularity, but in this renunciation it cannot find escape from corporeality. Rather, without being able to take flight from desires, passions, and will, the body is offered up to God through ritualistic fasting and mortification. In unhappy consciousness, passion turns against itself in self-abnegation and self-beratement. This self-sacrifice is orchestrated and sanctified by the mediating priest or minister, who promises that a life spent in imitation of the self-sacrificial passion of Christ will be rewarded with eternal pleasure and happiness.

Butler is right to stress that the mediating figure of the priest is essential to this sacrificial scene and to the critique of unhappy consciousness Hegel offers. The paradox Hegel exposes in unhappy consciousness is not quite that self-negating activity is itself a reassertion of the self negated, that the self-sacrificing subject is involved in what is itself an assertion of will, or that the sacrificial ideal functions to mask the will to power that set it in motion. This is Nietzsche's critique of the ascetic ideal. Rather, the problem Hegel exposes in unhappy consciousness is that this supposed self-sacrifice is itself mediated by another, endowed with positivity, meaning, and significance by the priest. Unhappy consciousness is the ritualistic withdrawal from concrete historical life and the dispassionate renunciation of the flesh. One wonders if unhappy consciousness is not quite "religious consciousness," as Charles Taylor suggests, but a consciousness that fails to appreciate that concrete historical life is the true stage for this self-sacrifice and that a genuinely sacred posture is one of passionate, reflexive immersion in the real.[90] Despair opposes unhappiness, not only for its resignation but for a cold dispassion that drapes itself in religious enthusiasm and righteousness.

If despair is not unhappiness, in the ordinary sense or in Hegel's specific usage, it is also not quite tragic vision. In her recent work on Hegel and the French Revolution, Rebecca Comay develops an interpretation of the Hegelian Absolute in connection with Lady Macbeth's pronouncement: "what's done cannot be undone."[91] It is undeniable that there is an irreversibility in the movements Hegel tracks. But I have also suggested that the *Phenomenology of Spirit* is a demonstration of what is always coming undone. I read this demonstration not as a meditation on "mourning sickness" or in terms of the tragic, but for the connection it establishes between reason and passion. And I am arguing that, in the "Bacchanalian revel in which no member is not drunk," the concrete experience of freedom— drenched in despair, aligned with the accidental and the nonsensical, felt as violence—spoils the "state of repose" that a sober philosophy of Spirit promises.[92]

I have hoped to recover that voice in Hegel's *Phenomenology* that speaks not of clear beginnings and certain endings, but of the forces set in motion by the restlessness of the negative. And I have gestured toward a buried idea of freedom in Hegel that is found in the play of passions. This is an order of freedom radically apart from reconciliation and remembrance, which does not soar above despair, but allows us to find our footing in it. It remains an undeveloped idea in Hegel, who took as an article of faith that philosophy must furnish a way out of despair.

Kierkegaard shares in this faith. If it seems that I have done interpretive violence to Hegel by shaping his text into an almost Kierkegaardian form, my treatment of Kierkegaard in the following chapter reenacts that violence in the opposite direction. Above all, I aim to retrieve Kierkegaard and the pseudonymous texts for contemporary critical theory. Few writers better appreciate the passions, the paradoxes, and the pathos of philosophy. And *The Sickness Unto Death* is perhaps the most rigorous and systematic analysis of despair in the Western philosophical tradition. Kierkegaard excavated a buried idea in Hegel and made it the foundation for an analytic of faith. But just as I have tried to think despair under and against the reconciliatory voice in Hegel, I want to think despair against the edifying voice in Kierkegaard. That he was a religious poet with bourgeois sensibilities and little interest in political questions is only a part of the picture. More important is how despair gets reinscribed as a spiritual sickness and a sickness of Spirit.

2
Kierkegaard's Diagnostics

You cannot refute Kierkegaard: you must simply read him, consider, and then get on with your work—but "with your eyes fixed on the exception."

—Paul Ricoeur, "Philosophy After Kierkegaard"

1

The writings of Søren Kierkegaard present a notorious challenge to the reader in search of definitive answers to the questions they pose about despair, anxiety, and other "wounds of Spirit." While Kierkegaard—under his own name or with his many pseudonyms—hoped to elucidate a Christian remedy to the seemingly intractable problem of modern despair, his reformulation of faith seems somewhat feeble in the face of it. Kierkegaard's texts simply cannot be measured by the solutions he offers, which are consistently inadequate to the questions he raises. Some of his readers have looked to the upbuilding discourses (the "religious" writings penned under his own name) for prescriptions that supplement the diagnostic writings (the pseudonymous writings on aesthetics and ethics). But if we take seriously Kierkegaard's own claim that his upbuilding discourses are "not sermons, because [their] author does not have the authority to *preach*, [but] 'upbuilding discourses,' not discourses for upbuilding, because the speaker by no means claims to be a *teacher*," then it seems that these texts will not furnish the type of instruction we have come to demand from philosophical critique.

Kierkegaard's rejection of the role of preacher or pedagogue produced in him a deep resistance to the institutions of academic scholarship, where much of the work of critical theory presently takes place. Professional philosophers—that hybrid between preacher and pedagogue—coined only lifeless and lethargic abstractions. Whatever forms of knowledge might be contained in these abstractions, Kierkegaard believed them to be far removed from real experience. (Whether his massive body of writing manages to get any closer is a different question. Pseudonyms are one way of dealing with this distance.) Kierkegaard was a deeply anti-political thinker in his aversion to the powers of collectivities, his resistance to any social or political forms that would assume priority over the subject, and his conviction that the value of individuality could be neither radically enhanced nor substantially impaired by any transformation in political life. He thought of himself as a "religious poet" and believed spiritual despair—not political oppression, economic exploitation, or social alienation—to be the plague of his present age. So, notwithstanding a theological turn in contemporary theory, Kierkegaard is a dicey source for contemporary critique. We know him mostly through the existentialist philosophies of the twentieth century, and even there as a thinker for whom freedom is a subjective and spiritual achievement, not a political or historical project.

That said, there is something in the way we have come to talk about despair that resonates with Kierkegaard's thinking. His lasting significance might be measured, for instance, in the prevailing suspicion that unbounded critique is a recipe for resignation. Like so many contemporary critics, he believed despair to be *the* sickness of the age. Where Kierkegaard departs from many of the present-day prophets of hope is in appreciating how the border patrolling between reason and its "other"—the paradoxical, the absurd, the extraordinary, the passionate—symptomatizes the despair from which critique is often presumed to need rescue. Kierkegaard's critique of reason was, of course, not a rejection of the powers of human rationality to upset entrenched traditions, conventions, and authorities. But he was insistent upon the limits of reason in clearing the pathway out of despair. In his elaborations on anxiety, fear, and despair, Kierkegaard advances a critical discourse on the passions, on those forces that circulate at the outer limits of rationality and resist philosophical disclosure.

The recovery of a Kierkegaardian voice in contemporary critical theory turns on what many scholars have now recognized as the ambiguous debt to Hegel contained in the inward dialectic of faith. In the previous chapter, I suggested that critical theory might tarry with the complex of passions that exceed dialectical synthesis in Spirit and frustrate Hegel's own confidence in the all-embracing historical force of reason. Kierkegaard took passion as the repressed source of any philosophical system. But Kierkegaard's break with Hegel did not free him from the urge to rescue consciousness from despair. Quite the contrary: as Hegel's dialectic falls into disrepair, the sickness unto death assumes epidemic proportions.

Kierkegaard calls Hegel's system an "essay in the comical"—its comic element being the author's failure to avow the system's condition of possibility, or the real existence of the man who thought it up. Hegel alleges that the system begins with no presuppositions, but on Kierkegaard's view, it begins with the principle passions of existence: faith and despair. Dialectical categories do not circulate in the ether, but derive from concrete and corporeal life. Hegel the philosopher—an existing individual—is systematically effaced in his philosophy. And his philosophy repeats that same gesture, subsuming individual experience into a speculative totality and synthetic unity. For Kierkegaard, this erasure of the real subject—without whom the system cannot find articulation in the first place—is the sleight of hand by which the dialectical system maintains itself as a totality of rational reflection and accomplished mediation. Forsaking the subjectivity that makes the system possible, Hegel never manages to get beyond it. Rather, despair and faith endure as the irreconciled passions that prevent the consummation of philosophical science. What is so funny about Hegel, for Kierkegaard, is that he always lands back where he begins, back to despair, back to a philosophical yearning that cannot be satisfied by reason alone. As Richard Bernstein puts it in his classic *Praxis and Action*, "Like Marx, but in a drastically different way, Kierkegaard wants to force us 'beyond' philosophy."[1]

Kierkegaard says that Hegel's speculative system promises a salvation that it cannot deliver, as the movements of consciousness are lifted from individual experience and abstracted into categories of abstract thought. The persistence of despair as a philosophical problem confirmed to Kierkegaard the extent to which reason can neither relinquish its "religious" residue, nor sublimate through concepts the all-too-human passions that rebel against rational reflection. Put differently, modern philosophical discourse taps a reservoir of faith that it cannot sustain within the system. What is more, Hegel mistakenly assumes that this faith is an a priori of natural consciousness, as opposed to what Kierkegaard says it is: the rare achievement of real individuals. The repetition of religious striving is no "simple" repetition, but it also does not conform to any given teleology. Contra Hegel, Kierkegaard reintroduces a radical discordance between thought and being, between consciousness and communication, between inner and outer experience. And he proffers a choice about how to live in the context of inevitable diremption, a choice between despair and faith.

This either/or, as I see it, does not so much resolve as restate the problem, in which the sickness of the age prepares the subject for faith, but also keeps faith forever out of reach. Despair energizes and it paralyzes. It trains subjectivity for a real leap of faith but also inhibits and undermines any real movement. Kierkegaard's account of faith, which substantially reworks and revises a Hegelian narrative as existential Christian drama, harbors its own secret promise of the Absolute. This Absolute can only find indirect, ironic, or absurd articulation in profane language. In a stunning twist, faith is to do the work that Hegel's philosophy had reserved for reason. Faith relieves subjectivity from despair.

In a lecture from 1963, Paul Ricoeur notes that when Kierkegaard's texts were first translated in the 1920s (into German) and 1930s (into French), "he was called upon to play a double role: on the one hand as a thinker of protest, on the other as a thinker of renewal."[2] And Ricoeur postulates that Kierkegaard's protest—against Hegel, against German Idealism, against the philosophical "system"—was more ambiguous than his early readers in France and Germany appreciated. He sees Kierkegaard's writings on anxiety and despair as the work of a thinker who transposed living experiences into a well-honed dialectic which was based not on experience but on abstractly imagined artificial stages of existence. These stages were then elaborated into a fractured dialectic of the finite and the infinite, the possible and the actual, the unconscious and the conscious, etc. And this fractured dialectic, we suspect, had rather more in common with [his] own best enemy—Hegel—than with his supposed intellectual heirs.[3]

Ricoeur is hardly the first to suggest the dialectical quality of Kierkegaard's stages of life's way, nor is he alone in his insistence that Kierkegaard's protest against Hegel was a complicated one. For Ricoeur, Kierkegaard's dialectic—like his own best enemy's—is *fractured*, which seems to have something to do with its abstract, artificial, and imagined quality. I think Ricoeur is right that the stages of life's way are not based on experience, that despair remains an abstraction in Kierkegaard's thought. Perhaps even more so than in Hegel, for recall that despair in the *Phenomenology* circulates in misrelations between selves and others, between subjects and objects. Kierkegaard's investment in the individual is chiefly a divestment in the world of others and objects. Despair at its heights: "to be unwilling to hope in the possibility that an earthly need, a temporal cross, can come to an end."[4]

The equally important point, as I see it, is that Kierkegaard's presentation of the passions exceeds the experiential—or, better, indicates what remains unavailable to direct experience and what experiences resist articulation. Despair, which haunts subjectivity at every "stage," is not an object of experience, though it may be felt through a range of emotions and affects. Despair is how the Kierkegaardian subject relates to itself and the world. It is an *orientation* to experience, not an object of experience. In this way, it runs parallel—though, importantly, does not overlap—with Marx's concept of social alienation.[5] The three distinct stages Kierkegaard describes—the aesthetic, the ethical, and the religious—do not automatically give way to one another according to a successionist logic. Instead, each represents a particular reckoning with subjectivity split between the finite and the infinite, the actual and the possible, necessity and freedom. If Kierkegaard's dialectic is permanently fractured, then this is because the struggle against despair is something that must be lived as a continuous and ongoing activity, not only understood and synthesized in rational reflection. Indeed, it is this diremption—between understanding and living the struggle against despair—that comprises the core of Kierkegaard's critique of Hegel's speculative system.

Also like Marx, Kierkegaard will proceed from Hegel's premises to indicate that which cannot be fully synthesized by philosophical reflection. Specifically, he will concur that the failure to achieve identity is the occasion for all despair and that the struggle *against* despair—which necessarily takes place *in* despair—is the most elevated task of consciousness. Kierkegaard ironically extends the Hegelian view of the subject to demonstrate the limits of philosophical science in securing hope. Kierkegaard's opposition to Hegel takes shape on markedly Hegelian grounds: despair is that condition born of the subject's mediating and reflective activity, but also that terribly destructive sickness for which the subject requires remedy. The suggestion that the subject might find escape from despair in and through the very activity that produced it is, for Kierkegaard, the system's comic conceit. If philosophy has made us sick, then philosophy can provide no remedy for our sickness. But the underlying assumption that some remedy is needed—indeed, that despair is a sickness—remains.

The etymology of the English term "despair" is Latinate: from *de-sperare*, it means literally to be without hope. Kierkegaard was aware of this Latin term and its significance in Christian thought, but writing in Danish, he used a term with a somewhat different set of implications. Kierkegaard's *Fortvivlelse*—like Hegel's *Verzweiflung*—suggests an augmentation or intensification of doubt, but also, as Alastair Hannay has suggested, "bears 'two' (*tvi*) on its face, so the suggestion of complexity is conveyed here even more directly than in the case of 'despair' and its cognates."[6] That said, the English "despair" is not as misleading a translation of Kierkegaardian *Fortvivlelse* as Hannay suggests, for Kierkegaard treats the sickness unto death as a condition without hope and is concerned throughout his writings to measure the implications of such hopelessness for a properly religious life. One might say that he brings the religious dimension of this doubling movement in despair to the forefront; the "doubts" upon which modern philosophical inquiry proceeds assume profound spiritual significance in Kierkegaard's rewriting. But Kierkegaard is not concerned with the rational proof of God's existence, so the predicament opened up by despair is quite different from the problem conventionally associated with doubt or philosophical skepticism. Doubts provoke a crisis in truth and knowledge. Despair provokes a crisis in experience. Kierkegaard's chief concern is not with the objective truth of Christianity, the obsessive pursuit of which he treats as precisely symptomatic of sickness. Kierkegaard is chiefly interested in Christianity as it relates to the existing individual, specifically, how a subject divided might hope to achieve a self-restoring faith.

Many scholars have suggested that Kierkegaard's existential analytic remains entangled in the condition Hegel calls unhappy consciousness, but this reading fails to fully appreciate the nuance of Kierkegaard's critical opposition to Hegel. Put simply, Kierkegaard wonders if the highway of despair described in the *Phenomenology* does not raise questions it cannot answer: toward what end does critical reflection aspire and how might the subject reach this end? Kierkegaard's critique of Hegel revolves around the precise ways that the speculative system intensifies and magnifies the despair it claims to overcome. Here is Johannes Climacus, the pseudonymous author of the *Concluding Unscientific Postscript*:

> How do I put an end to the reflection which was set up in order to reach the beginning here in question? Reflection has the remarkable quality of being infinite. But to say that it is infinite is equivalent, in any case, to saying that it cannot be stopped by itself; because in attempting to stop itself it must use itself, and is thus stopped in the same way that a disease is cured when it is allowed to choose its own treatment, which is to say it waxes and thrives.[7]

Reflection itself has no logical or necessary end; nothing puts a stop to it. For the system to have an end—and "system and finality are pretty much one and the same, so much so that if the system is not finished, there is no system"—requires an arbitrary termination of infinite reflection.[8] Movements (and their interruptions) do not inhere in logic or abstract rational categories, but in the dynamic conditions and conflicting forces that structure individual lives: "An existential system cannot be formulated. Does this mean that no such system exists? By no means; nor is this implied in our assertion. Existence itself is a system—for God, but it cannot be a system for any existing spirit."[9] Hegel's offense is hubris, that of the professional philosopher who imagines that he—an "existing spirit"—can somehow assume the place of the Absolute. To craft the "categories which mediate between the individual and the world-process" and "string them altogether on the systematic thread" is either immoral or comic. Either he believes himself God or he forgets himself to be all too human.[10]

Despair is such an important concept in Kierkegaard's fractured dialectic because it is the condition brought on by rational reflection that also most forcefully rebels against the conceits of rationality and the strictures of the system. Despair exposes aporia. As Johannes Climacus puts it, "despair is despair because it does not know the way out."[11] It is for this reason that Kierkegaard believes despair never really comes into view as a problem for speculative philosophy. Hegel presupposes what he purports to discover—a way out that retrospectively rescues subjectivity and heals the wounds of negativity. Kierkegaard sees faith as the only real way out of despair. And this is not the work of rational reflection and systematic knowledge, but extrarational will. Faith is not an a priori actualized in reality, but the highest state of subjectivity. For this reason, the individual cannot get at faith through phenomenological proof of God's existence or the rationality of the real. Faith is aligned with the absurd, the incommunicable, and the extraordinary embedded in ordinary life.

Here is Johannes Climacus again:

> If a dancer could leap very high, we should admire him. But if he tried to give the impression that he could fly, let laughter single him out for suitable punishment, even though it might be true that he could leap as high as any dancer ever had done. Leaping is the accomplishment of a being essentially earthly, one who respects the earth's gravitational force, since leaping is only momentary. But flying carries a suggestion of being emancipated from the telluric condition, a privilege reserved for winged creatures, and perhaps also shared by the inhabitants of the moon—and there perhaps the System will first find its true readers.[12]

Thinking, like leaping, is an earthly and human activity. Profound thinking is an achievement, to be sure, but it is still confined to the coordinates of the human mind. What Hegel accomplishes on the level of abstract thought demands "just and proper respect," but what he alleges to have discerned in reality is an absurdity. Johannes Climacus notes the "ungodliness" of the system, but does not play preacher or pedagogue. Instead, his response is laugher at Hegel's clownish claims to have unearthed a way to fly by virtue of the human capacity to leap. Climacus underscores, too, the physicality of existence, the manner in which bodies are set in motion through the restlessness of thought. Human bodies, too, are confined to terrestriality. Any temporary suspension of the earth's gravitational pull is simply that—temporary.

Like faith, despair is not a category of abstract rationality, but of earthly existence. Its antidote cannot be found in the elucidation of the concept or the philosophical reconstruction of the identity of subjective and objective spirit: "The systematic Idea is the identity of subject and object, the unity of thought and being. Existence, on the other hand, is their separation."[13] This is a succinct formulation of what proves to be Kierkegaard's most enduring contribution to the philosophical critique of Hegel in European thought. Existence means separation. And so, it means despair. What he inherits from Hegel is the conviction that despair is a problem to be cured, that one of life's primary passions is also a sign of sickness.

Despair mirrors and mimics its opposing force at every turn, which explains why Kierkegaard both struggles to name it with precision and seems to find it everywhere. It is elusive and pervasive. It consumes the individual so completely that full knowledge or disclosure of the condition is a nearly impossible task for the ordinary person. But Kierkegaard's diagnostics demand a way out. The way out cannot be taught or learned per se, since it is the singular achievement of only the most extraordinary knight of faith. Abraham is the obvious example: He cannot communicate the secrets of his faith. He remains a source of mysterious wonder for all ordinary individuals who seek to understand him, especially those who admire him. He is not an example to be followed. Instead, this prodigious knight stands as testimony to the paradoxes of a faith that cannot find its articulation in philosophical discourse, "because faith begins precisely where thought stops."[14] Both Hegel and Kierkegaard cast despair as that which presents itself to be overcome and the condition of possibility for this necessary overcoming. Both of them rest dialectics on the assumption that the doubling incurred through reflective activity must come to some end. Kierkegaard's critique of Hegel turns on the latter's claim to having discovered the way out in the rational reconstruction of reality. But he never abandons the idea of a way out—or the claim to have discovered it. Kierkegaard's afterlife in late modernity hangs on a variety of despair that resists the consolations of faith as aggressively as it disrupts the claims of reason.

2

The Sickness Unto Death, written under the name Anti-Climacus, provides the most comprehensive treatment of despair in Kierkegaard's corpus. It as an especially important text in his vast body of work, because despair is the primary problem to which all of Kierkegaard's writing is some response. The book is also one of the few in the Western philosophical tradition that takes despair as its explicit theme, this despite consistent and widespread anxiety about the effects of despair on our cultural projects. Kierkegaard considered publishing the book under his own name, but ultimately decided in favor of pseudonymous authorship. The three voices—Johannes Climacus (author of *Philosophical Fragments* and *Concluding Unscientific Postscript*), Anti-Climacus (author of *The Sickness Unto Death*), and Kierkegaard himself (who assumes responsibility for the publication of all three)—bear some relationship to one another. Kierkegaard glosses it this way:

> Johannes Climacus and Anti-Climacus have several things in common; but the difference is whereas Johannes Climacus places himself so low that he even says that he himself is not a Christian, one seems to be able to detect in Anti-Climacus that he considers himself to be a Christian on an extraordinarily high level. . . . I would place myself higher than Johannes Climacus, lower than Anti-Climacus.[15]

This passage confirms that the prefix "Anti-" does not mean opposition, but is an archaic form of "ante-" that connotes a relation of rank, order, or time. Anti-Climacus comes before Climacus, though not in a temporal progression, but in his standing before God as a Christian. That said, Kierkegaard does not quite assign a higher rank to Anti-Climacus. He says only that this "author" *regards himself* to be a Christian of the highest order. And Johannes Climacus considers himself so low that he is unworthy of the claim to be a Christian. Kierkegaard positions himself somewhere in between these two, perhaps detecting excess pride in the claim to "be" a Christian and excess denial in Johannes Climacus's claim not to be. Yet if a higher or lower rank here is determined according to the author's self-presentation, the classification itself remains suspect. If there is a single lesson that can be taken from Kierkegaard's experiments in multivocal writing, it concerns the profound unreliability of any self-presentation.

Despair intensifies this unreliability from all directions. Here is Anti-Climacus on the difficulties with diagnosing despair: "Despair is not only dialectically different from a sickness, but all its symptoms are also dialectical, and therefore the superficial view is very easily deceived in determining whether or not despair is present. Not to be in despair can in fact signify precisely to be in despair, and it can signify having been rescued from being in despair."[16] Diagnosis requires radical doubt about everything that is reported, as the risks of error and deception are extraordinarily high when it comes to a sickness that most often appears as health. The physician of the soul, to whom Anti-Climacus refers but whom he significantly *does not claim to be*, has a task that requires a hermeneutics of deepest suspicion. Almost a critic, "the physician, precisely because he is a physician (well informed), does not have complete confidence in what a person says about his condition."[17] And whatever could be said about a person's symptoms doesn't necessarily indicate, in any transparent or straightforward way, the status of his or her sickness. Even health and sickness become unstable, sometimes indistinguishable categories: "both health and sickness are critical; there is no immediate health of spirit."[18]

Note how Anti-Climacus deploys medical discourse in an analytics of despair.[19] The point is that despair must be treated as a sickness: "Everything essentially Christian must have in its presentation a resemblance to the way a physician speaks at the sickbed; even if only medical experts understand it, it must never be forgotten that the situation is the bedside of a sick person." Though he does not discuss Kierkegaard directly, Reinhardt Koselleck's influential *Critique and Crisis* helps to make some sense of these metaphors drawn from medicine.[20] He shows how critique emerges first in Greek juridical discourses, as a term for the art of cutting, sifting, separating, distinguishing, but also judging and deciding. Athenians saw critique, or *krinein*, as a response to crisis, or a disturbance, controversy, or disorder in the polis.[21] By the Middle Ages, the connection between critique and crisis shifted from juridical to medical discourses. Not the judge, but the physician came to determine whether a condition could be called "critical" or stable. Modern philosophical notions of critique developed at some remove from these jurisprudential and medical usages. And since Kant's inaugural *Critique of Pure Reason*, the term has come to designate the philosophical aspirations of the European Enlightenment to ground knowledge, moral autonomy, and human freedom in the foundations of reason. As I see things, a medieval genealogy is delicately preserved in the *diagnostic* ambitions of critique—and Kierkegaard's entire philosophy could be called critical in this respect.

With the unreliability and instability that come with despair, it is difficult to know how the physician does the necessary diagnostics, much less how health is restored to a sickened soul. Anti-Climacus insists that perspective is what matters most. Diagnostics must assume a "Christian point of view" or an "upbuilding" relationship to the individual. Upbuilding discourses emerge from and are immersed in life itself. He continues:

> It is precisely Christianity's relation to life (in contrast to a scholarly distance from life) or the ethical aspect of Christianity that is upbuilding, and the mode of presentation, however rigorous it may be otherwise, is completely different, qualitatively different, from the kind of scienticity and scholarliness that is "indifferent," whose lofty heroism is so far, Christianly, from being heroism that, Christianly, it is a kind of inhuman curiosity.[22]

The Sickness Unto Death is rigorous in form, meaning systematic and philosophical. But unlike conventional philosophical exercises, it springs from deep investment, passionate attachment, and earnest engagement. Though the presentation of despair may read as detached and disinterested, Anti-Climacus assures the reader that his perspective is Christian, meaning it maintains an authentic vitality. What Anti-Climacus cherishes in the Christian point of view is its "relation to life"—and its implicit critique of scholarly indifference. Anti-Climacus sees this as the only position from which despair properly comes into view, as the sickness that is also a sin.

This is a highly distinctive and idiosyncratic idea of Christianity and the result is an analytics of despair that is qualitatively different from what the Christian moralists understood in terms of virtue and vice. Sin, as Anti-Climacus presents it, is not a deliberate or volitional act contrary to virtue, but a conscious or unconscious condition contrary to faith. Despair is faithlessness in its variety of forms: faith absent, arrested, lost; faith that is insecure, uncertain, and incomplete; or faith that is too secure, too certain, and rests in itself. Despair says that there is no hope. From the moralist point of view, despair is an inability to live in accord with reason and goodness. In *The Sickness Unto Death*, it indicates a far greater misfortune. Anti-Climacus calls it the inability to die, "yet not as if there were hope of life; no, the hopelessness is that there is not even the ultimate hope, death."[23]

It turns out that this misfortune puts all others in perspective. Only the Christian can see it for the simple reason that only the Christian really knows it:

> Christianity has in turn discovered a miserable condition that man as such does not know exists. This miserable condition is the sickness unto death. What the natural man catalogs as appalling—after he has recounted everything and has nothing more to mention—this to the Christian is like a jest. Such is the relation between the natural man and the Christian; it is like the relation between a child and an adult: what makes the child shudder and shrink, the adult regards as nothing. The child does not know what the horrifying is; the adult knows and shrinks from it. Only the Christian knows what is meant by the sickness unto death. As a Christian, he has gained a courage that the natural man does not know, and he has gained this courage by learning to fear something even more horrifying.[24]

This passage reads as Kierkegaard's direct intervention in the philosophical discourse of the German Enlightenment. It draws upon the general motif of individual maturation, and the idea that the movement from childish naïveté to adult awareness is one that demands courage.[25] More specifically, it offers a critique of the figure of natural consciousness in Hegel. Natural consciousness may know lesser horrors—worldly miseries like slavery and warfare—but, contra Hegel, it does not know despair. Despair presupposes the faith that it also denies. The sickness unto death already indicates a rare achievement. Christian consciousness possesses a knowledge that is unavailable to natural consciousness. That Hegel follows natural consciousness on a journey toward the consummation of the system suggests that he is looking for passion in all the wrong places: Hegel ought to be chasing the Christian.

To determine what this something is, more terrifying than death itself, Anti-Climacus parodically assumes the Hegelian subject only to show how this subjectivity is constituted in such a way as to remain stuck in despair. Judith Butler is right to insist that "this is a parody that does not entail a thorough rejection of Hegel," that Kierkegaard "recirculates or preserves some aspects of Hegel's system and jettisons some others."[26] Where I want to dwell is in the place where Kierkegaard follows Hegel, where dialectical thought meets up with passion, where the restlessness of the negative keeps things moving. Kevin Newmark has noted, "Kierkegaard understood, more clearly than most of us today, that Hegel's true importance resides in the way his writings provide the fullest exposition of the capacities and limits of Western philosophical thought."[27] Kierkegaard understood that, after Hegel, *the* philosophical problem is despair. Kierkegaard imitates the formal features of Hegel's speculative philosophy in *The Sickness Unto Death* because this is the philosophical system in which the problem of despair takes its most acute form. Seen in this way, Kierkegaard proffers an immanent critique of Hegelian dialectics.

Despair comes in two basic forms—unconscious and conscious. All despair, "without regard to its being conscious or not," involves a fundamental "disequilibrium" in the self divided between two polarities: finitude and infinitude, on the one hand; necessity and possibility, on the other. Unconscious forms of despair are often the easiest to detect and diagnose in others, and the most difficult to see in one-self. The despair of infinitude, for instance, is volatile and fantastical, and indulges in an "abstract sentimentality that inhumanly belongs to no human being but inhumanly combines sentimentally, as it were, with some abstract fate—for example, humanity *in abstracto*."[28] This despair sends the individual "plunging headlong into fantasy" or keeps that individual in perfect conformity with an arbitrary and imagined fate. The despair of finitude is its mirror opposite, which Anti-Climacus connects more directly to the "secular mentality" of the age:

> The secular view always clings tightly to the difference between man and man and naturally does not have any understanding of the one thing that is needful (for to have it is spirituality), and thus has no understanding of the reductionism and narrowness involved in having lost oneself, not by being volatilized in the infinite, but by being completely finitized, by becoming a number instead of a self, just one more man, just one more repetition of this everlasting one and the same.[29]

Finitude's despair is that of the crowd, of mass man, of the primacy of quantitative over qualitative difference, what Marxist theorists would identify with the rationalities of bourgeois capitalism. Anti-Climacus does not pursue a materialist account of this variety of despair, but does describe its sufferer as a "circulating coin" who has "gained an increased capacity for going along superbly in business and social life."[30] This is a form of despair directly linked to the comforts and conveniences of bourgeois life and the attachments to worldly successes and calculable fortunes.

Despair of possibility and necessity is structurally similar to that of infinitude and finitude. Lost in the despair of possibility, the self becomes "unreal" to itself in frenzied pursuit of endlessly renewed potentiality: "these phastasmagoria follow one another in such rapid succession that it seems as if everything were possible, and this is exactly the final moment, the point at which the individual himself becomes a mirage."[31] Possibility, though, is also the distinctive promise of God, for with God "everything is possible at every moment," and so we see how every form of despair opens up its potential over-

KIERKEGAARD'S DIAGNOSTICS 73

coming.[32] The despair of necessity is essentially a rebellion against the infinite possibility harbored in the experience of faith. This despair says that everything has been decided in advance. Like the despair of finitude, the despair of necessity is linked to silence, "a mute capitulation" to powers and forces beyond any individual human control. Anti-Climacus also identifies this type of despair with the "philistine-bourgeois mentality" that reduces all possibility to quantifiable, calculable probability: "Bereft of imagination, as the philistine-bourgeois always is, whether alehouse keeper or prime minister, he lives within a certain compendium of experiences as to how things go, what is possible, what usually happens."[33] Philistine-bourgeois attitudes are those intoxicated by the trivialities of chance, which serves as spirit-numbing solace for the larger and more significant constraints of necessity. These are not historical or social types per se, though Anti-Climacus cannot wholly banish the historical and sociological element from his spiritual anthropology.

Our author notes that it is possible to live one's whole life in one or more of these basic varieties of despair, without ever being conscious of the precise nature of the sickness one suffers. Becoming conscious of being in despair is a necessary but insufficient step toward being relieved of it. But conscious despair is a more advanced form of sickness. It, too, comes in several forms (of all the pseudonyms, Anti-Climacus is the most unforgiving typologist): despair *in* weakness, a despair *over* weakness, and, finally, the despair of defiance. All three are forms of reflective despair, meaning they intensify in force as the individual grows in introspection and self-projection. But all three conditions—particularly the despair of defiance—open up into their antithesis. "In relating itself to itself and in willing to be itself, the self rests transparently in the power that established it."[34] Defiance is when the individual takes itself as an absolute, which is also precisely when the self is prepared to put itself into the hands of a power other than itself.

Anti-Climacus treats weakness and defiance as sexual symptoms, the former predictably associated with feminine "devotedness" and the latter with masculine egoism and intellectualism.[35] Despair in weakness involves the incapacity to will oneself as the individual one inescapably is. It is a retreat from oneself and the conditions of one's existence. It is fueled by fantasy and utopian reveries, since this variety of despair entails the desire for difference, the desire *to be different*. (Per usual, Kierkegaard never considers these desires in relation to systems of power or structures of domination.) A preoccupation with distant times, remote or imaginary places, and hypothetical situations are symptoms of weak despair. As with any conscious despair, weakness has several varieties and gradations. One can despair over something earthly and temporal, but this sickness can extend from particular objects to encompass the world in toto. And "the category of totality," as Anti-Climacus insists, "inheres in and belongs to the despairing person."[36] This shift—from despair over earthly particulars to despair over the world in its totality—is the disease of abstraction. Totality itself is a "thought category" where the mind "infinitely magnifies the actual loss and then despairs over the earthly *in toto*."[37] Thinking, no matter how rational, tends toward the catastrophic.

Defiance—or the will to be oneself as absolute—remains the individual's penultimate revolt. In anticipation of E. M. Cioran (among the few others to have written a philosophical study of despair), defiance is man's comportment at the heights of despair.[38] This is conscious despair in masculine form, in the mode of mastery, as the individual becomes "its own master, *absolutely* its own master." It appears in the world as arrogant self-satisfaction and a tendency toward unnecessary risk. This is not merely an autonomous self, in the sense that he gives himself his own law; this is a self who takes himself as the law. Here again, there are images drawn from society and politics. Defiance, in particular, assumes an unmistakably political cast. This is because defiance has a tendency toward action, toward expanding its domain of rule, toward self-assertion. "Upon closer examination," Anti-Climacus remarks, "it is easy to see that this absolute ruler is a king without a country, actually ruling over nothing; his position, his sovereignty, is subordinate to the dialectic that rebellion is legitimate at any moment."[39] With no power greater than himself, this master loses all of his real powers.

Defiance means strength and determination though, and for this reason it suggests to Anti-Climacus a subject ripened to recoup his real power. These are recurring themes in Kierkegaard: the idea of readiness, of things changing in an instant, and the idea that everything may be gotten back, that in the instant of the leap all things are restored. These themes dominate *Fear and Trembling*, where the real miracle is that Abraham *does* have it all, that in an instant he gets everything back—Isaac and God—without having to lose anything. But this gift comes only with the movement from defiance to compliance, from rebellion to submission, from despair to faith. Despair points to the "riddle" of human subjectivity—"something the Christian would call a cross, a basic defect, whatever it may be."[40]

Kierkegaard, under his own name or his pseudonyms, gets no further than this on the problem of despair. It is a "basic defect" that appears in various forms of individuated sickness. This is, of course, the problem with any serious attempt to recover Kierkegaard for social or political theory. Despair in Kierkegaard always points back to a spiritualized ontology. Lifted out of history and society, despair is simply another name for that basic human defect, sin. (Part 2 of *The Sickness Unto Death*, where abstraction and mechanical jargon reach absurd proportions, centers on this basic position: that despair is Sin and Sin is despair.) Whether sin or sickness, Kierkegaard consistently treats despair as a problem pertaining to the subject—an ahistorical and abstract subject—not a condition that structures relations between subjects and a world of objects and others. Passions, for Kierkegaard, are private and interiorized forces, which means the collective shape of despair and the historical forces that produce it fall out of view. What is more, Kierkegaard never abandons the Hegelian search for a way out of despair. He renders despair itself the vital means to that end. The result is a concept of despair that is at once instrumental and redemptive: despair becomes the instrument of its overcoming.

Michael Theunissen has suggested that "the joy of reading *The Sickness Unto Death* is spoiled mainly because the book is composed in a language that mystifies it subject matter. . . . Despair can inflate into the ostensible subject because a dialectic that, in the punishment of regression, condemns one to endure the process of sickness to the very end absorbs the real subjects."[41] Put differently, *The Sickness Unto Death* becomes a book about the concept of despair, as opposed a record of its experience. I have also argued that Kierkegaard imposes a teleological logic on an otherwise static picture of sickness. He charts an inescapable pathway through despair, a rigid determinacy that spoils the freedom suggested by the leap. As Theunissen has put it, "the leap sideways is not a possibility for the person in despair himself, because what Kierkegaard does state clearly enough is considered a foregone conclusion: to reach the truth, one must go through *every* negativity."[42] Individuals can move forward or backward along this highway, but like in Hegel before him, the Kierkegaardian subject "must be broken to become itself."[43] And paradoxically, this subject must not be consumed by a sickness that is consuming in its very nature. To remain in despair, says Kierkegaard, to get stuck there, is to be bereft of hope. To choose faith is to be saved. But there is no freedom in this choice, and no accounting for the agency required to make it.

3

Kierkegaard follows Hegel in treating despair as a *dialectical* passion. And Kierkegaard's fractured dialectic, like Hegel's, draws its energy from the passions that it also prohibits. He comes after Hegel in recentering the passionate side of philosophical activity. In thinking and writing at the limits of philosophy, he aims to do justice to our passions. And he goes beyond Hegel in casting passionate life as the real foundation of law, ethics, and the public use of reason.

If philosophy takes its flight from the individual's fear and trembling by way of a speculative system that purports to rationalize it, modern politics takes its flight from collective fear and trembling by way of an institutionalized order that claims to eliminate it once and for all. This seems to be the kernel of real insight in what Merold Westphal calls Kierkegaard's "politics in a nutshell."[44] And on occasion, the self-proclaimed religious poet gives this politics explicit articulation. Here is Anti-Climacus, from what Kierkegaard considered to be his most important work, *Training in Christianity*:

> Every individual ought to live in fear and trembling, so too there is no established order which can do without fear and trembling. Fear and trembling signifies that one is in a process of becoming, and every individual man, and the race as well, is or should be conscious of being in process of becoming. And fear and trembling signifies that a God exists—a fact which no man and no established order dare for an instant forget.[45]

This passage opens up the potential for inquiries that Kierkegaard did not undertake—investigations into the historicity of becoming, the objective conditions under which these processes takes shape, the frailty of our individual and collective projects, and the possibilities for freedom given the shared experience of finitude. Kierkegaard does not specify how fear and trembling testify to a process of becoming, though the position seems to anticipate what Judith Butler has elaborated as precarious life, or the shared vulnerability of our attachments and our projects in a world that keeps moving without us.[46] Still less does he talk about how fear and trembling confirm the existence of God, or what happens in the event that God is forgotten. Theunissen has suggested that "just as Kierkegaard's 'No' to any system is ambivalent, so too is his rejection of the philosophical proofs of the existence of God half-hearted. Secretly, he would like to prove the existence of God by way of the existence of despair."[47] I would add: both faith and despair become our surest evidence of God and of our own finitude and freedom. That *both* despair and faith are possible—indeed, that they presuppose each other and that the struggle between them *is* this mortal coil—becomes ontological proof of the existence of God. That this proof is a paradox does not much trouble the poet or the physician.

We can only wonder what the leap of faith would look like when assumed by the "established order," but Kierkegaard would not be the first to suggest that political communities might be invigorated and strengthened by a recollection of the primordial fear upon which they are built and maintained. (Machiavelli infamously called for a periodic return to beginnings, which has been repeated throughout the history of political thought. Freud's writings on religion, especially *Totem and Taboo*, make complementary claims from a different perspective.) Our institutions are fortified by the flexibility that allows them to adapt and change. Adaptation does not necessarily follow a progressive path, or any historical logic whatsoever, but it does signify that institutions exist in real time.

Kierkegaard does not advance an account of what might be called "objective despair"—despair embedded in social forms, political institutions, cultural practices, and economic life.[48] This silence is especially surprising in that he understood despair to be the "universal" epidemic of his age, resulting from religion on the cheap and an inflated investment in philosophical wisdom. Had he considered "objective despair" or despair as it circulates between subjects and objects, perhaps this "basic defect" would take on distinct historical shapes and his epoch would come into clearer focus. Perhaps a sickness of the soul would appear as a sickness in social conditions. Perhaps neither sickness nor sin would quite capture despair. And neither reason nor faith could quite banish it.

Kierkegaard's dialectic of faith demonstrates that, while the particular hopes sustained by critical theory may be secular and rational, the reservoirs from which we draw those hopes are not. Critical theory ought to maintain a hold on the deeply "religious" quality of hope, so that this element does not recede to the margins of our philosophical and political work. The point is not an uncritical embrace of the "return of religion" in contemporary political and intellectual life—as if religion had disappeared, as if the new forms of religious life are premodern residues and not themselves the result of present conditions and conflicts. The point is that critical theory finds its footing in the forces that circulate at the outer limits of reason. And it takes reprieve from the rescue operations of Reason (Hegel) or Faith (Kierkegaard), through which critique is spared the ordeal of despair. What's left of critical theory that is left to its despair? What does critique look like when it bears the wounds of negativity? Could the play of passions indicate new directions for critical theory? And do our remaining hopes for substantive freedom and concrete pleasures lie in the very condition that would seem inhospitable to all hope? These are the questions that guide the remaining chapters. From each of the thinkers that follow, contemporary critique learns something about how to take refreshment from the dialectical quality of despair.

Part 2

▼

DIALECTICAL
REMAINS

3
Theodor W. Adorno

APORETICS

1

I have exaggerated the somber side, following the maxim that
only exaggeration today can be the medium of truth.
—Adorno, "The Meaning of Working Through the Past"

Theodor W. Adorno comes to us in various ways—as a philosopher, a
cultural critic, a literary theorist, a sociologist—but *always* in despair.
Martin Jay, describing the famous profile photograph of Adorno
used by his German publisher, deciphers despair in the contours of
his downcast lips and eyes, in the "mournful expression on his face."[1]
This photo—the one Jay used on the cover of his own book-length
study of Adorno—is a portrait of the critic, a snapshot image of a
vast philosophical legacy, yet one that resonates precisely because it
captures the somber tones of so much of Adorno's writing. Jay writes:
"The cumulative effect produced by the photo is so powerful, showing us a man brooding in subdued sadness about the untold horrors
of his lifetime."[2]

This part of the story is, by now, familiar. A thinker best known for
the suggestion that poetry is not possible after Auschwitz has become
the archetype of mid-century European melancholia. His infamous, if
misunderstood, requiem for lyric poetry expresses felt historical grief

and regret, as well as a secondary mourning for a vanquished aesthetic. And there are good historical grounds for Adorno's despair: his
career as a social theorist and philosopher stretches from the late 1920s
until his death in 1969. His extended exile in America—an especially
fertile period of twelve years—may have deepened his interest and
involvement in popular culture, but it also intensified his experience
of alienation from dominant national cultures. The apparent failure
of European working classes to develop revolutionary consciousness,
the rise of fascism, the horrors of Nazism and world war, the merger
of authoritarian statecraft and bourgeois rationality, the entwinement
of culture and capitalism, and ever-developing technologies of mass
death and destruction will wear away at even the instinctual revolutionary. We would not expect an ambivalent aesthete to join in a false
and mandatory optimism. Despair is the passionate testimony to a
life witness to Auschwitz, exile, authoritarianism, the collapse of individuality and the triumph of mass conformity, and the rationalization
of all forms of life according to the logic of capitalist profit. And his
personal losses were mighty.

It goes without saying that Adorno's texts cannot be extracted
from their historical (and biographical) contexts. But I'm not sure
that more detailing of this history (and life) will get at the strange
timeliness of the texts, what Robert Hullot-Kentor describes as the
"paradoxical recent development of substantial interest in Adorno's
work in the United States."[3] Paradoxical, because Adorno speaks in a
philosophical language foreign to America, in a style at odds with the
perennial fashion of industrial entertainment and at a pitch too Germanic: "he antagonizes virtually everyone in a nation where the ear
is certainly the most stupefied, rawly integrated and exploited of the
senses."[4] Yet the very idea of critical theory—the aspiration to continue the "ruthless critique of everything existing"—is unthinkable
absent Adorno. It is a curious case in elective affinity: the unlikeli-
hood that a fiercely anti-intellectual national culture is also the one
that has claimed Adorno as one of its adopted intellectual treasures.

Hullot-Kentor, whose commentaries and translations are themselves part of this vast treasure, argues that Adorno's appeal is, in part,
an episode in comparative political history: "Americans during the
Bush presidency . . . [found] themselves in the midst of experiencing

what Germans themselves underwent more than a half a century ago . . . living in a country that has been seized by a minority that has drawn it into desperate circumstances."[5] But the end of the Bush presidency has not meant the end of Adorno, any more than it has meant the end of an episode in American empire. (Adorno may have something to tell us about the strange forgetfulness that has taken hold in post-Bush America and allows for the continuation of substantial parts of his foreign and domestic policy, even the intensification of the covert elements of the war on terror.) More substantially, Hullot-Kentor says that timeliness of Adorno lies in the fate of his philosophical project: "No other contemporary philosophy is able to set its finger with such precision, so unwaveringly, on the content of this historical moment."[6] I do not disagree, though I think there is more to say. No other contemporary philosophy is able to express, in its form and its content, in its theoretical rigor and poetic style, what is meant by *critique* at this historical moment. What is generally known about Adorno—that his was a critical theory *and* a melancholy science, an experiment in negative dialectics as critique and a restoration of thinking into the repertoire of radicalism—remains what is most significant. It answers the question of why critical theory after Hegel begins with Adorno.

Attacks on Adorno come from many quarters and are also, by now, familiar. Within the mainstream of cultural studies, for example, there is a shared sense that Adorno's modernist aesthetics fails to capture the complexities of cultural production, circulation, and consumption in everyday life. For thinkers of a post-Marxist or post-structuralist bent, Adorno's thinking is beset by numerous problems: his productionist bias, his aspiration to a theoretical view of the social totality, his attachment to concepts like contradiction and catastrophe, his residual subjectivism, his undisguised elitism. For radical thinkers of various stripes, there is too much in his work that rings of antiblack racism, liberal apologetics, and political reaction. And some of this is true. But I want to suggest that we approach his work in a way other than what Evan Watkins calls the "Adorno two-step"— an intellectual's dance in which the partner is "wrong in substance, but still relevant as a reminder of the dangers of uncritical engagement."[7] Instead, I aim to amplify the joyful wisdom in a melancholy science, the radical commitment that underwrites the respect for autonomy in art and culture, and the subjective comportment that insists upon the preponderance of the object. In taking negative dialectics more seriously, I also hope to take Adorno less seriously—or, better, read him with an ear to his laughter, his self-effacing humor, and his manic delight in the ordeal of aporetics. I suspect that we do Adorno some disservice in allowing the "somber side" to silence his slapstick. (That he reserves his rare esteem for Beckett's *Endgame* and Chaplin's Tramp suggests something of the importance of clowning for Adorno.) And I am not sure that we have adequately deciphered that somber side anyway, or its relation to the philosophy of negative dialectics. The following pages pursue the secondary argument that no other contemporary philosophy is able to set its finger with such precision, so unwaveringly, on the play of passions that accompany the restlessness of the negative.

Adorno's despair has been well established by his critics, but I will argue in the following pages that it has been poorly understood. For the second and third generation of Frankfurt School social theorists, the central project has been to rescue critical reason from the uninhibited despair of their predecessors, under the assumption that despair is corrosive of political vision. For Habermas in particular, Adorno betrays the "rational content of cultural modernity" to an unyielding logic of domination.[8] The result is a critique of Enlightenment without "any dynamism upon which critique could base its hope," hopeless critique, inimical to Habermas's deepest faith in communicative reason:[9] "*Negative Dialectics* reads like a continuing explanation of why we have to circle about within this performative contradiction and indeed even remain there."[10] Despair becomes a problem for philosophy to fix. In Habermas, despair becomes *the* philosophical problem, originating in a bad philosophy (which starts with Nietzsche) and resolved with good philosophy (which starts with Kant). The aim of his "postmetaphysical" philosophy is to repair broken faith in the powers of human reason.

The way I see things, Habermas's philosophical project—offered up as an alternative to the "uninhibited skepticism" of the first generation—doubles down on the instrumentalism of thinking and surrenders to philosophy's urge to be edifying. Habermas treats critical philosophy as a rescue operation—most of all, critique must be saved from itself. This move allows the objective history of despair to fall into obscurity and compels the passions to give way to the primacy of communicative reason. Another approach would be to follow Adorno to the places where negative dialectics is allegedly confined to its hopeless wheel spinning: the absurd, the aesthetic, the aporetic. Here we will not find resignation, or lingering on the lost cause, or betraying the present one, but a glimpse into the forms that critique takes at the heights of despair.

Again, Hullot-Kentor is instructive and right to insist that "Adorno's thinking as a whole is a materialist critique of historical despair."[11] But it is also true that this critique never gets wholly outside of or beyond the object. Put differently, this is the basic position: *the only philosophy that can be practiced responsibly in the face of despair is a philosophy that bears the face of despair.*[12] Critical theory after Hegel, after the collapse of any meaningful distinction between reason and barbarism, after the dialectic of Western modernity reveals itself as the wrong state of things, must learn to find renewal from real conditions. I read Adorno's aporetics—the form of thinking that establishes negative dialectics as a proposition and practice, more than a system—as adventures in despair. These adventures do not cohere into a sustainable ethics,[13] a weak metaphysics,[14] or a minimal theology,[15] but they do offer some surprising provocations for political thinking. Perhaps the biggest surprise is how Adorno permits us to steal happiness from a world that keeps it just out of reach.

What is important about despair, in particular, is its distinctive relation to the dialectic. Despair is the residue left by the restlessness of the negative. And despair always means its own negation and is, in this sense, a dialectical passion. With Adorno's help, I want to move away from an idea of despair that turns on subjective desire and its disappointment and toward one that dwells in the misrelations between subjects and objects. For example, in *Minimal Theologies*, Hent DeVries treats despair as a problem pertaining to the pathos of desire: "Because desire cannot, in principle, be satisfied, there clings to consciousness (which is primarily involved with conscience and in that sense is already conscientious, not unhappy) a trace of despair."[16] The distinction between unhappy consciousness and despair is germane to the argument pursued here and to my reading of Hegel's *Phenomenology*, but DeVries's argument suffers an excess of subjectivism at the expense of what both Hegel and Adorno appreciate as a dialectical condition. Despair, as I see it, has less to do with desire that cannot "in principle" be satisfied and more to do with the contexts and the conditions under which desire comes undone and forms anew. DeVries neglects how despair points to a potentiality, and not merely a regrettable facticity. Moreover, his efforts to wrest Adorno away from Hegel obscure Hegel's own contribution to thinking despair apart from unhappiness.

Minimal Theologies is the most ambitious and accomplished attempt to put negative dialectics to work for a *minima theologia*. My aims, which rely extensively on figures of thought DeVries opens up in his reading of Adorno, are modest by comparison: I do not seek in negative dialectics a ground for the rearticulation of posttheological theology, but only the horizon through which hope—in distinction from faith—might find indirect expression. All theology, however minimal, requires a move beyond what is made possible by negative dialectics. This is why DeVries must turn to Levinasian ethics and Derridean deconstruction to supplement Adorno's critique of secular reason. And I am not sure that religion retains its specificity in this turn. Put a different way, if "theology" is simply a generic term for all forms of thought, representation, and discourse that do not adhere to the strictures of reason, then what remains of the particular themes addressed by theology? What is distinctive about "religious" life and the faith upon which religion is built? Does religion involve something different from what we find in Levinas, Derrida, or any other philosophical discourse?[17] DeVries succeeds in the reconstruction of Adorno's critique of secular reason, but this critique need not carry or sustain a minimal theology. If there is a theological impulse in Adorno, it presumes the historical obsolescence of revealed religion and a disenchanted world. I suspect DeVries's minimal theology does as well. The crucial difference is that Adorno did not give the name of theology—minimal or otherwise—to an impulse that survives the death of God.

If I continue to exaggerate Adorno's somber side, as well as the joyful wisdom that may be found there, then I do so following the maxim that exaggeration remains a medium of truth. In her classic study *Critique, Norm, and Utopia*, Seyla Benhabib casts Adorno's critical theory as a "relentless pessimism," and, my quarrels notwithstanding, I do think she is right that his thinking "cannot be explained by the darkness of human history at that point in time alone."[18] What I reject in Benhabib—and in Habermas, in Honneth, in the very raison d'être of Frankfurt School critical theory after Adorno—is not the exaggerated image of Adorno as the figuration of despair, but the presumption that despair spells disaster. What if there are no rational grounds for hope? Does this mean there is no hope? Or does it mean instead that the proof of hope lies in the persistence of despair, that to speak of despair is also to bespeak of hope.

2

> Even inwardness participates in dialectics.
>
> —Adorno, *Aesthetic Theory*

Confirming what Edward Said calls his "late style" (a formulation Said borrows from Adorno's analysis of Beethoven's mature works), we don't really think of Adorno as ever having been young. But among other interests, the youthful Adorno was submerged in the study of Søren Kierkegaard. The book that resulted from it, *Kierkegaard: Construction of the Aesthetic*, would launch his academic career. It is also the place to look for Adorno's earliest efforts at mapping despair as a philosophical idea.

Kierkegaard enjoyed a spectacular afterlife in Weimar Germany. Martin Heidegger was at the center of the revival, developing Kierkegaardian themes for a fundamental ontology. Heidegger's lectures in the 1920s echoed and elaborated what many of students were also discovering in Kierkegaard.[19] Critics of Idealism took Kierkegaard's philosophy of existence to be a powerful assault on the postulates of German philosophy since Kant and Hegel. An existentialist philosophy emerged out the impulse in Kierkegaard to pay attention to how we live more than what we think. By 1933, when Adorno published his *Habilitation*, a new set of orthodoxies had emerged about how to read the melancholy Dane. Adorno challenges many of them. He reads Kierkegaardian concepts as elements of an Idealist philosophy of the subject. He treats Kierkegaard's ahistorical philosophy of existence as itself a historical expression of bourgeois existence. And he develops a dialectical critique of the mythical subjectivity that Kierkegaard calls Christian.

"The aura of the poetic," Adorno remarks, invoking the authority of Hegel, "surrounds every philosophical beginning."[20] Nevertheless, Adorno begins *Kierkegaard: Construction of the Aesthetic* with a restatement of the abiding difference between philosophy and poetry. Philosophy, quite apart from poetry, is measured "in the first place by the degree to which the real has entered into concepts, manifests itself in these concepts, and comprehensively justifies them."[21] In other words, philosophy dwells in that point of contact between reality and concepts, and Adorno aims to represent Kierkegaard, who begs to be read as a poet, *philosophically*. Reading him poetically, which is to say without regard for the real or the concept as it takes form in Kierkegaard's writings, is to "dishonor the poetry as well as the philosophy."[22] Reading him philosophically is to assess the clarity and purchase of Kierkegaardian concepts. Adorno sees the concept of despair as absolutely central to Kierkegaard's fractured dialectic.

Somewhat contrary to its own beginnings, which insist upon the boundary between philosophy and aesthetics, *Kierkegaard: Construction of the Aesthetic* is Adorno's earliest effort at the revaluation of aesthetic life. The book has two distinct objectives with respect to its explicit subject matter: to reveal Kierkegaard as the apex of Idealist thinking and to rescue aesthetic experience from Kierkegaard's ultimate derision. The first aim is to expose in the father of existentialism the philosophical antinomies he purports to overcome. This reading uncovers the shadowy Idealism lurking in the recesses of subjective inwardness. In this respect, this early book is best understood in terms of Adorno's larger critique of German existentialism.[23] The second aim of the work—to recover an aesthetic sensibility that Kierkegaard disparaged in his own dialectic of existence—anticipates Adorno's later writings on culture and aesthetic theory. For Adorno, Kierkegaard's tendency to reduce aesthetic life to its purely empirical or unmediated positivity squanders the real critical force harbored in aesthetic experience. So while Adorno reads Kierkegaard philosophically, not poetically, which is to say he subjects Kierkegaard's philosophy to

critique, what is unearthed from that critique is the supreme importance of the aesthetic. Aesthetic experience—presented by Kierkegaard
as shattered and in despair—harbors traces of difference at odds
with the positivistic affirmation of what merely is. Though scorned
by Kierkegaard, aesthetic individuality refuses the calm comforts of
inwardness. It preserves the interactions between subjects and objects
as sites of recollection, resistance, and possibility. In despair, which is
not overcome by a subjective leap any more than it results from a subjective failing, the aesthete refuses to trade the frustrations of concrete
freedom for the comforts of an illusory agency.

It is helpful to review Kierkegaard briefly, though chapter 2 offers
a more detailed treatment. *The Sickness Unto Death* is Kierkegaard's
most systematic analysis of the movements of despair, though the
concept is everywhere in the analytic of faith. In established Catholic
doctrine, despair is a voluntary condition of faithlessness, marked by
the absence of hope in the possibility of one's salvation. Since it is the
active denial of God's grace, Catholics also treat it as a mortal sin,
punished by eternal damnation. Kierkegaard, too, views despair as
sin, though, like Luther before him, he regards it as the principal condition of possibility for the experience of faith. Faith, for Kierkegaard,
is the enduring and passionate struggle with and against despair. Ever
haunted by the sickness unto death, the authentically religious life
meets its greatest threat and challenge in despair, but at its heights—
or, rather, in its depths—this sickness propels the subject toward God.

Despair, according to Kierkegaard, is a misrelation to the self that
occurs on two levels: on the first level, to be in despair is the failure to
will to be oneself; the second and more elusive form of despair is the
will to be oneself as an Absolute. The first form of despair is a flight
from the imperatives of subjectivity, motivated by jealousy, angst, fear,
or self-hatred. A wrongful use of one's freedom, this despair is a denial
of oneself as a responsible being before God. It is a form of despair
transcended as soon as one comes to accept oneself and will the realization of oneself as a responsible agent. In this initial overcoming, the
subject becomes self-conscious of himself as a finite being with the
capacity to make aesthetic, ethical, and religious choices, yet is entirely
dependent upon God as the supreme condition of possibility to whom
faith is owed. The second form of despair is more elusive, insofar as the

self in despair is rarely—if ever—fully conscious of being in the sinful state. On this second level, despair is the prideful will to be oneself as Absolute. It is a failure to recognize oneself as finite—therefore, not Absolute. And it is a failure to recognize oneself as the finite product of something infinite—the only power that truly can be called Absolute. What marks despair of this second sort is precisely that it often manifests as its opposite—self-certainty, poise, confidence, defiance, and even rage—in the world of appearances. This is why, for Kierkegaard, to *be* in despair is not necessarily *to appear* in despair, either to oneself or to others.

Though the sickness unto death defines us as historical and "fallen" creatures, and despair proves the condition of possibility for the leap of faith, it also inhibits a truly spiritual relation to ourselves and God. For Kierkegaard, to despair is to be without hope—in oneself, in God, or even in what might ultimately deliver him from this condition: death. Only the properly religious life can escape despair, and Kierkegaard's writings, if they can be taken as a whole, point to what is required of the Christian seeking escape. The human condition, especially in an age of Christendom that cares little for faith, means despair in one form or another. Faith is that which allows us to live, finally.

What Adorno so powerfully demonstrates is the desperation and frailty of Kierkegaardian faith. And he challenges Kierkegaard's Idealism about despair—despair Kierkegaard calls objective, but then treats in narrowly subjectivist terms. The first point, about Kierkegaard's desperate faith, is crucial in anticipating Adorno's later critique of sacrificial subjectivity in the dialectic of Enlightenment. Contrary to the official promise of the upbuilding discourses, Adorno discerns that Kierkegaardian transcendence does not come "bestowed as a miracle of faith" but is instead "despairingly demanded" as a way out of fractured and finite immanence.[24] God's grace is not given as gift; it is furiously petitioned by a subject who is rather ill equipped to receive it. It is not faith but *desperation*—or, despair that does not will to be itself—that compels subjectivity before God. Religious life, as Adorno interprets it, has less to do with the miraculous offerings of true belief than with the desperate measures taken by a life condemned to meaninglessness. Kierkegaardian faith is then a symptom of the sickness it purports to cure. It presumes a shattered subject for whom self-preservation involves surrender: "In fact his philosophy develops the cult of sacrifice with such tenacity that it finally becomes a gnosis, which Kierkegaard as a Protestant would have otherwise passionately opposed."[25] This cult, like the one that forms around Odysseus, is primarily about the sacrifice of the aesthetic. What is distinctive in Kierkegaard's sacrifice is that this is also, surprisingly and paradoxically, the place where Kierkegaardian philosophy offers the outlines of a dialectical image.

The general argument of the book, about the Idealist core of Kierkegaardian thought, is crucial in anticipating negative dialectics. As Adorno interprets it, the resolution to despair is found in that "mythical figure of idealism"—the will.[26] This figure serves two roles in Kierkegaard. First, the will is the seat of sinfulness and the source of all despair. Second, the will is the place Kierkegaard goes for a way out of despair. Leaping acts of will are what permit surrender to look like triumph. The will gives subjective desperation the consoling appearance of agency. In these acts of willing surrender, the Kierkegaardian self is endlessly thrown back toward sin, toward the shattered subjectivity that denies divinity, "toward the state of despair, toward total sinfulness." Though he calls despair an "objective" concept and says it is the sickness of his age, Kierkegaard can only place despair within the bowels of inwardness: "In Kierkegaard there is so little of a subject/object in the Hegelian sense as there are given objects; there is only an isolated subjectivity, surrounded by a dark otherness. Indeed, only by crossing over this abyss would subjectivity be able to participate in 'meaning' that otherwise denies itself to subjectivity's solitude."[27] Inward despair is lifted out of history, abstracted from the real relations that give rise to it and, therefore, from whatever meanings it may harbor for human experience. And an overweening will that is a symptom of despair is also its alleged cure.

This is not to say that Kierkegaardian subjectivity is itself without a historical shape. Even Kierkegaard's doctrine of despair participates in dialectics: "Despair disassociates the self, and the ruins of the shattered self are the marks of hope. In Kierkegaard's work, this remains the innermost (and hence from Kierkegaard hidden) dialectical truth, which could only be disclosed in the posthumous history of his work." The philosophy of inwardness is a reflex of the age—and Kierkegaard himself comes close to recognizing it, but for the spell of Idealism. Like Kafka and Beckett later, Kierkegaard's pseudonyms testify to fractured and alienated individuality in bourgeois society. Unlike Kafka and Beckett, however, Kierkegaard interiorizes both the experience and the problem of despair in such a way as to guarantee its reproduction. What is a historically constituted image of individuality, Kierkegaard treats as ontology. Adorno describes this image as the nineteenth-century European bourgeois *intérieur*, a death-like subjectivity. In contrast with Baudelaire's *flâneur*, for whom inward reflection is nourished by an estranged encounter with urban and public places, the *intérieur* is a figure of reclusivity and hermitage. His comfort zone is an apartment interior, with furniture assembled as lifeless objects, cut off from the outside. And the preference for inwardness is totally severed from the objective conditions that make it possible, meaningful, or desirable: "The image of the *intérieur* therefore draws all of Kierkegaard's philosophy into its perspective, because in this image the doctrine's elements of ancient and unchanging nature present themselves directly as the elements of a historical constellation that governs the image."[28] As the *intérieur* withdraws from social relations and his contemporaries, Kierkegaard's philosophy withdraws from society and history. And still, the philosophy of inwardness reads as the abstract documentation of real historical developments.

Adorno does not commit the error he identifies in Kierkegaard. Damaged life, as he details it in the aphorisms of *Minima Moralia* for example, is no refuge from history and society, but our only available point of contact with it. Where he is forced to choose between subject and object—a choice that no genuine dialectics can make *or* escape—Adorno consistently defends the primacy of the object. Reflections from subjective experience must be taken as an extension of that basic commitment, and never as its contradiction. And Adorno resists every ontologizing gesture, not because philosophy can wholly escape the claims of ontology, but because it is the task of critique to challenge and contest those inevitable claims. So, there is much that sets him apart from Kierkegaard. But perhaps something he says of Kierkegaard is true of Adorno's thought as well. Perhaps the "dialectical truth" in Adorno is disclosed only in the posthumous history of his work, in the decades-long effort to rescue critique from despair. What is clear enough from this history is a general prohibition on the passions, particularly those aligned with the negative. It is as if despair (or fear or hatred) is a subjective deformation and not an objective formation, as if it is something borne by subjects and not in interaction of subjects and objects. An alternative would be a materialist critique of despair, in which the complex of human passions is seen to emerge out of historical processes and social relations. But even this materialism will find its footing in objective despair.

Dialectics and despair are brought into explicit relation toward the conclusion of the Kierkegaard study. Here is Adorno again, bearing substantial debts to Walter Benjamin:

> No truer image of hope can be imagined than that of ciphers, readable as traces, dissolving in history, disappearing in front of overflowing eyes, indeed confirmed in lamentation. In these tears of despair the ciphers appear as incandescent figures, dialectically, as compassion, comfort, and hope. Dialectical melancholy does not mourn vanished happiness. It knows that it is unreachable. But it knows also of the promise that conjoins the unreachable, precisely in its origin, with the wish.[29]

Benjaminian themes are striking, from the preliminary idea of the dialectical image to the conviction that this image reveals its truth-content through dissolution. Refracted images bear secret truths, preserved as trace elements, and disclosed upon vanishing. Here is Edward Said again: "Lateness as theme and as style keeps reminding us of death"—and, in this respect, everything about the early Kierkegaard book is already late style.[30] Also striking is the refusal to mourn in "dialectical melancholy" and the implicit repudiation of a Freudian preference for mourning over melancholia. Adorno's position is neither nostalgic nor utopian. And the tears of despair are not dissolved in a subjective leap or a spontaneous act of will. As he remarks elsewhere, such ideas are "too optimistic, even as an expression of despair; one cannot conceive of a versatile spontaneity outside of its entwinement with society."[31] The best retort to the disappearance of things is not pessimism, but fidelity to the promise of happiness preserved in tears. (Bataille, to whom I turn in the following chapter, also invokes tears as a dialectical image, discussing at length the peculiar experience of happy tears. In both instances, tears denote a relationship to history and temporality. Adorno's tears of despair bring vanished beginnings into contact with the future. Bataille's happy tears signal something unexpected, a surprise within the present, an aleatory experience.) Note that Adorno's fidelity is bound from the start to the aesthetic; there is nothing of an "aesthetic turn" in Adorno that occurs when revolutionary praxis fails him. And he is explicit about the real political stakes: "*not to forget in dreams the present world, but to change it by the strength of an image.*"[32]

These stakes are very different from the ones Bernard Yack sees as the principle symptom of "terminal left-Kantianism" (which is also, as it turns out, an "unresolved" Left Hegelianism): the longing, or "empty wish," for total revolution.[33] Critical theory, for Yack, is the consummation of a naïve and simplistic philosophic discontent. The pathos is "to declare dehumanizing any constraint imposed upon us by our social institutions that does not embody our humanity and to unmask as false all claims to satisfy their longing for the realization of humanity. Permanent, hopeless longing seems to be the critical theorists' obligation as well as their fate."[34] Admittedly, Yack is not centrally concerned with Adorno and discusses him only briefly in the book. That said, it is difficult to identify a recent work in political theory that more directly opposes the spirit of Adorno. Even putting to one side Yack's dubious depiction of the antinomies of Left Kantianism/Hegelianism, Yack's reflex prejudice against longing itself and the scorn with which he treats social discontents betray his deepest moralism and his highest preference for reconciliation. Adorno says something very different about longing: that it is, in fact, "the dialectical substratum of the 'doctrine of reconciliation.'"[35] And he is substantially more critical of anything "total"—revolution or not—than Yack allows. For Adorno, the unreconciled and irreconcilable are more reliable sites for a real immersion in the world. Yack can only see the longing for total revolution as a flight from reality, and, at the same time, he fails to see his own investment in reconciliation as a different variety of escapism. Furthermore, he does not appreciate that harbored in this longing, in dreams deferred or wishes unfilled, is the negative trace

of what remains possible. This is not to endorse the view that Adornian negativity ultimately offers little beyond a rarefied and precious
humanity, at best a morality of human rights but neither a politics nor
a philosophy. Adorno does not stop at the longings still capable of stir-
ring humanity—the longing for freedom, for justice, for happiness—
and enshrine them as founding principles for total revolution or universal human rights. On the contrary: Adorno is mostly apprehen-
sive about the work of dreams and desires, especially as they take
shape under an administered culture, and never defers to them in
their immediacy.[36] The task of critique is to decipher these dreams in
terms of a crooked involvement with the real conditions of existence.

Moving abruptly from his beginnings in Kierkegaard to endings,
it seems to me that the controversial radio address from 1969, "Resignation," reiterates Adorno's promise "not to forget in dreams the
present world," as well as his unwavering commitment to changing
the world.[37] Here it must be admitted that the posthumous history of
Adorno's twilight years have done more to shape the received political wisdom about negative dialectics than anything he ever wrote
about the state, political economy, police powers, or revolution. But
one ought not to commit the interpretive misstep that conflates the
idea of "context" with only the most immediate political circumstances that shape a given text. The context for his remarks is only
partly accounted for by the designation "'68" or by the student movement that erupted across the German university system, only partly
explained by Adorno's declining health or the war of position over
his role in the student protests. A closer examination reveals, too, how
this melancholic self-defense also involves a reorientation to Marx's
celebrated eleventh thesis on Feuerbach. Here "late style" as practiced
by "the older representatives of what the name 'Frankfurt School' has
come to designate" returns to its revolutionary beginnings in Marx.[38]
But this aspect of the address has gone unremarked.

I will turn to resignation—and the "wounds" Adorno purports to
expose in Marx—in conclusion to this chapter. But first I must explain
what is meant by Adorno's aporetics. Geoff Waite has emphasized that
"for the ancient Greeks as for Nietzsche, the *aporía* (*a-poros*: no way)
was the *beginning* of a way *out* of a problematic," but it is too simplistic to say that "for most intellectuals today it remains yet another

dead-end street."[39] Adorno's thinking rebels against philosophical beginnings of this sort, as well as the tacit conceit that philosophy initiates a way out of aporia. Adorno's highway is no dead-end street. Instead, a constellation of potentialities appears right on the surface of contemporary society, though many others are admittedly foreclosed. Aporias are not simply philosophical problems, so they are not answered by philosophy alone. In aporia, the restlessness of subjective reflection comes up against dim reality of objective conditions. Adorno's aporias offer a dispersal of fragments, concepts, and dialectical images. But they do not deliver a way out. Critical theory today might take this as Adorno's rare achievement instead of his failure.

3

Dialectics is the self-consciousness of the objective context of delusion; it does not mean to have escaped from that context.
— Adorno, *Negative Dialectics*

Critique has always been about limits.[40] Kant developed the philosophical idea of critique as a reflection on the limits of knowledge, the inescapably finite quality of what we can know about the world and ourselves. Hegel further pressed the connection between critique and limits, first by noting that every limit implies the possibility of going beyond it and then by casting philosophy as a retrospective enterprise. Philosophical critique paints its gray in gray at dusk, bound to belatedness and the limits of time. For Marx, philosophical critique had been limited to the interpretation of the world, while the point was to change it. Adorno too dwells in liminality, in the "no-man's-land" where critical theory is permitted its utopian pleasures and prompted to its painful lament.

His most systematic account of critique comes in the essay "Cultural Criticism and Society" from 1949—where the infamous dictum about Auschwitz and poetry also appears. In it, Adorno elaborates on a practice of cultural criticism that is neither transcendent nor purely immanent: "either calling culture as a whole into question from outside under the general notion of ideology, or confronting it with the norms which it itself has crystallized . . . cannot be accepted by critical theory."[41] This essay suggests the partial error in standard representations of Adorno's thought as immanent critique. Adorno hesitates in an embrace of immanence, and his rejection of transcendence is reluctant.

"The transcendent method," he writes, "which aims at totality, seems more radical than the immanent method, which presupposes the questionable whole," while transcendence promises a view from beyond it.[42] Transcendent critique offers a view of the totality, fixed in time and frozen in space, from a standpoint outside a reified field of knowledge. It adopts Archimedean points, or grounds from which the critic can examine the whole without immersion in it. For these reasons, it seems more radical, more likely to get at the root of a cultural formation. Yet, as Adorno sees it, "the choice of a standpoint outside the sway of existing society is as fictitious as only the construction of abstract utopias can be."[43] Transcendent critique takes itself as objective, universal, and disinterested. It can't admit its deep and inevitable partiality, nor can the transcendent critic take pleasure from attachments to the world. Ultimately this critic bears no such attachments; "wishing to wipe away the whole as if with a sponge," transcendent critique betrays its "affinity to barbarism."[44] It arouses a dream-wish to escape the confines of a bad reality, but does so at the expense of maintaining contact with reality.

Immanent critique, by contrast, remains fully immersed in the world, confined to the coordinates of the existing order and settling on a standpoint within the structure of reality. Transcendent critique imposes a false totality upon culture from outside. Immanent critique reveals a true atonality that emerges out of culture from within. It points to "the idea of harmony negatively by embodying the contradictions, pure and uncompromised, in its innermost structure."[45] Drawing it concepts from extant things, immanent critique maintains both spontaneous and strategic relations with reality. Adorno undeniably prefers this form—"the more essentially dialectical"—to transcendent criticism. But immanence, too, has its limits. Though the standpoint of transcendence is rigid and apart from the object, immanence risks absorption in the object. Though transcendent critique takes flight from the real, immanent critique is captive to a bad reality. And what the transcendent critic lacks in spontaneity and solidarity, the immanent critic lacks in originality and courage. As a procedure, immanent critique points to its limits and its objective conditions. As Adorno puts it: "Immanent criticism holds in evidence the fact that the mind has always been under a spell. On its own it is unable to resolve the contradictions under which it labors."[46]

Critical theory is tragically bound to the conditions of its production. Max Horkheimer's celebrated essay "Traditional and Critical Theory" also makes this point, emphasizing the limits of the mind in breaking the spell of a bad reality. "The thinking subject is not the place where knowledge and object coincide," Horkheimer argues, "nor consequently the starting-point for attaining absolute knowledge. Such an illusion about the thinking subject, under which idealism lived since Descartes, is ideology in the strict sense, for in it the limited freedom of the bourgeois individual puts on the illusory form of perfect freedom and autonomy."[47] All theory must suffer the ruse of ideology in the general sense, even reproduce it through concepts and representations drawn from the world.[48] Critical theory concedes this complicity. What it rejects is a greater complicity with set of illusions about the thinking subject. For Horkheimer, and for Adorno, the thinking subject is itself an abstract effect of real relations of domination. This subject cannot be considered separate from its objective conditions of possibility. Further, the thinking activity of this thinking subject is an incomplete and insufficient episode in freedom. To accept that an illusory freedom of the mind is somehow freedom in its most perfect form is, in the strict sense, to advance the cause of domination. Thinking, no matter how radical, cannot escape the world. And what is true for thought is also true of action, no matter how militant: it bears the features of the force it opposes. What Adorno calls dialectical critique dwells in this double bind: "the dialectical critic of culture must both participate in culture and not participate. Only then does he do justice to his object and to himself."[49] To participate—without joining in—is the supreme challenge. In *Minima Moralia*, Adorno describes the comportment in connection with the figure of Münchhausen: "Nothing less is asked of the thinker today than that he should be at every moment both within things and outside them—Münchhausen pulling himself out of the bog by his pig-tail becomes the pattern of knowledge that wishes to be more than either verification or speculation."⁵⁰ The procedure is constant struggle against attachment and indifference.

Dialectical critique does not mean mapping a middle ground between extremes. As he argues in his lectures on Hegel, dialectics takes place at the extremes and points to a philosophy of experience energized by extremes.⁵¹ Experience is everything in Adorno. It brings the subject to the object. It opens thought to the passions. It joins Kant and Hegel. But even experience does not become a site of affirmation. Alain Badiou has proposed that Adorno's project "consists in retaining (simultaneously and at the same time going beyond) Kant's negative critique as well as Hegel's dialectical negativity . . . [joining] Kant's critical gesture, which is a gesture of separation, of limitation of the pretensions of reason, with the Hegelian dialectical negativity shorn of its affirmative absoluteness."⁵² Badiou is right. But importantly, Adorno's project also consists in combining a philosophy of experience with a real radicalism. He opposes any effort to moderate a melancholy science.

This aspect of Adorno's thinking—its contempt for the middle ground, its delight in the extremes—is crucial for any political interpretation of his work. It is also crucial for understanding what he retains from Kant and Hegel, and what he leaves behind. The discussion of Kant in *Negative Dialectics*, for example, cherishes the unrestraint in Kantian reason and centers on the concept of despair:

> The postulate [of immortality] condemns the intolerability of extant things and confirms the spirit of its recognition. That no reforms within the world sufficed to do justice to the dead, that none of them touched upon the wrong of death—this is what moves Kantian reason to hope against reason. The secret of his philosophy is the unthinkability [*Unausdenkbarkeit*] of despair.⁵³

Immortality as a postulate of practical reason is reinterpreted here as Kant's radical condemnation of historical death. As Adorno sees it, Kantian reason is moved by passion and by a refusal to join in a world gone mad. That there is nothing in this world that can bring back the dead, or even do justice to their memory, requires that life itself become a postulate—and spring from a source beyond the intelligible sphere. Kantian reason draws its nourishment from the unreasonable hope that objective despair does not have the final word. The postulate of immortality "resists all attempts of a desperate consciousness to posit despair as an absolute" and insists that "the world's course is not absolutely conclusive, nor is absolute despair."[54] The secret of Kant's critical philosophy is its desperate passion, its unreasonable hope of banishing the thought of despair.

Transcendence, deferred and postponed, allows Kant to preserve something nonidentical with injustice. Eternal life is his indirect assault on the wrong of death. It continues in a certain tradition of German lamentation, though distinct from the Baroque drama that interested Benjamin.[55] The postulates of practical reason point to what Adorno calls a "rescuing urge" at the heart of Kantian metaphysics—an impulse that Habermas also identifies in Benjamin's redemptive critique.[56] Adorno is sympathetic to it, and even invokes the language of redemption in clarifying the tasks of philosophy in the face of despair. But the secret of Kant's philosophy, the unthinkability of despair, also gets at the heart of the problem with the rescuing urge: invariably, it begins and ends in prohibition. For Kant, it means a ban on thinking the Absolute. Premised on this basic prohibition, what looks like a philosophy of freedom reveals itself as something quite different. "The Kantian system is a system of stop signals," Adorno observes, "obsessed with the apriority of its synthetic judgments," and averse to any thinking that would require substantial revision of its basic apparatus.[57] The unthinkability of despair, while a genuine revolt against an irredeemable reality, also indicates a tendency in Kant's system that sometimes turns "terroristic"—a tendency to set limits around what can be thought and exclude any experience that does not conform to its mandates.[58] "Irresistibly," says Adorno, "it drifts toward a ban on all thinking."[59] The deeper secret of Kant's critical philosophy is the wish to render *all things* unthinkable.

At least in this respect Hegel is just the opposite. The impulse in Hegel, as Adorno sees it, is to render things thinkable, to set static forms into motion and follow the interface between subjects and objects. Adorno describes the "spontaneous receptivity" in Hegel's dialectic, referring to its dynamism and its deference to a world of objects. "Hegel everywhere yields to the object's own nature," an exercise radical in immanence that permits him to bring concepts to experience.[60] Extending philosophical dignity to experience is one important way that Hegel's thinking represents, for Adorno, a genuine advance in the cause of critique. Furthermore, the very idea of the dialectic in Adorno is drawn from Hegel: "the dialectic, the epitome of Hegel's philosophy, cannot be likened to a methodological or ontological principle . . . the dialectic is neither a mere method . . . nor is it a *weltanschauung* into whose schema one has to squeeze reality . . . [it] is the unswerving effort to conjoin reason's critical consciousness of itself and the critical experience of objects."[61] It is in the spirit of Hegel that Adorno insists upon the preponderance of the object, the value of determinate negation, and the transcending powers of immanent critique. Throughout his major works, Adorno will invoke Hegel's authority in defense of negative dialectics and to clarify the melancholy science.

Adorno's critique of Hegel is well known and implicit in the idea of negative dialectics. Simply stated, Adorno rejects Hegel's affirmative ambitions for the system. In Hegel's positive dialectic, the restlessness of the negative inevitably gives way to a higher concept of the Absolute. Cracks in the system are filled in by the comforting assurance that reality is rational and rationality is real. Passions and experience are subordinated to a logic of identity that annihilates them both. For Adorno, Hegel's deepest investment in identity means the erasure of difference and the end of critical experience. This is how he puts it in one of the lectures on metaphysics: "Hegel's philosophy contains a moment by which that philosophy, despite having made the principle of determinate negation its vital nerve, passes over into affirmation and therefore into ideology: the belief that negation, by being pushed far enough and by reflecting itself, is one with positivity."[62] Negative dialectics refuses this passage and, with it, any hope of rescue from the highway of despair. Contra Hegel, the wounds of spirit do leave scars. As if to anticipate the difficulties with reading his work, Adorno posits that "the incomprehensible in Hegel is the scar left by identity-thinking." [63] Scars are also marks of struggle, sources of memory, and signs of life. The incomprehensible in Adorno is the scar left by objective despair.

Hegel concludes the preface to the *Philosophy of Right* with a celebrated statement on the limits of philosophy: "When philosophy paints its gray in gray, then has a shape of life grown old. Philosophy's gray in gray cannot be rejuvenated, only understood."[64] In a passage from *Negative Dialectics* that reads as if a direct retort to Hegel's gray scaling, Adorno maintains that "grayness could not fill us with despair if our minds did not harbor the concept of different colors, scattered traces of which are not absent from the negative whole."[65] Despair is a dialectical passion in its connection with work of determinate negation. This much Hegel understood. But it is also a dialectical passion in that it contains its negation. It signals to its other. Passions in general have a dialectical quality; seemingly opposed forces exchange energy and move in the same direction. "The capacity for fear and for happiness are the same," for example, which Adorno describes as "the unrestricted openness to experience amounting to self-abandonment in which the vanquished rediscovers himself."[66] And the power of critical reason depends upon the force of passions. "Sense can only endure in despair and extremity"—which is also to say, critical reason lives in unreason, and avoids objective madness to the extent that it remains receptive to absurdity, nonsense, and experience at the extremes of knowledge.[67] Despair reflects real conditions, and registers a revolt against them. The conclusion to Walter Benjamin's essay on *Elective Affinities* provides Adorno with a version of this passionate dialectic: "Only for the sake of the hopeless ones have we been given hope."[68] Hope without hope—or, the formula for critique that retains the "color of the concrete."

4

For thought there is really no other possibility, no other opportunity, than to do what the miner's adage forbids: to work one's way through the darkness without a lamp, without possessing the positive through the higher concept of the negation of the negation, and to immerse oneself in the darkness as deeply as one can.

—Adorno, *Metaphysics*

Some of the most powerful "dialectical images" in Adorno are drawn from darkness, examples of the immersion cited earlier. These images are everywhere in Adorno, but three in particular stand out for the hope without hope suggested in each. The first comes from the famous "Culture Industry" chapter of *Dialectic of Enlightenment*, when Horkheimer and Adorno consider what, if anything, could be said on behalf of the cinema. Would anything be lost if the movie house was burned to the ground? It is a remarkable moment in the text, one of several that interrupt the generally negative movements of the critique and demonstrate the fugitive experiences of freedom preserved in mass culture. The second image is drawn from *Aesthetic Theory*, and it contains one of Adorno's answers to the question concerning commitment, art and politics, politics and pleasure, and the potential forms of a radical aesthetic. Third and finally, there is *Endgame*—or, more specifically, Adorno trying to understand *Endgame* and contemporary critics trying to understand both. Adorno's analysis of Beckett is complex and far reaching; I will focus in particular on the experimentation with dramatic form, the interaction between laughter and disgust, and parody as aesthetic praxis. These images are only some of the joyful remains of Adorno's aporetics, where thinking goes to take refreshment and everyday experience furnishes its unexpected felicity.

First, the critique of the Culture Industry: this chapter from *The Dialectic of Enlightenment* remains one of the most widely read and referenced of the early Frankfurt School texts. Its powerful and comprehensive assault on mass culture, while jarring to late modern sensibilities, remains a classic in Marxist cultural theory. More recent scholarship also demonstrates that its time for a serious rethinking of this critique, of Adorno's attitudes toward American popular culture, and of the posture that critical theory assumes toward cultural production.[69] That Horkheimer and Adorno cite in celebration a number of popular eccentricities—Chaplin, Greta Garbo, Betty Boop, clowning, slapstick, brothels, peep shows, and the circus—suggests that their critique is rather different from a mandarin contempt for the popular. If anything, the text clears a terrain of investigation—popular song, film, cartoon, physical comedy—that hitherto seemed beyond the boundaries of theoretical critique. And it demonstrates an erudition in the popular, which cannot be attributed entirely to the demands of scientific analysis. Their critique confesses the real pleasures of its object and betrays a secret affection for at least some of what goes by the name of entertainment.

The movie theater is no exception. Not what appears on screen per se, though there we occasionally find those images—Garbo's melancholy smile, for example—capable of bringing dialectics to a standstill. But the place that is the cinema, where audiences gather in the dark to participate in the reproduction of Hollywood dreams: Would it be better if these places did not exist? What if "the use of these institutions was no longer made obligatory by their mere existence"?[70] Here is how the authors respond:

> Shutting them down in this way would not be reactionary machine-wrecking. Those who suffered would not be the film enthusiasts but those who always pay the penalty in any case, the ones who had lagged behind. For the housewife, despite the films which are supposed to integrate her still further, the dark of the cinema grants a refuge in which she can spend a few unsupervised hours, just as once, when there were still dwellings and evening repose, she could sit gazing out of the window. The unemployed of the great centers find freshness in summer and warmth in winter in these places of regulated temperature.[71]

From the perspective of cultural consumption and criticism, it matters little whether the theater survives. Film has no essential relationship to freedom or happiness, only a contingent and artificial link. Enthusiasts will find other venues for their entertainment, and technology is set to transform the cinema by its own accord. Still, though it would not be reactionary to shut down the movie house, the authors find good reason to keep it open. The darkened theater offers the housewife respite from the watchful eyes of her family and provides the homeless with needed shelter. These are not the champions and protectorates of the entertainment industry, but anachronistic figures on the margins of cultural consumption. They exist within structures of domination—the household, the system of private property—and their presence in the theater cannot be thought apart from those structures. But they are nevertheless the inadvertent and real beneficiaries of cinema. Horkheimer and Adorno find a genuine happiness in this most unlikely place.

Another image of darkness appears in *Aesthetic Theory* and suggests a complement to Adorno's notorious critique of "commitment" in art—or art that advances an explicit political content or message. Here is Adorno on a vastly preferable aesthetic:

> Radical art today is synonymous with dark art; its primary color is black. Much contemporary production is irrelevant because it takes no note of this and childishly delights in color. The ideal of blackness with regard to content is one of the deepest impulses of abstraction. It may well be that the current trifling with sound and color effects is a reaction to the impoverishment entailed by the ideal of black.[72]

Note that the potential for a radical aesthetic remains Adorno's guiding concern.[73] Elsewhere, Adorno will insist that art with a political message is reactionary more than radical, no matter its content, because it renders aesthetics a mere instrument.[74] Political art tends toward the propagandistic, not for any inherent disposition to dishonesty, but for its sacrifice of the aesthetic. And whatever political program may be justifiably served by such art would be still further degraded by it. Against committed art stands the true radicalism of the ideal of black, which is not given to use-value. In this specific passage, it is aligned with abstraction and what was "established by the surrealists as black humor," though the ideal of black finds occasional champions in popular culture as well.[75] The ideal of black opposes the mandatory optimism of contemporary production and "the injustice committed by all cheerful art."[76] Darkness, at least since Baudelaire, also suggests a "sensuous enticement" to the dissonant and discordant, and the vague outlines of a critical hedonism: "Negation may reverse into pleasure, not affirmation."[77]

Negation may reverse into pleasure. Adorno could have been more emphatic about this, and elaborate its implications beyond the sphere of art.[78] *Negative Dialectics* reads differently as a document of immanent pleasures. Adorno's sustained interest in Freud and psychoanalysis takes on a greater significance. The apparatus of wage labor and the ideology of leisure look like direct assaults on the very possibility of pleasure. And certainly the analyses of astrology, regressive listening, baseball, and jazz seem to beg for a critical concept of pleasure.

Emphatic or not, Adorno shows what critical theory could look like in pursuit of the pleasures of the negative rather than the good reasons for the affirmative.

The pleasures of trying to understand *Endgame* inspire Adorno's plan to dedicate *Aesthetic Theory* to the memory of Samuel Beckett. Though he is resistant to the idea of masterpiece, "an idea which itself reflects the idea of creation and totality," Adorno sees *Endgame* as an aesthetic achievement of the first order.[79] Adorno's approach to the drama is the inverse of his approach to Kierkegaard. Understanding Beckett is not a philosophical project. Recall that Kierkegaard begs to be read aesthetically, but must be considered philosophically—that is, in terms of the concept and its fate. By contrast, the study of *Endgame* cannot proceed philosophically—that is, in terms of an abstract ontology or a moral imperative. *Endgame* stages the poverty of philosophy and its radical critique: "Understanding it can mean nothing other than understanding its incomprehensibility."[80] And the incomprehensibility of *Endgame* is the scar left by social conditions: "The irrationality of bourgeois society in its late phase rebels at letting itself be understood; those were the good old days, when a critique of the political economy of this society could be written that judged it in terms of its own *ratio*. For since then the society has thrown its *ratio* on the scrap heap and replaced it with virtually unmediated control."[81] Understanding *Endgame* means deciphering the dramatic enactment of sociohistorical conditions and the parodic critique of how we have learned to live with these conditions. Beckett demands that we interpret him *critically*—that is, in terms of historical processes, social forms, and the degradation of experience. This is not the same as political judgment, nor does it mean pulling Beckett into the service of a cause. "Just as it would be ridiculous to impute an abstract subjectivist ontology to Beckett and then put that ontology on some index of degenerate art," as Adorno alleges Lukács does, "so it would be ridiculous to put Beckett on the stand as star political witness."[82] *Endgame* sets to stage a specific historical moment, and is for that reason more profoundly political than the existential philosophies that make an ontology of our history. But it does not exist apart from the catastrophic situation it presents. Beckett is not the source for a politics that puts an end to objective despair. Instead, he is best understood in terms of a radical aesthetic that can do justice to it.

This radical aesthetic takes the form of parody—"parody of the philosophy spit out by his dialogues as well as parody of forms"—and, as parody, elicits laughter as its response.[83] Parody is crucially different from ridicule, which presupposes distance and hierarchy. Beckett's parody involves the misuse of dramatic form, the "use of forms in the epoch of their impossibility"—or, comic anachronism.[84] Beckett's humor is more clownish than contemptuous. It transforms the stage into a zoo, converts dialogue into sounds and noise, and reduces humans to their animality. It delights in deformity and disfigurement, the terrors of somatic experience, and the nonsense that passes for communication. Beckett's parody arouses the laughter of immanence. This laughter "ought to suffocate the ones who laugh," but *Endgame* arouses laughter still: "This is what has become of humor now that it has become obsolete as an aesthetic medium and repulsive, without a canon for what should be laughed about, without a place of reconciliation from which one could laugh, and without anything harmless on the face of the earth that would allow itself to be laughed at."[85] The historical obsolescence of humor is not the end of laughter, but it does demand comic forms equipped to handle the revolting and repellant. What looks like regressive infantilism takes on a sharp critical edge.

Beckett lingers on the irrationality harbored in reason, and renders in this obsolete dramatic form a theoretical position staked out in *Dialectic of Enlightenment*. His drama demonstrates that a *ratio* confident in it powers would not be so desperate to prove them. *Endgame* shows how reason cannot escape its lapse into absurdity. "*Ratio* itself sprang from the interest of self-preservation," Adorno notes, "hence its compulsive rationalizations demonstrate its own irrationality."[86] As Horkheimer and Adorno argue in *Dialectic of Enlightenment*, the concept of reason finds its beginnings in fear—the fear of nature and the desire to preserve oneself against the fearsome force of nature. The force of the passions lies at the origins of the dialectic of reason. And just as *ratio* harbors the irrational fear that engulfs it, absurdity maintains a secret alliance with dialectical critique. Here is how Adorno puts it in *Minima Moralia*:

Dialectical reason is, when set against the dominant mode of reason, unreason: only in encompassing and canceling this mode does
it become itself reasonable. . . . The dialectic cannot stop short before
the concepts of health and sickness nor indeed before their siblings
reason and unreason. Once it has recognized the ruling order and
its proportions as sick—marked in the most literal sense with paranoia, with "pathic projection"—then it can see as healing cells only
what appears, by the standards of that order, as itself sick, eccentric,
paranoia—indeed, "mad."[87]

If dominant rationality is shot through with madness, if the order it
re-creates and legitimates is not simply irrational but paranoid and
murderous, if sickness seems like health and unreason like reason,
then these categories lose their stability and certitude. The absurd in
Beckett is not "an 'existential situation' diluted to an idea and then
illustrated," as it is for Sartre, but a sociohistorical condition given to
aesthetic representation.[88]

We can appreciate why Adorno has been accused of aestheticism,
but what he claims to find in *Endgame* is "something like a *philosophical anthropology*."[89] Like Bataille's anthropology, this project pivots on
waste—on what becomes of the superfluous or obsolete, on how culture treats the refuse, garbage, and waste to which it has been reduced.
"Beckett's trash cans are emblems of the culture rebuilt after Auschwitz,"
and, in this way, he goes beyond Bataille to capture the catastrophic
conditions of this anthropology.[90] *Endgame* presents a world where
everyone and everything "waits to be carted off to the dump"—stumps,
fragments, clichés, names, everything is mutilated and thrown away.[91]
This is a form of humor that draws much of its force from horror:
"*Endgame* prepares us for a state of affairs in which everyone who lifts
the lid of the nearest trashcan can expect to find his own parents in it."[92]
Yet, it is also here, in the complete disposability of all things, where the
critical purchase of this philosophical anthropology is measured. What
is thrown away—in a culture that throws everything away—is seen to
matter. Again, a passage from *Minima Moralia* details the position:

If Benjamin said that history had hitherto been written from the
standpoint of the victor, and needed to be written from that of the

vanquished, we might add that knowledge must indeed present the fatally rectilinear succession of victory and defeat, but should also address itself to those things which were not embraced by this dynamic, which fell by the wayside—what might be called the waste products and blind spots that have escaped the dialectic.[93]

The idea that our waste may tell us something about our history and culture links Adorno to Bataille, as does the investment in what escapes the dialectic, which is not quite the same as a divestment from the dialectic.[94] In Adorno, this project involves the revaluation of obsolescence, and an enthusiasm for the outmoded, untimely, and anachronistic elements of society. (This enthusiasm occasionally lapses into an uncritical nostalgia, but most often indicates Adorno's real affection for difference.) Adorno's addition to the Benjaminian doctrine does something more: it invites critical theory into drama that is not primarily about loss and defeat. That "fatally rectilinear" drama continues, with the brutality and blindness that Benjamin attributes to it. But a different drama also takes form, a story not of our losses, but of our excess and those experiences that escape the laws of victory and defeat.

5

> Already in Marx there lies concealed a wound. He may have presented the eleventh thesis on Feuerbach so authoritatively because he knew he wasn't entirely sure about it.
>
> —Adorno, "Resignation"

Toward the conclusion of his life, Adorno gives explicit consideration to a claim that had been made about his work for some time, but that had intensified during the cultural conflicts of the 1960s. During these turbulent times, he was thought by many student radicals to be Frankfurt's knight of resignation. It was said that he and "older representatives" of the Frankfurt School "had indeed developed elements of a critical theory of society . . . [but] were not ready to draw the practical consequences from it."[95] And the charge was not simply that the professor had failed supply programs for action, but that he "did not even support actions by those who felt inspired by critical theory."[96] Critical theory, so the accusation went (and still goes), is theory with no praxis, theory that harbors a hidden distaste for praxis, theory that is *generously* called resignation, but is probably closer to reaction. Adorno's reply to his accusers was delivered just before his death and in the immediate context of protest actions on the university campus—at times, in his lecture hall. What is especially fascinating about his reply is how much of it involves Marx, how the Frankfurt School here returns to its radical origins in Marxist critique and reiterates that the point is to change the world. Adorno inquires into the value of a theory that bears openly Marx's concealed wounds.

Marx's lessons structure the entire analysis. To begin, Adorno underscores the social significance of the division of labor as described by Marx, especially the process through which mental labor was set in distinction from other kinds of work activity. "Theoretical thinkers" are themselves produced through a system of social relationships and "the purpose that has fallen to them in a society based on the division of labor may be questionable; they may be deformed by it."[97] But maintaining even the very basic elements of a Marxist social theory is to appreciate that theoretical types "could not by sheer will abolish what they have become."[98] Voluntarism is always a feeble response to structures. Further, and more importantly, "the much invoked unity of theory and practice has the tendency of slipping into the predominance of practice" and an antipathy to theory.[99] This is in direct violation of the dialectical approach that Marx takes, in which theory and practice name equally necessary and mutually dependent forms of human activity. Marx's critique of capitalism centers on the practical consequences of our theories and the theoretical assumptions that guide our practice. And Marx's revolutionary activity followed from a theoretical analysis of the crisis tendencies in capitalist society. What the unity of theory and practice meant for Marx it no longer means: "In Marx, the doctrine of this unity was inspired by the real possibility of action, which even at the time was not actualized. Today what is emerging is more the direct contrary. *One clings to action for the sake of the impossibility of action.*"[100] Marx's demand to change the world was inspired by the real possibility of revolution, which even then was a failure. Now the call to action expresses the opposite: the impossibility of changing the world. If the buried truth in Marx is that he is never wholly persuaded of the primacy of practice, now the lie is that we believe we are changing anything.

There is a point at which the primacy of practice becomes the prohibition on thinking—and Adorno stands guard at that point, whether facing Kantian postulates or student radicals. When theory is forced to be practical—to speak to the demands of practice and to speak in a practical voice—it is typically forced to give up on that aspect of theory that involves actual thinking. "Many movements defame theory as a form of oppression, as though practice were not much more directly related to oppression," Adorno remarks, contrasting theory's benign elitism to the murderous egalitarianism of so many practical programs.[101] Totalitarian regimes are defined by their founding assault on any thinking that does not enhance and enlarge the power of the state. But what he sees in the lecture hall is not a movement of this type. Adorno calls it "pseudo-activity: action that overdoes and aggravates itself for the sake of its own publicity, without admitting to itself to what extent it serves as substitute satisfaction, elevating itself into an end in itself."[102] It is political theater in the crude sense, with the caveat that this actionism also expresses psychosocial drives as well. It is suggestive of anxiety—anxiety about powerlessness, about the inability to act, and about acting in error. The antitheoretical reflex is symptomatic of the anxieties of actionism. Pressing the psychoanalytic point, Adorno wonders about the ego that surrenders to the power of a collective with which it is also identified. One of the satisfactions of collective action—on the ground and apart from whether objectives are met—is the feeling of being among the few who seem to be many. Adorno suggests that a powerless ego chases after these satisfactions. And all the drama and the noise smack of regress: "At this time no higher form of society is concretely visible: for that reason whatever acts as though it were in easy reach has something regressive about it."[103]

This is not to say that a higher form of society is beyond reach, only that Adorno opposes those who contend that this society is right in front of us. What is more, he shows how pseudo-activity is the real resignation; the struggle to change the world is traded for the satisfactions of signing on. Its dominant affect is rage, for the reason that the pseudo-activity registers and reflects powerlessness. But justifiable rage is unjustifiably turned toward theory. The revaluation of critique—forms of thought that do not come with positive programs, so their value must reside elsewhere—is resistance against the pressures to resign. Negative critique preserves a noninstrumental relationship to a world of objects and others, and in the context of late capitalism, this is its highest value. Critique that is impractical or inactionable, without clear uses, has significance nonetheless. It challenges an order of things measured by utility. It points to the wasteful elements of contemporary overproduction, not to extend the empire of efficiency but to honor what escapes it. Critique advances the cause of individuality, not as an unfinished project of European modernity, but as a potential site of nonidentity.[104] And what Hegel describes in connection with the nega-tive—restlessness, but also patience and seriousness—is what permits us to reach for a different world. Critique opposes resignation in "its insatiable aspect, its aversion to being quickly and easily satisfied."[105] Pseudo-activity is quickly and easily satisfied by forgery and fakes.

The politics of critique inheres in its forms: "Prior to all particu-lar content, thinking is actually the force of resistance."[106] The anti-theoretical position that demands something positive and practical from critique harbors a desire to dominate, to quash all resistance, to eliminate all trace of difference. An equally antitheoretical position measures the value of critique only by its particular political com-mitments or the actions of the critic. We are now in a position to appreciate why Adorno's most radical and political works are so often considerations on (and experiments with) form. "The Essay as Form" is the most obvious example. Nowhere does he provide a more pow-erful statement on the connection between philosophical writing and political commitment. And the text enacts its argument; the form is the defense of its content. *Minima Moralia*, too, has ambitions that come before its particular content. Aphorisms, in the context of dam-aged life, read as fragmentary episodes in freedom. The melancholy science draws the force of resistance from these episodes—and the experience of friendship that makes them possible.[107]

Asad Haider and Salar Mohandesi remind us that serious challenges to the eleventh thesis on Feuerbach are rare in the history of criti-cal theory.[108] Adorno's late reflections on resignation are remarkable in this respect. The primacy of practice in Marx falls under suspicion and theory is finally unrepentant for its role in "the ruthless critique of everything existing." Adorno takes aim at a bourgeois tendency, repeated in Marx, now almost second nature: to measure the value of an idea by its "use-value" for action. And he questions part of Marx's revolutionary conviction, or at least introduces the possibility of a pathos that governs it. But this is also a critique that upholds the truth-content in Marx's command. And it radicalizes a line of argument found even in Lenin: "Without revolutionary theory there can be no revolutionary movement. This idea cannot be insisted upon too strongly at a time when the fashionable preaching of opportunism goes hand in hand with an infatuation for the narrowest forms of practical activity."[109] Practiced in freedom and permitted to be what it is, thinking shows why a "higher form of society" is something worth striving for. Changing the way we think will not change the world. But what we think about thinking—what we expect critical theory to be and do—says everything about the world we live in.

"Thinking that follows trails is narrative thinking, like the apocryphal model of the adventure story about the journey to a utopian goal," Adorno remarks in connection with the thought patterns of Ernst Bloch.[110] By contrast with narrative thinking, aporetics derives its sense of adventure from the fugitive traces of freedom that do not follow charted trails or pathways. Like the essay, aporetic thinking "abandons the royal road to origins, which leads only to what is most derivative," as well as plotted futures and ordained objectives, which lead only to what is most speculative.[111] Paradoxically, though, it does point to new directions for contemporary critical theory. I have tried to show that Adorno's philosophy finds its footing in despair and that this is not the problem he bequeaths to us but the value of his thinking for contemporary critical theory. I have hoped to indicate some of the places critical theory is permitted to go—the forms it takes, the postures it assumes, and the pleasures it offers—once released to the negative. And I have aimed to clarify how the concept of despair works in Adorno's thought. Bataille and Fanon allow us finally to take some welcome relief from the concept. But they also confirm that negative dialectics names a rich and varied project.

4
Georges Bataille

ALEATORY DIALECTICS

1

> Being, says Hegel, is the most impoverished notion. Chance, I
> say, is the richest.
>
> —Bataille, *Guilty*

If chance is, for Bataille, the richest of notions, this is for the havoc
it wreaks on human projects, on being *as project*, and on any philosophical system that posits the pursuit of a project as the highest
expression of freedom. Even those thinkers from whom Bataille took
philosophical nourishment—Hegel, Marx, and Nietzsche, to name the
most important—failed to exploit the richness of chance to the extent
that they pinned their fortunes to projects. Spirit, Communism, Will
to Power—each of them variations on a more fundamental theme, of
directing feverish passion toward specific and often practical ends, of
displacing desire for interests and freedom for necessity, of gather-
ing the disordered elements of human existence into a coherent set
of reasons, motivations, and explanations, of subordinating the eruptions of chance to the reign of knowledge. Chance sends projects into
ruin, leaving their architects to despair. Chance rips our designs to
shreds. But chance, says Bataille, also restores to the human condition that *play-element*, without which knowledge, community, and

the sacred are scarcely possible. The human being becomes sovereign, in Bataille's idiosyncratic and shifting sense of that term, only as the dice are falling.

Given Bataille's aversion to projects and disdain for use-values, it is no small difficulty that part of my project involves putting his texts to use for political thinking.[1] In particular, I aim at deciphering the paradoxical formula he names the "will to chance" and elaborates in the 1930s and 1940s as fascism takes hold of Europe. Here the difficulty lies not simply in making sense of Bataille, of writing that often induces silence and ideas that seem to conspire against their transmission, but in making *political* sense of Bataille.

Though his legacy looms large in literary circles, in aesthetics and visual culture, among scholars of sexuality, and even in some quarters of critical anthropology and religious studies, Bataille figures marginally in social and political theory—and, perhaps, for good reason. Notwithstanding his prominence in radical intellectual circles in Paris before the war, his consistent efforts to clarify the tasks of social science, his distinctive contributions to critical theory, political sociology, and philosophical anthropology, and his influence on a later generation of French thinkers,[2] we are still not quite sure what to *do* with Bataille. His prose is cryptic, though no more so than other "continental" thinkers in regular rotation. Substantial portions of his complete works remain unavailable to English readers, but even his translated texts have received scant attention from those trained to think and write about political ideas.[3] Politics were not his exclusive concern, for his interests were as eclectic and far reaching as his day job as a librarian and archivist at the Bibliothèque Nationale would suggest. But Bataille was attracted to revolutionary ideas and drawn in the 1930s to the uprisings of the Popular Front and the eruptions that take place *in the streets* and *among the poor*. Though he is not a theorist of democracy per se, and though he is a fierce opponent of democracy in its "bourgeois" form, these elements of Bataille's thinking resonate with radical strains in democratic thought. Jacques Rancière's formula for democratic equality, for instance—"the part with no part"—recalls Bataille's idea of the heterogeneous, even if the latter does not designate a political theoretical concept as such.[4]

Where he does deal with political questions directly and at length, for instance in his essay from 1933, "The Psychological Structure of Fascism," the results are powerful and incisive. This essay complements and complicates the more familiar investigations into fascism from the first generation of Frankfurt School critical theorists, blending Marxist social theory and Freudian psychoanalysis, developing a distinctive political anthropology, and gesturing toward a novel theory of the state.[5] The essay also contributes to a critique of what Sara Ahmed has recently described as the political economy of affect, for Bataille speaks to the processes and mechanisms by which the political apparatus grabs hold of the affective forces that make and destroy human communities.[6] Anticipating the "affective turn" in recent social and political theory, his analysis tracks the psychic energies that constitute military and religious orders, showing how these energies circulate to produce and maintain systems of hierarchy, domination, and control. The essay even gives a provocative, though disconcerting, account of political Islam, which he compares to fascism in its "sudden formation of a total power" that combines military, religious, and political dominion.[7] But this essay is not much discussed. And Bataille's reflections on materialist method—what he called "base materialism" and linked to the low, the degraded, the fallen, the unemployed, and the poor—have faded into some obscurity, despite a "new materialism" afoot in critical political theory and political-economic conditions ripe for this reorientation in perspective.[8] Those of us aligned with "continental" traditions, with critical theory in its broadest sense, with approaches and perspectives that Bataille helped to shape, haven't had much to say about his texts.

Admittedly, there is a whole lot of nonsense in them, a feature of his communication that readers might appreciate as part of the philosophical point but still view as a distraction from the difficult work of theorizing contemporary political formations. It is not my aim in the following pages to reclaim the whole of Bataille for political thinking. That said, I hope to resist two familiar and dominant representations of Bataille: one that identifies in his thinking a variety of "Left fascism" and another that presents the development of his thought as a movement away from politics toward eroticism, hypersubjectivity, and mysticism.[9] To this end, I pull at a single thread in his theoretical work, a term that, I will argue, links his engagement with Hegel, Marx, and Nietzsche, and connects the "political" Bataille of the prewar period to the "mystical" Bataille of the postwar years: *chance.*

Chance makes its first appearances in Bataille's essays of the 1930s, most notably in "The Sorcerer's Apprentice," an important document from 1937 that deals with questions of politics, the fragmentation of the human being, the limits of action, and the aleatory experience of freedom. (I will come back to this essay, and others from the period, in the next section.) With the outbreak of war and the German occupation of France, chance resurfaces as a dominant motif of his writings, reaching its apogee in the unfinished *Somme Athéologique.* Though written and published individually, Bataille envisioned *Inner Experience, Guilty,* and *On Nietzsche* to comprise the first three volumes of this magnum opus, and each contains extensive but elusive remarks on chance. Sylvère Lotringer has suggested that these works indicate that Bataille had been "released from the political fervor of the prewar years" and "had come to view any effort (any action) as a symptom of 'decline.'"[10] But "decline" is itself an ambiguous category for the proponent of "base materialism." I take Bataille's rejection of actionism to stem instead from the critique of calculative rationality, the assault on projects, and the refusal to subordinate the play of chance to the empire of profit.[11] And I read the texts that compose the unfinished *Somme Athéologique* as attempts to push political thinking to the outer limits of reason so that praxis may come back into contact with the fugitive principle of freedom. Though it can be taken as a philosophical doctrine, an interpretive device, a poetic experiment, and an ethical comportment, the will to chance is also a political formula.

This argument—and especially the claim that *On Nietzsche,* written in 1944 and published in 1945, is Bataille at his most political, even as it is also his most intensely personal book—confronts significant challenges in the text. As he puts it in the preface: "Following [Nietzsche's] paradoxical doctrines, you are forced to see yourself as excluded from participating in current causes. You'll eventually see that solitude is your only lot."[12] Bracketing for a moment whether this is, indeed, the only way to follow Nietzsche, does it not indicate Bataille's withdrawal from a world with others? What could be the political purchase of a formula that Bataille explicitly thematized as the *repudiation* of political causes? And does this apologia for solitude not reinforce conventional wisdom concerning the trajectory of Bataille's life and writing: his turn away from (misguided and ill-fated) revolutionary politics in the streets to the mythic rituals of secret societies to, finally, the interiority of mystical experience?

In this chapter, I will look more closely at the finer points in Bataille's treatment of Nietzsche, specifically his reformulation of the will to power as will to chance and his reinterpretation of the eternal return and *amor fati*. For now, it is worth underscoring the point that Bataille's effort to rescue Nietzsche's philosophy from fascist oblivion—if only for himself and, as he puts it in the opening lines, only for fear of going crazy—is deeply motivated by political concerns, notwithstanding Bataille's consistently unorthodox radicalism. *Current* causes, the causes that dominate the European political landscape in 1944, the causes that claim Nietzsche yet know nothing about him, causes that include European fascism and anti-Semitism, must be excluded. Such causes are hardly preferable to solitude—or, we might add, more meaningfully political, if by politics Bataille means something that pertains to the experience of freedom. This is the essential point: in Bataille, the will to chance amounts to something rather different from an ontology of contingency or a metaphysics of chaos, though it may depend upon both ultimately. It is an invitation to radically refigure the politics of freedom, the result of a strategic reading and representation of Nietzsche fueled by a resolute and consistent antifascism. I see the will to chance as the extension of Bataille's "base materialism" (chance is what falls or is fallen) and his critique of the Hegelian dialectic (chance is what falls from or out of the system). There is continuity in his impossible efforts to grab hold of chance, a secret flirtation with systematicity in the defiantly antisystematic.

As he would put it years before in the pamphlet launching the Contre-Attaque group (one of several he formed in the 1930s, this one after his first fallout but before his final break with André Breton): "What to do? Faced with fascism, given the insufficiency of communism?"[13] One answer, I am suggesting, is Bataille's aleatory dialectics—or "the world as seen from the night of nonknowledge . . . which is different from *laws* obeyed by the world as its gambled."[14]

This answer takes refuge neither in the rules of probability, by which we strive toward the *elimination* of chance in human affairs, nor in the sagely wisdom of philosophy, by which we *subordinate* chance to our individual projects. Neither can do justice to the world as it's wagered.

Jean-Michel Besnier has usefully suggested that Bataille furnishes an "impossible politics"—one that aims at "subverting a politics which limits itself to a 'discourse of the possible.'"[15] Habermas, too, dwells in the theme of impossibility attached to Bataille: "the salient attribute of 'the impossible one' . . . refers to the philosopher and scholar who tried to take up the impossible heritage of Nietzsche as critic of ideology."[16] But Habermas draws a very different political lesson from Bataille. This impossible enterprise, says Habermas, is a colossal failure, which does not break through the limits of any discourse as much as it offers up a "philosophy of history with a Manichean turn," premised on hierarchy, distinction, rank, and violence.[17] If there is a coherent politics in Bataille's writings from the 1930s, it is too close to "what fascist power would like to be" and too enamored with what fascist power had become.[18] And Habermas sees Bataille's eroticism as the poetic proxy for his failed political project.

This has become the conventional wisdom. From a different perspective, Geoff Waite casts Bataille as the founding father of a confused Left Nietzscheanism. Waite concedes that the view of Bataille as "attracted to and repelled by fascism" is a "sweeping generalization," failing to do justice to the finer points in his reading of Nietzsche and his critique of fascist power.[19] Waite offers an alternative story, in which Bataille stands at the beginnings of an unfortunate appeal to Nietzsche for Left politics. Though I think Waite himself fails to do justice to specific details of Bataille's Nietzsche—especially the crucially important reinterpretation of will to power as will to chance—his critique is at least refreshing in its appreciation of a political voice that reverberates throughout. Waite aims to discredit this "Left Nietzschean" voice, as well as the technocultural apparatus that has amplified it in the contemporary period. I aim, by contrast, to revalue the political concepts still buried in Bataille's corpus.

This task is made difficult by the undeniable instability in Bataille's thinking and even in his terminology. For instance, an important term like "sovereignty" seems to mean one thing in an early text and the precise opposite in a later work. These instabilities can be taken for confusions or errors, or more generously as considered and thoughtful revisions. They might also be taken to indicate the paradoxes that permeate his "negative dialectics" and the impossible effort to liberate philosophical discourse from the strictures of logic.[20] Indeed, the will to chance bears paradox on its surface, for chance is precisely that force which frustrates, thwarts, and defies the will. Willing, as Bataille insists, belongs to the domain of the personal, while chance has to do with the impersonal. Willing is a capacity of subjects, while chance cannot be but an objective force. Willing connotes something deliberate and directed, while chance suggests the disruption of deliberation and direction. Bataille, who described himself as a "paradoxical philosopher," might be compared in this respect with thinkers like Rousseau or Kierkegaard, both of whom place paradox at the center of human freedom. Bataille's formula signals the radical *exposure* of the subject to the other, to others, to heterogeneous forces, to the force of heterogeneity. It expresses and avows the vulnerability—in the etymological sense of a wound or a tear—that inheres in this exposure. And it points to a concept of sovereignty premised not on unity and homogeneity, not on the disclosure of identity, and not on the postulates of reason or the laws of nature, but on fragmentation and abandon, on excess and expenditure, on the incommunicable in human experience and the inassimilable in human history.

Though it refuses subordination to a cause, chance in Bataille also bears witness to the condition of possibility for politics as such: "Chance wagers people as they join—when two by two or in larger groupings they sometimes dream, act, make love, curse, dominate, and kill each other."[21] Chance is the potentiality for politics, structuring the field of relations between individuals and groups. And here we might begin to think with Bataille, though he never thought this possibility himself, of an aleatory dialectics that could do justice to this play of chance. This would involve theorizing political life not centrally in terms of its agonistic element, or the play of competition that structures the field of politics, but in terms of the aleatory element, or the unexpected and surprise encounters that create worlds in common. Notwithstanding the volatility of his thought, if there is a project (or

antiproject) in Bataille, one that goes by various names (base materialism, a general economy, a philosophy of play) and marshals a host of
concepts (expenditure, waste, the sacred, filth, violence, sacrifice), the
whole of it would appear to hang on chance—on the figure of the gambler, a roll of the dice, and the fortuitous placement of a hook.

2

> On a roof I saw large, sturdy hooks placed halfway up. Suppose
> someone falls from a rooftop . . . couldn't he maybe catch hold
> of one of those hooks with an arm or a leg? If I fell from a roof-
> top, I'd plummet to the ground. But if a hook was there, I'd come
> to a stop halfway down! Just a little later I might say to myself:
> "Once an architect planned this hook, and without it I'd be dead. I
> should be dead, but I am not at all—in fact, I'm alive. A hook was
> put there." Let's say my presence, my life are inescapable. Some-
> thing impossible and incomprehensible would still be its prin-
> ciple. I understand now—picturing the momentum of falling,
> that there's nothing in this world unless it meets up with a hook.
> —Bataille, *Guilty*

At least since Pascal, thinking about chance has been intimately connected to exercises in probabilistic reasoning. Bataille does not wholly
break with this Pascalian tradition in French philosophy; mathematical theory was never, for him, an object of derision, though he did hold
in contempt the "practical attitude" he attributed to the mathemati-
cian.[22] His important early essay "The Critique of the Foundations of
the Hegelian Dialectic" deals briefly with the modern history of mathematics and Engels's effort to bring elementary mathematical symbol-
ism to dialectic thought. Here is Bataille's assessment of these efforts:

> Thus mathematics—whether higher or not—underwent, during the
> nineteenth century, an evolution that in every way was contrary to
> Engels's program; it eliminated every appearance of a dialectic. Rigor
> in demonstrations, noncontradiction in principles, constant accord
> with logic; those are the ends pursued, and on the whole attained,
> by mathematics. One could object, certainly, that new difficulties
> reappeared with set theory and that the transfinite could give rise to

developments having the appearance of the dialectic. But the mathematicians' attitude (their *practical* attitude) toward these new paradoxes is the same as their attitude toward the old ones: far from seeing them as a result of a superior mode of thought, they examine them with horror. A new labor of logical reduction starts.[23]

The problem, as Bataille sees it, lies with a tendency among mathematicians, and not precisely with mathematics itself. The will to chance stands in stark opposition to a "practical attitude" that strives at the elimination of noncontradiction and paradox. While set theory and the concept of the transfinite may, indeed, open up mathematics to alternative modes of thinking, what is needed is a different posture, hopelessly *impractical*, that sees the paradox not as a scourge to be calculated away, but as an opportunity to liberate thought from the strictures of practical reason.[24]

This posture, says Bataille, requires a turn away from part of the project undertaken—and ultimately abandoned—by Engels in the *Anti-Dühring*. What was Engels's failure, if we bear in mind that a great failure is also a certain achievement for Bataille? The attempt to establish dialectical materialism in the natural sciences, which he says even Hegel understood to be resistant to dialectical categories:[25] "The failure of Engels, who worked for eight years preparing a dialectical theory of nature, . . . has not yet been the object of the studies that the considerable efforts of this great pioneer of the Revolution so richly deserve. Many people prefer to speak of dialectical materialism as if it were not an incomplete project, but a constituted doctrine."[26] Incomplete projects may be the only sort worth attending to, for Bataille absorbs Engels's failure as a provocation. He suggests not quite that dialectical materialism surrender its tie to nature "for phantoms that would be absolutely heterogeneous to it," but rather that it be recast in the light of lived experience, somatic and psychic struggle, and the concrete shapes of historical life.[27] Bataille never abandons these ideas. And so Engels's misstep is also an opportunity, not to be missed: the restoration of human experience to the dialectic, which is itself reacquaintance with nature. "The objects of dialectical investigation represent only the most complex products of nature"—namely, humans and their historical conditions.[28] Bataille calls his procedure a "dialectic of the real" and places historical agency at its center.[29] In 1932, when this essay was published, this meant paying particular attention to "the immediate terrain of class struggle"—there is no denying that class recedes from the later works as the dominant mode of enframing human experience.[30] Struggle becomes play.

Like Pascal, Bataille understood the human being as a creature *obliged* to play. (As Pascal would put in *Pensées*: "you must wager. It is not optional. You are embarked.") But Bataille gives this obligation not an existentialist cast, but rather an anthropological, psychological, and sociological significance. Human cultures, psychological processes, and everyday life, says Bataille, are constituted by play, by the nonproductive expenditure of "wasteful" energy, by the various games and rituals that permit human contact with excess and superfluity. And probability and statistics, though they represent dominant modes by which human reason has been *put to work* against the play of chance, cannot exhaust the affective forces unleashed by the compulsion to play, the imperative to take chances, to place bets, to enter a field of relations with others.

At the betting table, calculation and instrumental reasoning play only a minor role. What Bataille cherishes in gambling is an abyssal experience that separates actions from their ends, where each instant is unhinged from a logical sequence or chain of events and severed from any larger plans or purposes, where all that matters is the present moment and dice as they are falling. This capacity to *demotivate* the instant links gambling to the doctrine of the eternal return, to which I will return in the next section. For now, note the "base materialism" of chance and its opposition to any idealist heroics. As John Lechte has noted, "chance is what falls or is fallen" and in this way is linked in Bataille with the impure and the obscene, with what is base and lowly, with the banished, hidden, and wasteful elements of human culture.[31] Though he preferred brothels to casinos, Bataille, much like the compulsive gambler, was often broke and drawn to the play of chance for its secret alliance with poverty (confirmed by the mystics, as well as the *lumpenproletariat*). Chance is linked to that which falls, but also to things due, especially payments and rents. He connects chance to deadlines, and notes that both of the French terms—*échoit* and *échéance*—find their common root in the Latin *cadentia*, "falling."[32]

In picturing the momentum of falling, Bataille goes beyond the rather serene Epicurean image of the "swerve" among atoms dropping like rain (cited by Althusser in his late writings on aleatory materialism) to tarry with the body torn and shredded (*déchirement*) by chance, the violence done to the flesh when catching an arm or a leg on a hook. The image presses beyond Hegel, to whom it undoubted alludes. "The life of Spirit is not the life that shrinks from death and keeps itself untouched by devastation," Hegel insists, "but rather the life that endures it and maintains itself in it."[33] In Hegel, the subject "wins its truth only when, in utter dismemberment [*Zerrissenheit*], it finds itself"—a sentence from the *Phenomenology of Spirit* that draws explicit commentary from Bataille and encapsulates for him the sacrificial project presupposed by the Hegelian system, its fixation on death, and its effort to render negativity *serviceable* to philosophical eschatology. But Bataille never abandons the "utter dismemberment" connected with Hegelian negativity. Indeed, the impossible effort at writing chance may be seen as an attempt to do justice to it. It is here that Bataille's critical theory ventures to the heights of despair. The doubling movement in Hegelian despair, in which natural consciousness comes undone, becomes a more radical and total disintegration in Bataille.

Recall that for Hegel a properly *philosophical* view of the world precludes its surrender to the play of chance. This is nowhere more evident than in the introduction to the *Lectures on the Philosophy of History*, where chance is designated the enemy of reason and the end of philosophy. A philosophical orientation to world history both *presumes* and *demonstrates* the supremacy of reason, says Hegel, not as an abstract and unseen force, but as something *actually existing* in the world: "The only Thought which Philosophy brings with it to the contemplation of History, is the simple conception of Reason; that Reason is the Sovereign of the World; that the history of the world, therefore, presents us with a rational process."[34] This, Hegel argues, is the ruling principle of philosophy since Socrates inherited it from Anaxagoras, the idea that nature moves in harmony with reason. Philosophy, as Hegel understands it, is that systematic form of thinking that unearths the "determinate application" and "concrete development" of reason in the world.[35] To those unfamiliar with this philosophical project, Hegel notes:

I may fairly presume, at least, the existence of a belief in Reason, a desire, a thirst for acquaintance with it, in entering upon this course of Lectures. . . . If the clear idea of Reason is not already developed in our minds, in beginning the study of Universal History, we should at least have the firm, unconquerable faith that Reason *does* exist there; and that *the World of intelligence and conscious volition is not abandoned to chance*, but must show itself in the light of the self-cognizant Idea.[36]

Hegel will go on to insist that he needn't make any precursory demands on this "unconquerable faith" in reason, that his lectures will confirm what faith suggests: a rational process, a plan, a project, without which the world would indeed be given over to the "empire of chance."[37] His philosophy of history, Hegel assures us, will show how reason governs and has always governed the world, not as an abstract ideal, but as *manifest* in historical phenomena. He concedes that there is some intimation of this conviction in the religious doctrine of Providence, insofar as it encourages "pious persons to recognize in particular circumstances, something more than mere chance; to acknowledge the guiding hand of God."[38] But theology too often limits the reach of this "guiding hand" to individuals and their affairs, leaving peoples, states, and history untouched—what Hegel regards as a "peddling" version of Providence and divine wisdom insofar as it is tailored to suit the needs of individual believers and satisfies only the desire for solace and comfort, not the thirst for knowledge. Reason is a world-historical force, that which gives human history its direction and purpose, retrieving contingency from the abyss of pure accident.

Hegel's mature philosophy of history makes explicit the prohibition on chance that is largely implicit in the earlier works. Bataille limits his direct commentary on Hegel to the *Phenomenology of Spirit*, but the question of chance—how it rips human projects to shreds—is crucial to his critique. For Bataille—and in this respect he owes much to Alexander Kojève, whose seminars on Hegel in the mid-1930s he credits with leaving him "broken, crushed, killed ten times over, suffocated and nailed down"—the singular achievement of Hegel consisted in the weight he attached to the negative in the dialectic of history.[39] But he departs from Kojève (and from Hegel ultimately) in his attention to "unemployed negativity," or that which cannot be put to work for the system and frustrates any triumphant pronouncement of the end of history or the ends of man. Though his encounter with Hegel is informed by Kojève, he does not parrot this approach. Bataille underscores what falls away from the dialectic, or frustrates the teleological ambitions of the *Phenomenology*. He lingers on the pathos of the dialectic, the violence and excess unleashed by the restlessness of negativity. "[If] Kojève sets aside vulgar satisfaction—happiness—he now also sets aside Hegel's 'absolute dismemberment': indeed, such dismemberment is not easily reconciled with the desire for recognition."[40] *Déchirement*, the torn and shredded body suspended on a hook, is at odds with a politics of distinction and the heroic disclosure of authentic individuality. This is not only Kojève's error, but the surrealist misstep as well. The secret of Hegel's philosophy lies not in the cunning of reason or the ruse of recognition, but in the complex of passions unleashed in the play of chance.

Politically speaking, Bataille's negative dialectic is more circumspect. He takes the philosopher-sage (Hegel) to task, not quite for the liquidation of difference at the summit of self-sacrifice (this is Adorno's critique), but for his failure to wrest "absolute dismemberment" away from the arbitrary rule of accident. This failure, as Bataille sees it, is less the result of an error on Hegel's part and more a consequence of the "incomparable scope" of his project—namely, the philosophical representation of historical life as it meets up with a hook. By virtue of his faith in the project of philosophy, Hegel could not help but presume an architect (Spirit) put it there: "It is not a stroke of fate, a piece of bad luck, which would forever be deprived of sense. Dismemberment is, on the contrary full of meaning."[41] In sagely manner, Hegel rescues *déchirement* from the nonsense of the accidental and delivers it to dominion of the rational, where dismemberment can be given a purpose and the highway of despair can be given an end. But for Bataille, "this meaning is unfortunate. It is what limited and impoverished the *revelation* which the Sage drew from lingering in the regions where death reigns."[42] The point here is not the absence of meaning, as if the dialectic portends the nihilism it prohibits, but rather its *excess*. Nonsense is not senseless. Reason is too limited a concept for all that Hegel reveals, which is the restless dialectic of chance and fate, contingency and necessity, or—to borrow Althusser's

formula—how chance encounters "take hold" as necessary. In a val-
iant effort to escape the empire of chance, sagely wisdom suppresses
the "accident in the ascent" of sovereignty and surrenders instead to
the tyranny of project. Despair is the collapse of our projects—and an
opportunity to delight in aleatory experience.

Bataille's relationship to Hegel remains a point of substantial disagreement in the scholarly literature. Richard Wolin claims (wrongly
in my view) that "Bataille's relation to Hegel and dialectics is largely
scornful," while Asger Sørensen reads him as a dialectician in a certain
spirit of Marx, but still without a "practical" politics. Jacques Derrida's
treatment of Bataille constitutes the most substantial effort to tear a
general economy away from Hegelian dialectics, and his approach is,
in some ways, closest to my own. Here is Derrida:

> In interpreting negativity as labor, in betting for discourse, meaning,
> history, etc., Hegel has bet against play, against chance. He has blinded
> himself to the possibility of his own bet, to the fact that the conscien-
> tious suspension of play . . . was itself a phase of play; and to the fact
> that play includes the work of meaning or the meaning of work, and
> includes them not in terms of *knowledge*, but in terms of *inscription*:
> meaning is a *function* of play, is inscribed in a certain place in the con-
> figuration of a meaningless play.[43]

Derrida is right to counterpose Bataille's idea of play to the Hegelian
procedure, though I see this idea connected to the superabundance
of meaning rather than meaninglessness. This is important because
inscription occurs not on a blank tablet but in crowded field of forces.
Meaning is not a "phase" of play, or a "function" of play, or a moment
within the larger trajectory of meaninglessness. On Derrida's reading,
play seems to bear an uncanny resemblance to the sagely order that
it opposes.

I am suggesting that Bataille's reflections on Hegel and the Marxist
tradition provide the necessary context to appreciate his more ellipti-
cal intimations of a "philosophy of play" and the idea of the will to
chance. In the aporia between *déchirement* and sovereignty, between
the night of nonknowledge and the dusk of knowledge, there is
chance—the force upon which all of our projects depend, but which

nevertheless tears them to pieces. Chance figures in another early essay, "The Sorcerer's Apprentice," in connection with political action, but also with love and the world created by lovers: "what determines the election of the loved one—so that the possibility of another choice, represented logically, inspires horror—is in fact reducible to a series of chances."[44] This chance-element in the experience of love, for Bataille, gives force to our creativity and our will to exist, but this is no solitary ordeal. Chance is coincidence, or that which allows subjects to coincide. As he puts it: "the *isolated individual* never possesses the power to create a world. . . . Only the accord of lovers, like that of gamblers at a table, creates the living reality of still shapeless correspondences."[45] This living reality, intimated in love (and even in the sorrowful experience of love where there is no "accord"), rebels against calculations of merit, refuses considerations of usefulness, and defies rational intentions. The beloved appears as the figure of destiny, not for any specific and measurable qualities determined in advance, but for the "extreme luck" that arranges random moments into a series of chances. If chance establishes a world *in common* and animates the avid will to exist, this is "in no way similar to the will that deliberates and intervenes"—which is to say, the will that seeks to arrange the cards in advance or disclose their arrangement in the midst of play.[46] Here Bataille points to a noncommunicative—and incommunicable—intersubjectivity. Indeed, the effort to ground intersubjectivity in communicative practices—which is to say, subsume aleatory encounters under subjective intentionality and discursive necessity—would seem a betrayal of worlds created in common.

"What looks like politics and imagines itself to be politics, one day will show itself to be a religious movement." This was the inscription to the front page of *Acéphale*, the journal Bataille formed with Pierre Klossowski and devoted mainly to studies of Nietzsche. It is a line not from Nietzsche, but from Kierkegaard, responding to the revolutions of 1848. The epigraph might be said to herald Bataille's retreat from streets, where politics takes place, his flight inward. The problem with this view, beyond its exaggeration of the conflict between Bataille's politics and his atheology, is that *On Nietzsche*—the document of his efforts at averting madness during wartime—suggests a sort of strategic solitude that is not without political content.[47] Further,

the encounter with Nietzsche reads as deeply motivated by histori-
cal-political concerns, containing a critique of the will to power and
its radical reformation in light of worldly experience. Though he
well understood the extent to which Nietzsche's writings had been
perverted to serve the "cause" of Hitlerism (and remains underap-
preciated for being among the first among the French Left to wrest
Nietzsche's legacy from the Nazis), Bataille also recognized that
the doctrine of the will to power risked such perversion in ceding
human freedom to a specific set of goals—those of cultural renewal,
the rebirth of the tragic vision, and the restoration of strength, nobil-
ity, and vitality in the human animal. In being tethered to projects,
the will to power is easily poached by those with contrary aims and
objectives, no matter how consistent Nietzsche's rejection of German
anti-Semitism or how complete his rejection of the German state. By
contrast, the will to chance—for Bataille, the revolutionary residue of
Nietzsche's philosophy—cannot be made to serve any cause and, for
precisely that reason, sustains as paradox and passion the experience
of human freedom. Bataille's attraction to Nietzsche revolves around
the question of chance—and the disconcerting possibility that the
best bet against fascism lies in a roll of the dice.

3

> And truly, we're guided to that point by a commonly noted light
> proclaimed by the word FREEDOM. To which I am deeply
> attached.
>
> —Bataille, *On Nietzsche*

Martin Jay reminds us that *being at war* is an enduring frame for
Bataille's thinking, and it is in this context that we can appreciate
what attracts Bataille to Hegel: the portrait of life as risk and human
experience as life-and-death wagering. But in wartime, for almost
all of 1944, Bataille devoted his energies not to sagely wisdom but to
the writings of Nietzsche.[48] This was not his first encounter with the
writer of such good books.[49] An early essay, "The 'Old Mole' and the
Prefix *Sur* in Words *Surhomme* and *Surrealist*," drafted at the heights
of his feud with Breton in 1929 and 1930, is decidedly more ambivalent.

Base materialism, as Bataille had conceived it then, was closer to Marx's "old mole" than to Nietzsche's Icarian flight. This early essay develops an important critique of Nietzsche that he would never fully abandon. But by the 1940s, Nietzsche would appear as the only figure standing between Bataille and madness. *On Nietzsche* is Bataille's collection of theoretical ruminations, journal entries, poems, quotations, and aphorisms from 1944, or "the day-to-day record of what turned up as the dice were thrown."[50] This includes the chronicles of a "truly comical year of personal interests," for which he extends his reader due apology. He adds: "They are not a source of pain, and I'm glad to make fun of myself, knowing no better way to lose myself in immanence."[51] He had hoped to debut the work for the centennial of Nietzsche's birth in October 1944, and notes that he wrongly anticipated German retreat. The point here is that politics seems to always get in the way of our predictions and expectations, and insert itself into our most private cares and concerns in ways that exceed our calculations. Even with its intimate excursions into love, loss, and solitude, I read *On Nietzsche* as among the most significant experiments in radical antifascism and the beginnings of a poetics of freedom.

The text would seem at one level incomparable to *Minima Moralia*, which Adorno also begins in 1944 but takes many more years to "complete." The latter is, in some respects, the more profound and ambitious rewriting of *The Gay Science* in wartime, what Adorno calls the melancholy science. And it is the greater success. That said, when considered as a part of the larger *Somme Athéologique* and in terms of the impossible attempts at putting an aleatory dialectic into words, Bataille's text assumes an added weightiness. The reader comes to feel some gratitude for the author's laughter, his love of error, his esteem for failure, especially his own.[52] And like the aphoristic form of *Minima Moralia*, this writing is indecipherable apart from the political commitment that animates it. As I read it, this commitment is to a practice of freedom and an unyielding opposition to the forces of fascism. I take one of the more personal journal entries from June 1944 at its word: "The light of my life is missing and I'm desperately working, I'm studying the unity of humanness and the world, I'm making interconnected outlines of knowledge, political action, and unlimited contemplation."[53] Here readers catch a glimpse of despair in Bataille, a productive desperation that demands that he study and write. Like Hegel before him and Fanon after him, Bataille presents work as our best expression of despair and our surest defense against its damages. Work, done in desperation and performed with passion, offers a fugitive freedom under inhuman conditions. This freedom is imperfect, bearing the wounds of war. And a life measured by forms of labor that oppose play is a life of servility. But philosophical work—or "the seriousness, the suffering, the patience, and the labor of the negative"—is an indirect experience of freedom nonetheless. *On Nietzsche* is precisely an investigation into the mode of living that embodies a commitment to freedom in knowing, willing, and thinking. This commitment also carries Bataille to nonknowledge, a repudiation of the will to power, and an embrace of the unthinkable. He will not permit this commitment to become "servile"—that is to say, to articulate itself as a positive program or on behalf of a political party. Bataille's mature reacquaintance with Nietzsche is also the revaluation of thinking that refuses to render itself serviceable to a cause or a system. This spells not retreat from political life, but its reordering: "It's the positive practice of freedom, not the negative struggle against a particular oppression, that has lifted me above a mutilated existence. Each of us learns with bitterness that to struggle for freedom is first of all to alienate ourselves."[54] The negative struggle for freedom presupposes unfreedom and consolidates it. As several decades of feminist and antiracist theory have shown, identity-based struggles against oppression often work to reinforce precisely the conditions they contest, or they establish new forms of subjection. This does not mean such struggles are abandoned; Bataille concedes that the negative struggle for freedom is a part of him, albeit the "mutilated" part, the part formed and deformed by the very oppression he opposes. Struggle is inevitable, appropriate even, but it is still to see freedom as a project or end. In this way, the struggle for freedom is also the perpetual postponement of freedom. Play, by contrast, is the experience of freedom undeferred.

For Bataille, the postponement of freedom is implicit in the will to power—a point that Bataille would make in his varied reflections on Nietzsche. Will to power does not overturn this logic, but founders in it. In the early essay, which expresses a militant Left "friendship for the proletariat" that Bataille regrets is absent in Nietzsche, he calls the will to power a "regressive" formula in its flight from the real conditions of bourgeois society:[55] "It is not the masters who need such a morality: exploiters are not going to seek their values in an unbalanced philosophy. When their values are given to them immediately by the economic conditions of exploitation, American bankers dispense with *The Will to Power*."[56] Already Bataille appreciates the opportunism that surrounds Nietzschean morality, not Nietzsche's morality (ironically evidenced by the fact that he was no friend to the proletariat, or any class of his time) but those with plans and projects all their own. Will to power becomes "imbecilic" in the world of American bankers, French surrealists, and German Nazis, a clownish reenactment of a moral system that bourgeois society renders obsolete. Bankers will take or leave the will to power as it accords with the project of exploitation. Bataille even wonders if the will to power does not harbor "the unconscious pathological desire to be struck down violently like Icarus and Prometheus," if this is a will that lives for its defeat.[57]

On Nietzsche pursues the possibility that the will to power might be reformulated as will to chance: "Chance, as it turned out," he suggests, "corresponded to Nietzsche's intentions more accurately than power could."[58] It also recalls the "accident in the abyss" at the unwritten center of Hegel's *Phenomenology*, which similarly thwarted sagely systems. Bataille's reinterpretation focuses on some familiar Nietzschean themes: the will to power, as mentioned, the doctrine of the eternal return, and *amor fati*, to name only those of particular importance to the revaluation of chance. Of the will to power he says, again, that it is "regressive" as long as it is "considered as an end" or "another duty" that overwhelms the infinite lightness "expressed in Zarathustra's laughter and dancing"—and Nietzsche never fully averts this regress. And again, the theme of failure is attached to the thinkers for whom Bataille reserves his deepest admiration: "His last completed work, *Ecce Homo*, affirms the absence of goals as well as the author's complete lack of a plan. Considered from the standpoint of action, Nietzsche work amounts to a failure (one of the most indefensible!) and his life amounts to nothing—like the life of anyone who tries to put these writings into practice."[59] At times, Nietzsche succumbs to the alleged supremacy of this standpoint, of action and the value of a life measured according to one's action, only to discover "the profound nonviability of this doctrine"—

for Bataille, its distinctive virtue.[60] Chance is an assault on viability itself as the measure of an idea or an action.

Of the eternal return, Bataille suggests that it frees each instant from the tyranny of ends. Return is not the infinite repetition of a wound, but the refusal of a life in which each moment is motivated by some deferred dream: "Return unmotivates the moment and frees the life of ends—thus first of all destroys it. Return is the mode of drama, the mask of human entirety, a human desert wherein each moment is unmotivated."[61] Return breaks the addiction to ends and releases human experience to the real intoxication of historical existence: "To want chance is *amor fati* (love of fate). *Amor fati* signifies wanting chance, signifies differing from what was."[62] On this view *amor fati* is no posture of resignation to what is. It is not the endless reproduction of the same. Quite the contrary, as Bataille interprets it, *amor fati* is the love of things becoming different, the passions set in motion by difference.

With chance comes a play-element that radically refigures the field of politics: "the possibility of exploring the far reaches of possibility and no prejudicing the results, of giving to the future alone and its free occurrence the power usually assigned to choosing sides (which is only a form of the past)."[63] The will to chance is an invitation to danger and a real renunciation of life as measured by the calculus of probabilities and coordination of interests. But it also means extending thought and practice to those places they can't go when weighed down by ends. If Bataille's experimentation occasionally seems too reliant on futurity, risking again the subordination of freedom to the principle of postponement, it is nevertheless a provocation to seize upon a certain sovereignty at the heights of despair. This provocation is caught in paradox: to communicate it is to betray it; to offer it up as an example to be followed—in the manner of the mystics as they approached sovereignty—is to defile it; to chase it is to find it always beyond reach. Yet the distinctive freedom that is harbored in aleatory experience—"taking risks, going looking for chance—this requires patience, love, and total letting go."[64] Of course, this is no permanent political posture, and consistency is not its litmus test: "Each of us sometimes belongs to one, sometimes to the other"—sense and nonsense, reason and the nonknowledge, servility and sovereignty, freedom as a calculus of ends and freedom as the will to chance.

To this point, I have said nothing of *The Accursed Shared*, the third volume of which contains some of Bataille's most pointed observations on revolutionary politics, the Marxist tradition and actually existing communism, and the Nietzschean alternative to the Stalinist assault on sovereignty. There is much to be said for and about this work, which further develops Bataille's distinctive approach to heterogeneity, nonproductive expenditure, and sovereign subjectivity. For the purposes of the argument developed in this chapter, I want to limit my attention to two crucial themes that emerge in this text, particularly its final sections. The first concerns *play*, which Bataille juxtaposes against the communist (and bourgeois) exaltation of work. The second has to do with the relationship between the miraculous and sovereign freedom, which Bataille sees as subordinated under communism to the empire of necessity. It is in relation to the unexpected and unanticipated—the realm of the sacred miracle—where human beings escape this empire. Here, the reign of knowledge gives way to the force of nonknowledge and sovereignty is enlivened by the play of chance. Bataille's political thinking, I am suggesting, lives here.

In referring to communism, Bataille means Stalinism, appreciating more than so many of its contemporary advocates the extent to which the term bears the horrific imprints of the Soviet dictatorship. This is not to say that Bataille conflates this dictatorship with Marx's political project, for he reads Marx (and Hegel) in terms of the opposition between labor and freedom. He puts it this way: "The point is that labor is the exact opposite of the sovereign attitude. For Hegel, in an aspect of this doctrine that was at the origin of Marx's, labor is the action of the man who, rather than *die* free, chose to *live* in servitude."[65] For Bataille, both Hegel and Marx cast labor as servility; freedom begins where labor ends. Where Stalin develops and distorts Marx's doctrine is in the acceptance of labor as life itself, as if the choice to live in servitude is not only inevitable and inescapable, but also noble and righteous. The result is not the elimination of death, but the prohibition on dying freely—which is to say, the imperative to die as a continuation of the unfree life. Communism renders servile labor the highest principle of life and death, and no activity is permitted that does not advance the cause of labor itself. For Bataille, this means the interdiction against play and against human experience conceived in terms of play. A footnote from the text proves crucial:

> Under the current leadership, communist humanity cannot conceive itself in terms of play but only in terms of labor. Play alone uses up the resources produced by labor (in its essence, war is a horrible game, from which the world of work, which meant to eliminate it, has taken away as much of its playfulness as possible). In any case, humanity is finally a game but the "man of renounced humanity" places it within the perspective of labor: this is why he seems to me to be condemned, as I already said, to that game which is no longer a game, to the most demanding form of depletion, to war.[66]

Linking war and play, Bataille is openly flirting with danger. The point is not any romanticism about war, but an appreciation that warfare was one of the practices through which human beings escaped the empire of utility. Indeed, in that it serves no purpose and is without meaning, war can be called play. (Indeed, work too can also be called play, suffused with playfulness, though this is precisely what is prohibited by Stalinism.) Communist (and bourgeois) leadership aspires to a world made entirely of labor, of purposive activity, and so theoretically should also aim at the elimination of war. But instead, war is grafted onto the work-imperative, its playfulness renounced as the game goes on, now with purpose, meaning, and ends beyond itself. The paradoxical result is that war *becomes* work—work that is not only inevitable and inescapable, but also noble and righteous. And all of humanity is forced, in servility and bondage, to participate in this game that is no longer a game, this most demanding depletion.

Bataille's remarks leave open the possibility that, under some other leadership, communist humanity might conceive itself in terms of play—and liberated forms of work. To be sure, this would not mean the end of war, an aspiration that Bataille suggests will only guarantee its continuation and intensification. But it could mean the restoration of its playfulness—and, perhaps, the pluralization of forms of play such that warfare is one game among many and hardly the primary force that gives us meaning. Refusing moralism about war, Bataille lends himself to misunderstanding and misrepresentation. But his real insight is that the effort to remake the world by the supremacy of work means complete annihilation. The attempt at banishing the playful element in violence means that what is violent becomes purposive and all purposes become violent. The prohibition on unnecessary expenditure means total and absolute expenditure.

Sovereign freedom is the opposite of servile labor and an antidote to life reduced to the principle of utility and the pursuit of knowledge. Such freedom cannot itself become the basis of a project, but is instead intimated in the human encounter with the miraculous: "This *miraculous* quality is conveyed rather explicitly by the expression: *impossible and yet there it is*"—an appearance that defies reasonable expectations and anticipations.[67] Indeed, it is the surprise that constitutes the miracle as miraculous, that aligns aleatory experience with the sacred. Bataille treats happy tears—the tears that signify not sadness or agony, but the ecstatic rush of euphoria that is the highest happiness—as expressions of the sacred. And these tears are nothing if not responses to chance: "there is no reason at all for thinking that tears of happiness signify gratified expectations, because the object of these tears is itself unanticipated; like death, it is only, all of a sudden, the impossible coming true, becoming *that which is*." All desire, which Bataille sets against anticipation, contains an aleatory dimension. It is not that desire fails to arrange possible and coveted outcomes; rather, it is that desire necessarily gives rise to that which escapes the order of the possible. As he puts it: "desire gives rise to unjustified hope, to hope that reason condemns, which is different from the anticipation of the desired object or of its duration."[68] This unjustified hope—and all hope, to the extent that it is hope and not expectation, is unjustified and unjustifiable—is the affective material that maintains human contact with the miraculous, linking sovereign freedom to the reign of the moment.

4

> Last hope: to forget, to come back to innocence,
> to the playfulness of despair.
>
> —Bataille, *Inner Experience*

In what sense can despair be called playful? Following Bataille, we can conclude that despair is playful, in part, because it does not permit the pursuit of ends at the expense of experience. Despair refuses the imperative to productive expenditure and servile labor. Despair is passion and without purpose. It refuses subordination to a project that is other than itself, even as it carries and preserves itself as a last hope. Despair is the repetition of a movement that is without telos, the amnesic return to the miracle of beginnings without ending, the forgetfulness required to start anew. This is patently Nietzschean, of course, but in Bataille, the playfulness of despair is also intimated in Hegel. Again, from the final pages of *The Accursed Share*:

> The difference between my *dialectical* thought and that of Hegel is difficult to formulate, since contradiction can constantly resume the development of both. There is nothing that I do not follow in the overall movement that Hegel's thought represents in my eyes. But the autonomy of Hegel's "absolute knowledge" is that of discourse unfolding in time. Hegel situates subjectivity not in the object's disintegration (always begun anew) but in the identity that the subject and object attain in discourse. But in the end, "absolute knowledge," the discourse in which the subject and object become identical, itself dissolves into the NOTHING of unknowing, and the vanishing thought of unknowing is in the movement.[69]

The "nothing" of unknowing is no absolute nothingness, but the determinate nothing that is opened up by negative dialectics—a dialectic that refuses, in Bataille's language, the sleep of the Absolute.

Here we can distinguish Bataille's will to chance from Gilles Deleuze's affirmation of chance in *Repetition and Difference*. The Deleuzian project is explicitly antidialectical, though it implicitly gathers the eruptions of chance into an order of necessity in a way that unwittingly reproduces sagely wisdom. Here is Deleuze:

> Chance is arbitrary only in so far as it is not affirmed or not sufficiently affirmed, in so far as it is distributed within a space, a number and under rules destined to avert it. When chance is sufficiently affirmed the player can no longer lose, since every combination and every throw which produces it is by nature adequate to the place and the mobile command of the aleatory point. . . . The whole of chance is

then indeed in each throw, even though this be partial, and it is there
in a single time even though the combination produced is the object
of a progressive determination. . . . Once chance is affirmed, all arbi-
trariness is abolished every time.[70]

Bataille's will to chance is no affirmation, if to affirm chance is to abolish precisely the excess and heterogeneous elements secreted by aleatory experience. What is key in Bataille is that the player can lose, that
the risk of loss is what aligns the will to chance with the struggle for
freedom, and that freedom itself is bereft of significance without the
risk that accompanies it. Bataille is substantially less hostile to what
is arbitrary in human life and, for this reason, more attuned to the
single throw of the dice that is not reassembled into a totality—or, as
Deleuze puts it, "the distribution of singular points which constitute
a structure."[71] If human beings catch a glimpse of sovereign freedom
in aleatory experience, this does not mean they occupy a "blind spot"
from which problems might be taken up and resolved.[72] Chance is
no fixed point at all, no place that may be occupied, no horizon from
which the whole comes into view. For Bataille, it is the interruption
of time and space, where momentary vision—not blindness—may be
restored before it vanishes once again.

"Nietzsche's position is the only one apart from communism."[73] By
this, Bataille is not saying Nietzsche's position points to a way out
of the standoff between bourgeois and communist forms, as if his
position may be reintegrated into a telos that, at his finest moments,
Nietzsche rejects. Bataille concedes that Nietzsche himself surrenders
to the temptation of this self-representation, but it does not constitute the real significance of Nietzsche's position. This position is not
an esoteric truth veiled by exoteric writing or a recipe for action, as
much as it is an idea indicated, but not elaborated—an idea that I am
calling aleatory dialectics. This idea has other antecedents in Western
thought, and other French Marxists, most notably Louis Althusser in
his later writings, will develop it more fully and systematically as a
political-theoretical position (though even Althusser's mature reflections on aleatory materialism forgo the scientific claims of his earlier writings on ideology). Bataille's remarks on chance are mostly
gestural and indefinite, as if to highlight how aleatory encounters

disrupt our attempts to write and record them. And they do not form a coherent doctrine or position as much as they press against the impulse to organize all thinking, writing, and communication into some useful project. Chance indicates not escape from aporia or exit from the highway of despair, but a manner with which to play amid the restlessness of the negative.

5

Frantz Fanon

CRITIQUE, WITH KNIVES

1

When the colonized hears a speech about Western culture he pulls out his knife—or at least he makes sure it is within reach.
—Fanon, *The Wretched of the Earth*

In the *Philosophy of Right*, Hegel considers how modern warfare differs from ancient forms and how the modern weapon of choice—the gun—both reflects and reinforces these differences. Warfare for the moderns means the depersonalization of conflict and the mechanization of killing. The gun marks this shift from a personal expression of bravery to a universal expression of courage. Hegel is certain that its invention can be "no accident."[1] Frantz Fanon is more interested in knives—the knife held to the throat of the silent Arab prisoner, the knife used by two boys to kill one of their European classmates, the knife used by a member of the Front de Libération Nationale (FLN) to murder his wife, the belief held by colonial magistrates that the knife is the Algerian's favorite weapon. There is nothing accidental about this, either: "Any colony tends to become one vast farmyard, one vast concentration camp where the only law is that of the knife."[2] If the gun for Hegel is mechanical and abstract, the knife is physical and concrete. It points to the immediate brutality and bloodletting of the colonial system. It reflects and reinforces the specific order of violence that Fanon sees as elemental to colonial power. And it also suggests the forms of critique—or, for the Greeks, the art of cutting—that scratch away at a system where violence is at once direct and atmospheric. For Nietzsche's philosophy with a hammer, there is Fanon's alliance with an Algerian reaching for his knife.

This alliance is complex, raising all of the most difficult questions in Fanon's work, on violence, identity, and the demands of critique. On the question of violence, Fanon has been judged too harshly and read too carelessly.[3] *The Wretched of the Earth* proffers a powerful and notorious argument for the role of violence in transforming the colonial subject and destroying the colonial system. But Fanon's approach to the question of violence cannot be considered in abstraction from the colonial system that lives on it—and this includes the practice of colonial medicine, in which he played a part. Fanon also treats violence as colonial symptom. What *Wretched* offers is neither a defense of violence (as if violence ceases once we cease in defending it) nor a denunciation (as if denouncing violence will not ensure that some remain its permanent victims), but an analytic of violence. Fanon's analytic of violence does not oppose as much as it *includes* the doctrine of nonviolence—or, better, it explains the strategic emergence in political time of a class-specific call to nonviolence. It is also a critique of the world produced by colonialism, a "Manichean" world, a world cut in two and divided by domination. Violence in this world becomes critical.

On the question of identity, Fanon has also been judged too harshly, even when read much more carefully. What some scholars describe as Fanon's disavowal of Creole Martinique and divestment from home and identity, I see as experimentation with political subjectivity rooted in the places and people that we see everyday. This investment in everyday life is also how I interpret Fanon's attachment to revolutionary Algeria, an attachment forged in ambiguity and difference, maintained through affinity and experience. Françoise Vergès reads it differently. For Vergès, the identification with Algeria is primarily a disavowal of Creole identity, of identity forged in ambiguity and difference. Here is Vergès: "The Creole filiation, a site of anxiety and ambivalence, was displaced and a revolutionary filiation took its place: the heroic fighters of the national struggle become his fathers and brothers. But upon his disavowal he created a theory of masculinity and of a black-white relation suffused with attraction, repulsion, denial, and anxiety."[4] This is a powerful claim, though matters are complicated by Fanon's attention to the active role of Algerian women in advancing the revolution. As Vergès presents it, the Fanonian drama is one that transpires between men, with women's bodies as "hostages" to the conflicts that unfold between men.[5] If *Black Skin, White Masks* turns on the disavowal of a Creole descent and the wounds of an emasculated masculinity, then Vergès suggests a reading of *Wretched* in terms of a fantasy filiation: "Algeria gave Fanon his dreamed filiation. It embodied the future of emancipated mankind and could claim, Fanon imagined, a precolonial past untainted by the whites. Algeria was the authentic scene of recovered virility."[6] I don't think Fanon is ever much interested in recovering an authentic and uncorrupted past, and several passages from both of his major works demonstrate how these recovery missions sap energy from the more pressing political demands of the present. And this scene of authentic virility gets far more interesting once it is admitted that Fanon saw women there too. I will consider Fanon's portrait of Algeria's revolutionary female in the final section of this chapter, but for now suffice it to say that Vergès underestimates the "muscularity" of Algerian women in her critique of Fanon's phallogocentrism. Where Vergès sees disavowal in Fanon's departure from Martinique, I see avowal of the forms of life opened up in exile—and, in this, he shares more with Adorno than with any of the French thinkers with whom he is often identified.[7]

Though her perspective is feminist and psychoanalytic, Vergès follows in the spirit of Albert Memmi's critical account of what he describes as the "impossible life" of Fanon. Memmi glosses this impossibility as follows: "Fanon's life has been accepted as a matter of course. Yet it is scarcely believable. A man who has never set foot in a country decides within a rather brief span of time that this people will be his people, this country his country until death, even though he knows neither its language nor its civilization and has no particular ties to it. He eventually dies for this cause and is buried in Algerian soil."[8] Memmi also casts this life as one of denial and failure, fueled by an admixture of revolutionary romanticism and apocalyptic fantasy. For Memmi, the impulse to identify so completely with an Algeria that is not his own is a symptom of Fanon's "total despair"—which is also indicated by the passionate and lyrical quality of his rhetoric.[9] In the pages that follow, I aim at a revaluation of what Memmi sees as "the extraordinary passion and the latent despair that permeate Fanon's work"—but which I see as precisely the qualities that make this work so compelling still.[10] Passion is the most basic element of Fanonian critique, and what draws him to various traditions, schools of thought, lyrical forms, and political projects. Phenomenology, psychiatry, Négritude poetry, and revolutionary politics, as well as Fanon's experiments in writing, indicate his persistent efforts to give form to the passions. Consider, for example, how the formal features of *Black Skin, White Masks*—a text Fanon describes as a "prayer" though its author is "wary of being zealous"—are linked to its content. The quick shifts from poetic and highly stylized prose to dry and more detailed engagement in specialists' debates, from personal anecdotes and case studies to literary and philosophical sources, the proliferation of archetypes and examples, and the fragmented and unfinished quality of the analysis are distinctive to this early text. These features of the book tell us something about the problem it addresses, about the diremption and disrepair that result from racial domination, about the difficulties of finding a consistent way of speaking to effects of race on psyche and society. *Wretched* represents yet another form of critique, more analytical and systematic, but also more profoundly partisan. Fanon's diverse rhetorical strategies revolve around a different set of objects—the process of decolonization, the fate of the nation, the distinctive set of challenges faced by peoples determined to chart their own futures. I am also interested in Fanon's use of the epistolary form: his letter of resignation as medical director of Blida-Joinville Hospital, the largest mental institution in colonial Algeria; the "Letter to a Frenchman," concerning his occupation in—and departure from—Algeria; the "Letter to the Youth of Africa," on their responsibilities in the anticolonial struggle; and the epistolary techniques that Fanon employs throughout his texts. The forms of Fanonian critique are part of its substance.

I speak of the elements of Fanonian critique rather than what Henry Louis Gates has described as "Critical Fanonism"—though I am in full agreement with Gates's insistence that "we no longer allow Fanon to remain a kind of icon or 'screen memory,' rehearsing dimly remembered dreams of postcolonial emancipation," that understanding Fanon means actually *reading* him.[11] To read him is to take seriously that *writing* is his most meaningful work, that which joins the work in the clinic to the work in the FLN. Writing is his "absolute praxis."[12] Reading Fanon is also to discover the forms that critical theory takes when moved by despair. Unlike Memmi, I do not believe that despair renders Fanon's thinking delusional or deranged. (Memmi himself can't decide whether to portray Fanon as the opportunistic colonial elite or the willfully repressed revolutionary romantic.) I believe that tonalities of despair in Fanon issue from a residue in his thought left by Hegel. Reconstructing the elements of Fanonian critique involves tending to what he accepts and what he rejects in Hegel's dialectic and the radical philosophical projects that Hegel inspired. It also requires following Fanon into the clinic, where the sickness of the colonial system is concentrated and where critique finds its diagnostic voice.

Seeming to contradict Memmi's account, Neil Lazarus has described Fanon's political ethic as "revolutionary optimism" and has challenged this optimism in light of the subsequent "setbacks and defeats" of the postcolonial period.[13] But Lazarus shares with Memmi, and with so many readers of Fanon, a representation of his thinking as politically and philosophically naïve. Fanon appears so singularly driven by a revolutionary doctrine that he is blind to contradictory cultural formations and to the pathos in his commitment. His authorship is treated as if it is a primitive cry for revolution, transparent, and without a need to be interpreted or deciphered. Lazarus, like Memmi, represents Fanon as exemplary of the pitfalls of messianic consciousness:

> Fanon speaks adamantly of the "awakening" of "the people," of their "intelligence and the onward progress of their consciousness." One is led increasingly to the conclusion that what is at issue here is either an intellectualistic romanticization of "the people" as spontaneously revolutionary or, more likely, a messianic misreading of their political

bearing during the anticolonial struggle. . . . In spite of the proselytizing work of the revolutionaries like Fanon, the peasants were not
aiming their actions at the "Algeria of tomorrow," but seeking, rather,
to restore that of yesterday.[14]

It would be absurd to contradict Lazarus's point that anticolonial
conflict did not herald a postcolonial period of freedom and equality.
Fanon would not be the first to overestimate the revolutionary potential of the peasantry, or even overstate its revolutionary aspirations. If
Fanon believed the people to be spontaneously revolutionary, surely
he would not have devoted so many pages of *Wretched* to the meaning of popular political education—a pedagogy of the oppressed, to
invoke Paulo Freire. The impulse that holds Fanon responsible for
the violence and corruption of authoritarian regimes in postcolonial
Africa, which Lazarus sometimes seems to do, is both mysterious
and highly questionable.[15] And the very idea of "setback" reinforces
an imaginary telos that postcoloniality has thrown into disrepair.
More importantly, though, the pages that follow advance the position
that Fanon's political thinking proves more sophisticated than what
is suggested by the idea of optimism. Fanon is far more mindful of
political strategy than any messianism would suggest. And reading
Fanon requires remaining sensitive to his rhetoric—and the diversity of voices in his authorship, of which the "proselytizing" voice is
just one among several, hardly the loudest.[16] Besides, Fanon "had long
given up shouting" by the time he left Martinique.[17]

"Despair" is a good term to use in connection with Fanon, but
Memmi uses it disparagingly and not in a dialectical sense. Ato
Sekyi-Otu refers to Fanon's "anguished eloquence"—of which I aim
to give a theoretical and political interpretation.[18] What is extraordinary about Fanon is not his revolutionary optimism or his impossible attachment to an imaginary Algeria, but how he permits ruthless
critique to finally abandon its attachment to hope and find its dynamism elsewhere. Fanon's dialectic is not "hope without hope" or a last
affirmation, but steady and spontaneous receptivity to experience. A
world consumed with sickness and loathing is also one that furnishes
refracted images of freedom, justice, and democracy. The following pages take up Drucilla Cornell's recent challenge to decolonize

critical theory, to expand the aims of thinking and sharpen critical vision, providing the context for a truly transformative politics.[19] It may well appear that I recolonize critical theory when I purport to do otherwise, that I recenter dead Europeans—Hegel, especially—in a story about Fanon. I am alert to this problem. But my intention is to show how Fanonian critique can enrich contemporary political thinking. What we learn from Fanon is that critique gathers its real political force from the passions, that critical theory today demands a militant politics, and that militancy draws its strength from despair.

2

> As long as he has not been effectively recognized by the other, it is this other who remains the focus of his actions.
> —Fanon, *Black Skin, White Masks*

Fanon's explicit engagement with Hegel comes in his first book, *Black Skin, White Masks*. In it, Fanon challenges Hegel's master-slave dialectic from the perspective of the real hell of the Middle Passage and the racial order born of it. On Fanon's retelling, Hegel's parable obscures more than it reveals about bondage. It does not account for the epidermalization of inferiority, the process by which racial hierarchy is scratched into the surface of the skin. Hegel cannot comprehend the actual effects of subjection on the body and spirit of the enslaved. For Fanon, racial formation in this context is no simple failure of recognition. It involves a more fundamental assault on subjectivity. Fanon is interested, too, in "the form[s] of recognition that Hegel never described"—the desire not to be seen, the desire to be seen as other than what you are, the desire to *be* the other, the desire to be *everything*. But even as Fanon takes aim at Hegel, the pages of *Black Skin* turn on Hegelian themes: desire, consciousness, work, slavery, freedom. Curiously, there is no mention of Hegel in *Wretched*, neither the *Phenomenology* nor the mature philosophy of history and the state. Sekyi-Otu has suggested that the unnamed dialectician is everywhere in *Wretched*, that the first chapter on violence "paraphrases Hegel's *Phenomenology* and parodies his *Logic*," and that the whole of the book advances a "dialectic of experience."[20] Nigel Gibson has also emphasized the importance of Hegel for Fanonian critique.[21] If Sekyi-Otu's Fanon vacillates between Hegel and Aristotle, tethered to the dialectic but suspicious of mediation, Gibson's Fanon is the supreme dialectician. He depicts Fanon's break with Négritude as a refusal of unhappy consciousness. And he glosses Fanon's critique of Sartre as schooled in a true Hegelianism. Black consciousness, for Gibson, is the work of determinate negation.

I, too, read Fanon as a "deviant Hegelian" for whom the experience of freedom is bound to the fate of the dialectic.[22] Fanon is part of a venerable tradition in twentieth-century critical theory that recasts this dialectic as negative—broken, fractured, damaged, or in some way thrown into irreconciliation. But this, in itself, does not set Fanon apart from so many thinkers of his age and milieu. Fanon is also in the distinguished company of Black theorists drawing from Hegel to map the antinomies of consciousness and the task of liberation.[23] What is unique to Fanon, I would argue, is his joining of the work of liberation to a negative dialectic. Freedom is fastened to a rupture, to things coming undone and breaking apart.

What I find in Fanon is something radically different from what Homi Bhabha discards as his lingering debt to Hegel: a "desperate, doomed search for a dialectic of deliverance."[24] Wherever Bhabha detects the remains of Hegel, he sees this dialectic of deliverance and Fanon's longing to escape indeterminacy, contingency, and the ambiguities of identity. For Bhabha, it is Fanon's Hegelianism that gives "hope to history" as the march of freedom, a humanist conceit that also blinds him to the "distinctive force of his vision."[25] Bhabha recommends that contemporary cultural criticism find its resources from a different side of Fanon, where the "Hegelian dream for a human reality in-itself-for-itself is ironized, even mocked, by his view of the Manichean structure of colonial consciousness and its non-dialectical division."[26] I admire Bhabha's interpretive feat: Hegelianism appears as the reverse image of Manicheanism and postcolonial irony discards both in the same gesture. In the passage from *Wretched* that Bhabha reads as a mockery of the dialectic, Fanon claims: "The 'native' sector is not complementary to the European sector. The two confront each other, but not in the service of a higher unity. Governed by a purely Aristotlean logic, they follow the dictates of mutual exclusion: There is no conciliation possible, one of them is superfluous."[27] Undeniably there is a critique of (Hegelian) conciliation in this passage, and the operations of "mutual exclusion" replace those of reciprocal recognition. Fanon demonstrates how a Hegelian logic applied to "this compartmentalized world, this world divided in two," becomes Aristotelian: this world becomes "inhabited by different species."[28] Only one of these species can survive a life-and-death struggle. But much of Hegel's basic architecture remains in tact. Fanon only refuses the idea that a higher unity might be born out of this divided world, that there is something about these compartments that complement or complete each other, that there is something that *makes sense* about colonialism. The colonial relationship serves no higher unity: it is a military occupation to serve the economic and political interests of the occupying force. And Fanon will resist all forms of rationalization for colonial oppression.

As I see things, though, it is also Fanon's Hegelianism that *rules out* hope in history. Or, more precisely, his negative dialectic is what keeps things moving, without regard for our hopes. It leads him to favor work and passion over hollow hopes, permanent risk and unending struggle over the satisfactions of salvation: "During the colonial period the people were called upon to fight against oppression. Following national liberation they are urged to fight against poverty, illiteracy, and underdevelopment. The struggle, they say, goes on. The people realize that life is an unending struggle."[29] Fanon's negative dialectic restores the fullness and complexity of passion to human history. Love, rage, envy, pride, grief, shame, and hatred are all at play in this messy dialectic. His controversial call for a "new humanism" might be considered in this context as a political and philosophical alternative to a conciliatory Hegelianism. This humanism is not "philosophy as the wisdom of love" but critical theory as the force of our many passions.[30] There is a tragic dimension to Fanon's reading of Hegel that also rules out the ironic ambivalence of postcolonial discourse, as if the wounds of hybridity do not leave scars. But there is no dialectic of deliverance in Fanon. Indeed, the primacy of politics is demonstration that his dreams remain resolutely of this world.

Hegel is all over *Black Skin*, but direct commentary comes in the context of Fanon's reflections on sexual desire and lived experience, in the critique of Sartre, and in a brief section of the book just before its conclusion titled "The Black Man and Hegel." At a critical point, Fanon explains why Hegel matters for his analysis: "Since the black man is a former slave," there is good reason to consult the master-slave dialectic and Europe's premier philosopher of freedom.[31] Fanon turns to Hegel to test the limits of a dialectic of freedom and demonstrate how European philosophy remains oblivious to the abjection that European power produces. He also wants to show how a structure of white supremacy becomes impervious to challenges and resistances that inevitably form in reaction to it. On this point, note my minor disagreement with those who criticize Fanon for "a wilfull misreading of the history of resistance and insurrection under plantain slavery."[32] I agree that Fanon underestimates the force and intensity of opposition to the slave system. But this is, in part, because he is interested to show how Black resistance gets neutralized and erased by a system that "grudgingly decided to raise the animal-machine man to the supreme rank of *man*."[33] Hegel's master-slave dialectic, from the perspective of the Black man who is always seen to be acted upon, is the parable of what was never permitted to be. Sartre's dialectic does worse: he condemns Black experience to a "weak stage of a dialogical progression," passed over and left for dead as swiftly as it came to life. "For once this friend, this born Hegelian," Fanon remarks, "had forgotten that consciousness needs to get lost in the night of the absolute, the only condition for attaining self-consciousness."[34] The point is that the Sartrean subject never gives itself over to the object or the other; it never gets "lost" in the negative. Sartrean consciousness, *pace* Hegel, remains in full possession of itself. And therefore, it can have no knowledge of itself—or the other. As Adorno says of Kierkegaard, Fanon will say of Sartre: history, society, and corporeality recede from view and what remains is a timeless and abstract ontology. This "born Hegelian" neglected the concrete wisdom in Hegel's *Phenomenology*: consciousness "wins its truth only when, in utter dismemberment, it finds itself."[35]

Fanon's analytic of violence is unthinkable absent this patently Hegelian formula. But before turning to the question of violence, I want to pause on two ideas that emerge out of Fanon's direct encounter with Hegel: *aporia* and *work*. "There is at the basis of the Hegelian dialectic an absolute reciprocity that must be highlighted"—this, for Fanon, is what will separate Hegel from the lived experience of the Black Man.[36] The postulate of "absolute reciprocity" means that Hegel avoids all the real challenges introduced by a master-slave relationship. Recall that Hegel launches the master-slave dialectic with an initial encounter between two: "Each sees the other do the same as it does; each does what it demands of the other, and therefore also does what it does only in so far as the other does the same."[37] Recognition *is* reciprocity: the other is the same as me; the other is my equal and my rival. Absolute reciprocity means no actual aporia; a "way out" of impasse or conflict is built into the system. The Hegelian dialectic might be said, in this way, to rig its results. This dialectic cannot account for the forms of subjection that do not find their beginnings in the solace of sameness. It says nothing about failed recognition or misrecognition, or those relationships of exploitation and bondage that are not principally about recognition in the first place. It is silent on the distortions and deformations that interrupt the development of independence and self-certainty. This silence is deadly, for slavery is reproduced through these very distortions and deformations. Slavery is only possible under conditions of nonreciprocity; every other narrative is a fairy tale. As Fanon represents it, Hegel's master-slave dialectic has no slaves; everyone acts as a master, believes himself to be master, and regards the other as having a proper claim on mastery. Hegel's sanguine picture of bondage means that its pathos falls out of view. If Hegel's dialectic has no slaves, the greater absurdity is that a centuries-old system of racial domination built and maintained on the backs of slaves would "one day" decree that there would be no more masters. "It is not the sort of announcement you hear twice in a lifetime"—here Fanon's mockery, not of Black passivity but of White cynicism, is critical.[38] Once again, German Idealism works in tandem with European ideology. From both sides, the real effects of a slave system, maintained by the epidermalization of inferiority and the spiritualization of material violence, become imaginary figments: "You can imagine the temperature in such a jungle. *No way out*."[39]

Fanon proposes that this aporia is both enervating and energizing, in the way we tend to feel both fatigued and fired up in the heat. "For the black Frenchman," on the one hand, "the situation is unbearable.

Unsure whether the white man considers him as consciousness-in-itself-for-itself, he is constantly preoccupied with detecting resistance, opposition, and contestation."[40] Of course, he detects resistance, opposition, and contestation everywhere, but accompanied by the peculiar feeling that the fight has been postponed or called off, that he is "too late" or has arrived in the wrong place.[41] "As long as he has not been effectively recognized by the other," Fanon notes, "it is this other who remains the focus of his actions."[42] The tragedy is not that man was once a child, but that one man should be in the position of having to prove himself to another, while still being denied the dignity of a fight. But on the other hand, in its constant preoccupations, Black consciousness also experiences the "alterity of rupture, of struggle and combat."[43] An aporetic and unbearable situation, a jungle from which there is no way out, becomes the cracked and uneven terrain of struggle. Against Sartre's exit options, Fanon makes a plea for aporia: "I needed to lose myself totally in *négritude*. Perhaps one day, deep in this wretched romanticism. . . . In any case I *needed* not to know. This struggle, this descent once more, should be seen as a completed aspect."[44] Of course, the primacy of struggle—risk and conflict, staking one's life, the tremble unto death—confirms Fanon's deepest Hegelianism. Work is the other key ingredient. But Fanon's dialectic of rupture resists deliverance at every turn. We live and struggle in this broken world we have made for ourselves: "*And the war goes on.*"[45]

Hegel's master-slave dialectic is propelled forward by the desire for recognition: "Self-Consciousness exists in and for itself when, and by the fact that, it so exists for another; that is, it exists only in being acknowledged."[46] Work is derivative of this more fundamental need for recognition. For Fanon, what masters want from slaves is "not recognition but work"—and what may look with Hegelian specs like a two-way street is exploitation in one direction.[47] "Likewise, the slave here can in no way be equated with the slave who loses himself in the object and finds the source of his liberation in his work," and this is for two reasons.[48] The first, as Fanon will clarify in *Wretched*, is "that slavery is the opposite of work, and that work presupposes freedom, responsibility, and consciousness."[49] In short, work presupposes everything that slavery negates. No liberation can be found in slave labor. Second, a master-slave relationship means a diminishing world of objects and others. All focus tends toward the figure of force. "For Hegel, the slave turns away from the master and toward the object," Fanon notes. "Here the slave turns toward the master and abandons the object."[50] Donna Jones puts matters this way: "The Hegelian Dialectic simply does not seem to fit the experience of African slaves in the New World: it is nonsensical that chained and whipped slaves could see in work a vehicle for self-realization, much less in their whips and chains the necessary conditions for the compulsion of the labor by which their humanity is to be achieved."[51] Nonsensical, indeed, but this does not mean that Fanon will dispense altogether with the concept of work. If bondage means the abandonment of the object, among the most important rhetorical aims in *Wretched* is the recovery of a world of objects and others—and, with it, the reappraisal of work. The concept of work becomes crucial in defining political militancy, distinguishing between the colonizer and the colonized, and destroying the colonial apparatus. Though I am sympathetic to his treatment of Fanonian ambiguity, I think Ross Posnock misinterprets this aspect of Fanon's thinking. Posnock claims that "Fanon's commitment to a dialectic of the universal and the particular is in tension with what would short-circuit it—his Nietzschean leap of invention."[52] But Fanon's declaration—"*the militant therefore is one who works*"—resonates with a restless negativity as much as any joyful science.[53] What will separate a Nietzschean leap of invention from the Hegelian work of negation? In the case of Fanon, the idea of freedom seems not to depend on a leap that short-circuits the dialectic (this is his critique of Sartre) but on steady and patient labor: "The questions which the organization asks the militant bear the mark of this vision of things: 'Where have you worked? With whom? What have you accomplished?'"[54] The real concern when reading Fanon is not with a spontaneous leap into creation, but with the routine expectations of work and commitment. For Fanon, we are defined by our work, not as discrete individuals called to a particular vocation, but as classes and social groups. The colonizer is defined by his work—"to make even dreams of liberty impossible for the colonized"—just as it is the job of the colonized "to imagine every possible method for annihilating the colonist."[55] This also explains why "violence is invested with positive, formative features" for oppressed, enslaved, and occupied peoples: "it constitutes *their only work.*"[56]

Lest the empire of toil and drudgery fall over the resistance too, *Wretched* offers an astute defense of strategic slack. It wreaks havoc on a system that demands work. It prepares the people for a General Strike. Even when unmotivated and unthinking, there is an active principle in colonial apathy. We might speak, under certain conditions, not just of a right but also of *a duty to be lazy.* On the legendary "laziness" of the native, Fanon remarks:

> The colonized's indolence is the conscious sabotage of the colonial machine; on the biological plane it is a remarkable system of auto-protection; and in any case it is a sure brake upon the seizure of the whole country by the occupying power. . . . The duty of the colonized subject, who has not yet arrived at a political consciousness or a decision to reject the oppressor, is to have the slightest effort literally dragged out of him.[57]

This image of the idler, unwilling to hand over even minimal energy, is the perfect complement to the muscular exertion of the militant. What masters want from slaves, what the colonizer wants from the colonized, is not recognition but labor. There is an immense power in work, immanent to a structure in which some work on behalf of others, which can be harnessed to reproduce or destroy that structure. The refusal of work can be a physical defense against a definite harm. It can also bring an entire social structure to a standstill.[58] The refusal of work may be the sign of a revolt that has not yet come to pass. Or, like Fanon's resignation from his post at Bilda, it may be to join an insurrection already underway.

3

> It is necessary to analyze, patiently and lucidly, each one of the reactions of the colonized, and every time we do not understand, we must tell ourselves that we are at the heart of the drama—that of the impossibility of finding a meeting ground in any colonial situation.
>
> —Fanon, "Medicine and Colonialism"

How we read Fanon's work depends on what we are reading for. "Few historians of colonial medicine have engaged deeply with Fanon," the historian of colonial medicine Richard Keller laments, "leaving him to the clutches of postcolonial literary critics."[59] But critics would be well served to accompany historians into the clinic, for here the diagnostic ambitions in Fanonian critique have full command. Keller is interested in how "a colonial politics of race and exploitation constantly crept into the clinic," and Fanon's work gives him "at least partially an insider's perspective."[60] I am interested in how the clinic constantly creeps into Fanonian critique. By this, I mean how sickness and health circulate across Fanon's clinical practice and his critical theory, how systematic oppression erases the boundary between reason and madness, and how the politics of freedom promises moments of temporary sanity.

His best biographer, David Macey, tells a rich and complex story of Fanon's clinical experience, which draws from extensive archival material. Placing Fanon's psychiatry in a scholarly and professional context, Macey arrives at two surprising conclusions. First, psychoanalysis is not central to Fanon's work in the clinic and probably not so important for his critical theory.[61] The diagnostic strand in his thought hangs on a different set of referents, this notwithstanding some studied reflections on Lacan's "mirror stage" and the announcement in the introduction of *Black Skin* that he would advance a "psychoanalytic interpretation the black problem."[62] Second, Macey argues that Fanon's clinical practice is consistent with an established history of conventional medicine in the colonies. Fanon is implicated in this thorny history. Though compassionate in his treatment of patients, he is conservative in his techniques and treatments. According to Macey's more restrained portrait:

> Fanon was not a Laing-style anti-psychiatrist *avant la lettre* but a pragmatic psychiatrist working within the mainstream paradigms of his day and in the difficult environment of psychiatric hospitals. The revolutionary was not a psychoanalyst but an ambitious young doctor who wrote up his clinical experiences for the medical press and presented scientific papers to conferences on neuropsychiatry. Had he lived, it is not difficult to imagine him prescribing Ritalin and Prozac.[63]

This Fanon bears little resemblance to the incendiary subversive passed down in the hagiographic records. Fanon, the consummate professional, is a disturbing image even without the myth of the revolutionary Saint Frantz.[64] But had he lived, it is also not difficult to imagine Fanon detailing how attention disorders, hyperactivity, and clinical depression reflect the maladies of our social relations. It is not difficult to hear him reflect on the "affective disorders" that come with systematic abjection and ask after the objective origins of subjective illness. It is easy to see him in occupied territories, combat zones, or prison hospitals.

Fanon's basic disagreement with psychoanalysis—and, though basic, it's decisive—concerns the unconscious. This most elemental premise of psychoanalysis, that which gives content to the theory and purpose to the practice, also gives Fanon pause. He proposes that the conflicts psychoanalysis buries in the depths of the unconscious are not so deep after all. Much of the "psychic life of power" unfolds on the surface of social relations and behavior:[65]

> Since the racial drama is played out in the open, the black man has no time to "unconsciousnessize" it. The white man manages it to a certain degree because a new factor emerges: i.e., guilt. The black man's superiority or inferiority complex and his feeling of equality are conscious. He is constantly making them interact. He lives his drama. There is in him none of the affective amnesia characteristic of the typical neurotic.[66]

This passage is remarkable on a number of levels. Fanon stretches out the stage on which the racial drama transpires and condenses the time. Race is played out in the open but pressed for time, constantly on the move. Guilt, itself a racial mechanism, is the "new factor" that stops the clock. If there is an unconscious, there is a subject with the time, repose, forgetfulness, and guilt that this edifice requires. Such a subject cannot be a black man. With his fantasy of a virile and rugged black masculinity, Fanon insists that the black man "lives" his drama and doesn't bury it. He remains conscious of his conditions. "Ask any Antillean and he will tell you"—the refrain repeated in *Black Skin* might also read as a sideswipe at the idea of the unconscious.

Though he challenges the founding narratives and concepts of psychoanalysis, Fanon ventures toward this tradition with the aim of throwing light on the madness of a racist culture: "Racism is not the whole but the most visible, the most day-to-day and, not to mince matters, the crudest element of a given structure."[67] One of the real and most visible effects of racism is mental illness, both individual and collective. Another effect is that racial difference itself gets pathologized, as seen in the so-called North African Syndrome.[68] Fanon does not dispense with the basic distinction between health and sickness, but operates in world in which these are highly unstable and unreliable terms: "Psychoanalysis is a pessimistic view of man. The care of the person must be thought as a deliberately optimistic choice against human reality."[69] The critique of human reality dwells in the day-to-day, what Henri Lefebvre and Michel de Certeau call everyday life and Thomas Dumm describes in connection with the politics of the ordinary.[70] Here the critic ineluctably finds despair.

If ideas of health and sickness have been thrown into confusion and disrepair, there is no refuge in the idea of reason. Just knives: "I felt the knife blades sharpening within me. I made up my mind to defend myself. Like all good tacticians I wanted to rationalize the world and show the white man he was mistaken."[71] But reason would not be the referee to this fight. Against a philosophical discourse of (European) modernity, the problem for Fanon is not that reason has taken flight or that rationality has been supplanted by barbarism. As Cedric Robinson clarifies, we are "not faced with a rational order gone awry, but the exhaustion of a rationalist adventure in the wilderness of an irrational (i.e., racial) civilization."[72] We are faced with ideas of reason that not only are products of this racial order, but are produced for the purposes of legitimating it. Reason is not merely tainted by madness; it can be seen to conspire against freedom: "I had rationalized the world, and the world had rejected me in the name of color prejudice. Since there was no way we could agree on the basis of reason, I resorted to irrationality. . . . I am at home; I am made of the irrational; I wade in the irrational; Irrational up to my neck."[73] Fanon's critique of colonial reason works on this poetic front. A poetics of political thinking will resort to the irrational—and, on occasion, make a home there.[74] Yet there is a clinician in Fanon who suspects that the irrational harbors madness and knows that "madness is one of the means man has of losing his freedom."[75] Poetics is a site of anxiety and opportunity. Though Robinson heaps scorn on the "petit-bourgeois stink" of *Black Skin, White Masks*, it is this text that does poetic justice to the limits of reason.[76]

Fanon's critique of colonial reason moves on the tightrope that joins ideology critique and critical history. As ideology critic, Fanon considers how the philosophical discourses of European modernity serve and protect European oppression. Western values—at once particular and universal, depending on what the expansion or conservation of colonial power requires—never announce their alliance with oppression. But oppressed people are not so easily misled: "every time the issue of Western values crops up, the colonized grow tense and their muscles seize up. During the period of decolonization the colonized are called upon to be reasonable. They are offered rock-solid values, they are told in great detail that decolonization should not mean regression, and that they must rely on values which have proven to be reliable and worthwhile."[77] And this is the point at which the knives come out again. Fanonian critique defers not to the unreconstructed immediacy of experience, but to the capacity of oppressed peoples to reflect critically on their lived experience and respond to the structures that condition that experience. Values, principles, and ideals become sites of contestation and struggle. This is how ideology critique becomes critical history on a Hegelian register:

> Sometimes even these politicians declare: "We blacks, we Arabs" and these terms charged with ambivalence during the colonial period take on a sacred connotation. These nationalist politicians are playing with fire. As an African leader recently told a group of young intellectuals: "Think before speaking to the masses, they are easily excitable." There is therefore a cunning of history which plays havoc with the colonies.[78]

So, for Fanon, there is reason in the history of decolonization, even when it seems only the mad fury of destruction.

We are now in a position, at long last, to frame the question of violence in Fanon. Violence is not the sign of the irrational, the unreasonable, or the insane, though Fanon admits that every form of violence rebels against the boundaries of reason. Violence is, first of all, a symptom. It marks the absolute impossibility of finding consensus or conciliation in any colonial situation. It is the sign of a sickness, or *dis-ease*. And wherever there is violence, there is an underlying disorder. No matter how rational or instrumental, violence always contains more than a touch of madness. Colonial violence is the institutionalization of an insanity that imagines itself to be civilized. Anticolonial resistance is the rational violence that rebels against official madness. No form of violence—or nonviolence—can be considered apart from the objective conditions that produce it. At times, violence is an effort at diversion or denial: "By throwing himself muscle and soul into his blood feuds, the colonized subject endeavors to convince himself that colonialism never existed, that everything is as it used to be and history marches on."[79] Here we see a "restorative nostalgia" at work in the fury of destruction.[80] On other occasions, violence finds outlet in ritual activity: ceremonies, festivals, sacrifice. "During the struggle for liberation there is a singular loss of interest in these rituals," Fanon suggests. "With his back against the wall, the knife at his throat, or to be more exact the electrode at his genitals, the colonized subject is bound to stop telling stories."[81]

Some forms of violence resemble narrative, and they are ways of telling stories and communicating without words. Violence is, secondly, a symptom that is also a therapy. It is the sign of sickness that is also a treatment for sickness. Fanon describes its effects as detoxifying and cathartic: "At the individual level, violence is a cleansing force. It rids the colonized of their inferiority complex, of their passive and despairing attitude. It emboldens them, and restores their self-confidence."[82] This is an unsettling position. In an effort to blunt its force, Patrick Taylor says that the argument is not for "the act of violent struggle [as] the key to decolonization but, rather, the revolutionary leap, the 'willed' entry into history, the consciousness of the categorical imperative."[83] And Taylor regards this as Fanon's debt to Hegel: "What moves the Hegelian dialectic from a situation of mutually exclusive protagonists to one of mutual recognition, is the recognition of the other and the recognition of oneself as an active, freely creative being."[84] This somewhat sanitized reinterpretation forgets the part of Hegel that has to do with risk, and staking one's life, and facing death—all so crucial for Fanon. The act of violent struggle *is* key because it preserves the risk and responsibility that are elemental to freedom. And just as narrative and storytelling bring people into dialogue, violence establishes the bonds of camaraderie between some as it severs the connection and subjection to others. An atmospheric violence reminds the people that they are not alone—that, and a radio.[85]

Violence is a form of collective therapy that is also a political strategy. It must be harnessed and channeled, but also disciplined and restrained according to the imperatives of politics. The strategic element of violence is nowhere clearer, oddly enough, than in Fanon's interpretation of nonviolence. He sees nonviolence, too, as a product of the colonial context:

> At a critical, deciding moment the colonialist bourgeoisie, which had remained silent until then, enters the fray. They introduce a new notion, in actual fact a creation of the colonial situation: nonviolence. In its raw state this nonviolence conveys to the colonized intellectual and the business elite that their interests are identical to the colonialist bourgeoisie and it is therefore indispensable, a matter of urgency, to reach an agreement for the common good. Nonviolence is an attempt to solve the colonial problem around the negotiating table.[86]

These attempts are doomed: the colonial problem is fundamentally nonnegotiable and the doctrine of nonviolence "enters the fray" too late, once the vital effects of violence have been felt by the people. Political historians and analysts often tell the story of violence a different way. They depict resistance movements that begin in nonviolence and "fall" or "lapse" into violence when initial hopes are disappointed. Fanon presents something else entirely, not only an alternative temporality of political resistance, but also a materialist critique of violence. He describes a social structure built on systematic and institutionalized violence, a resistance movement that begins in sporadic and volatile fits of violence, a political organization that emerges to give form and direction to violence that is spontaneous and unpredictable, and *then* the introduction of nonviolence as a reactionary and desperate appeal for compromise. The doctrine of nonviolence does not exist apart from a dialectic of decolonization that is drenched in violence.

Even "raw state" nonviolence is a reaction-formation that reflects particular class interests and alliances. A colonial bourgeois, sensing the threat of battle and the urgency of the moment, joins forces with the intellectual and economic elites of the colony. The doctrine of nonviolence appears at a critical and decisive "stage" in a process of decolonization. Like the colonized subject, the colonial bourgeois "is aware of the exceptional nature of the current situation" and "brandishing the threat of violence . . . intends to make the most of it."[87] Nonviolence is not a pure or timeless moral doctrine. It is a political strategy that emerges within a larger history of violence, and is itself the product of colonial violence. Nonviolence doesn't mean keeping clean, but dirtying one's hands differently, through the force of compromise. For Fanon, the question concerning violence is neither ontological nor moral, but historical and political. A materialist critique of violence traces the history and class character of diverse political strategies.

Fanon does worry about perpetual violence and the unending cycle of revenge encouraged by every violent action. Admittedly, he worries more about ending colonial violence, about dismantling a system that has infected every social relationship with sickness. But part of what motivates his reflections on the pleasures of violence is recognition of its pathos. This born Hegelian appreciates that the fury of destruction threatens even the most righteous of projects. Or those especially. A materialist critique of violence maps the multiple political forms that appear and disappear amid the madness: "We do not expect this colonialism to commit suicide. It is altogether logical for it to defend itself fanatically. But it is, on the other hand, its awareness that it cannot survive which will determine its liquidation as a style of contact with other peoples."[88] Fanonian critique discerns the rationalities of violence—and treats violence as a rationality that contains its suspension or temporary armistice. Fanon believed, in the 1950s, that the structure of organized violence that goes by the name of colonialism could not go on forever, or even much longer. This does not does commit him to a dialectic of deliverance as much as it frees his thinking from the prison of colonial fate. An open and indeterminate future, for Fanon, recenters the question of action: "Placed in this world, in a real life situation, 'embarked' as Pascal would have it, am I going to accumulate weapons?"[89]

4

Monsieur le Ministre, there comes a moment when tenacity becomes morbid perseverance. Hope is then no longer an open door to the future but the illogical maintenance of a subjective attitude in organized contradiction with reality.

—Fanon, "Letter to the Resident Minister"

In 1956, when he was just thirty-one, Fanon tendered his formal resignation as medical director at Blida–Joinville Psychiatric Hospital in Algeria. Some of his readers have highlighted that he signed this letter as a "French citizen" and conclude from this that Fanon had not yet established a fantasy filiation with his beloved and imaginary Algeria.[90] The signature authorizes Fanon's wounded attachment to the French nation. I tend to see Fanon's signature as confirmation of a point also made by Thomas Dumm: "resignations are evidence of the fact that there are no clean slates in life."[91] Fanon's resignation is the continuation and the culmination of this experience, signed with dirty hands. Five years later, he would be dead.

"It does not matter how happy the occasion of any resignation might be," Dumm continues, "every resignation is connected to disappointment in that every resignation marks a rupture, a quitting, the ending of something, that places someone Nowhere in respect to where they were before."[92] Nowhere is the place Dumm goes with Stanley Cavell, not quite Utopia, but the place of disappointment, or the birthplace of philosophy.[93] Here Dumm, as well as Cavell, is hoping to preserve a refuge for a specific kind of philosophical inquiry— "hoping, against hope" for a place for thinking about ruptures and ordinary disappointments.[94] Fanon's resignation breaks with hope and rejects a politics sustained by a "hope against hope" that is in "organized contradiction" with the real. Hope is narrowly subjectivist, while reality is objects and others. Hope is an attitude, illogical in the face of reality, but not a position. Hope even has a death wish, a morbid determination to take flight from what exists.

This alliance between hope and death is captured in one of the case studies Fanon presents in the final chapter of *Wretched*, "Colonial War and Mental Disorders." The case involves a European police inspector whose evenings were increasingly given over to episodes of extreme violence toward his wife and children. His everyday work activity as a police offer had been redefined since "the troubles": his job was now the routine torture of Algerians. Fanon recounts the officer's "golden rule" of torture: "The golden rule is never give the guy the impression he won't get out alive. He'll then wonder what's the use of talking if it won't save his life. In that case you'll have no chance at all of getting anything out of him. He has to go on hoping. It's hope that makes them talk."[95] This torturer's moral code rests on the foundations of hope, on the confirmed desperation of hope, on the acquiescence of hope, on the treason of hope. He knows it to be a passion easily exploited and turned against the prisoner. After a ten-hour workday devoted to the routine business of crushing the human spirit, this officer sought overtime violence against his family. And this is the part that prompted his concerns and sent him into therapy. The goal in seeking therapy was *not* to stop the torture: "he asked me in plain language to help him torture Algerian patriots without having a guilty conscience, without any behavioral problems, and with a total piece of mind." The goal, as this officer understood, was to learn how to torture more effectively and efficiently—and how to avoid bringing his work home. Under these circumstances, if Fanon were to continue in employment for a colonial state that also claims this officer as one of its own, the principle of hope would be in alliance with inhumanity.

For this reason, I am reluctant to embrace an otherwise elegant reading from Nelson Maldonado-Torres, who defends what he calls a restorative philosophy of love in Fanon.[96] Hope and love are different, and Fanon is much more favorable in his handling of love. And there are passages in *Black Skin* that support an interpretation of New Humanism as a philosophy of love. My reluctance is based on a concern I have about reading Fanon in terms of any single passion, especially one that requires that the people set aside their hatred.[97] If every resignation is connected to disappointment and despair, then these too must find place in our political thinking. Against an affirmative philosophy of love that stands in organized contradiction with reality, I am proposing a critical theory premised on a *spontaneous receptivity* to reality. This is the spontaneous receptivity that Adorno discusses in connection with Hegel and links to a philosophy of experience. I see it as the comportment indicated in Fanon's letter of resignation and suggested by his emphasis on lived experience. This receptivity is neither a leap of invention nor pure passivity. Once again, Dumm is helpful: "Almost all resignations, forced or otherwise, are inflected with a certain passivity; indeed, this sense inheres in the meaning of the word. To be resigned is to accept one's fate. Both those who resign and those who accept a resignation can be led to feel as though events are beyond their control."[98] Fanon's resignation, too, concedes that the situation in Algeria, a systematic dehumanization and depersonalization of the Arab, has made it impossible to perform his professional duties. Psychiatry, or "the medical technique that enables man no longer to be a stranger in his environment," is powerless in the face of a colonial system that functions by alienating human beings from their surroundings.[99] In this context, the psychiatric focus on the individual and individuated illness is complicity with alienation. "The social structure existing in Algeria," Fanon explains, "was hostile to any attempt to put the individual back where he belonged."[100] This is a situation in which proceeding with business as usual is the real and more dangerous passivity. In resignation, Fanon accepts the inhuman reality of a French occupation in Algeria, as well as the fate of psychiatry under these conditions. In not resigning oneself to resignation, one submits to the rule of inhumanity and injustice.[101] The politics of resignation rebels against abstract notions of activity and passivity.

Fanon's resignation is dictated by reason and passion. Reason is critical. It furnishes the infinitely demanding imperative to speech and action: "It is the duty of the citizen to say this. No professional morality, no class solidarity, no desire to wash the family linen in private, can have a prior claim. No pseudo-national mystification can prevail against the requirement of reason."[102] Reason cuts through the fog of pseudo-familial loyalty and national attachments. It makes secondary our professional associations and other identifications. As Habermas also appreciates, the requirements of reason condition our speech acts. As Habermas could also appreciate, Fanon offers his resignation as a refusal of despair: "For many months my conscience has been the seat of unpardonable debates. And their conclusion is the determination not to despair of man, in other words, of myself."[103] The categorical requirement of reason ends in the determination not to despair. And not to hope. So on what basis do I justify the argument that this is a resignation dictated by both reason *and* passion? With Fanon, reason is locked in a relationship with the passions. And this relationship gets expressed in work, in the work we do and how we give account of that work to ourselves and others.

In that resignation often comes by letter, the politics of resignation also presents an occasion to reflect upon the politics of the epistolary form. The signatory matters, but so does the addressee. Is the letter public or private? Does the author anticipate a response? What sort of response? How does the letter establish a relationship between its author and its recipient? What sort of relationship is this? Why might a particular kind of political speech come in the form of a letter? How might the open letter be like or different from other rousing genres of political writing—for instance, the manifesto or the declaration? It seems Fanon had a certain fondness for the epistolary form and a recognition of its political uses. Paying attention to Fanon's complex rhetoric, the strategies he employs in narrating the colonial drama and the anticolonial struggle, requires consideration of the letter as form. Substance is also important. A section from "Letter to the Youth of Africa" underscores the importance of the concept of work for Fanon:

> In the fine hours of French imperialism, it could be a kind of honor for a colonized person to be a part of the French government. This honor without responsibility or risk, this childish complacency about being a minister or Secretary of State, could, in an extreme case, be forgiven. In the past ten years, however, it has become truly intolerable and unacceptable for Africans to hold a post in the government that dominates them.[104]

Note how the "honor" bestowed upon the colonized person who works for French government is a slave's honor, in Fanon's sense. Freedom is responsibility and risk; work without these cannot be called work in Fanon's more exalted (and idealized) sense. Note also how Fanon here dwells in the point of contact between work and politics, between one's everyday activity "on the job" and a social structure that is reproduced through ordinary life under extraordinary conditions. Fanon is also pointing to the place where theory meets practice and personal biography meets world history.

5

This is why we must watch the parallel progress of this man and this woman, of this couple that brings death to the enemy, life to the Revolution.

—Fanon, "Algeria Unveiled"

I do not conclude with this image from the opening essay from *A Dying Colonialism* to raise the vexed question of gender in Fanon at this late stage. Other have done some of this work and, while there is more to say, I have not treated the passions in connection with gender and have pushed the question of sex to the very margins of my analysis.[105] For better or worse. Nonetheless this image captures some of the elements of Fanon's work that assist us in charting new directions for critical theory. And I think it helps to recenter the question concerning the politics of critique. The essay is extraordinary in its own right, for developing the Fanonian themes of embodiment and corporeality, for its considerations on the still timely political question of how Muslim women dress, and for its focus on the Algerian woman as heroic revolutionary.[106] Fanon indulges his typical tendency to idealize the anticolonial freedom fighter, but here the fighter is a woman—and this fact is not irrelevant to a critique of the misogynist sexual economy in Fanon.

In the couple that brings "life" to the struggle, there is the trace of a revolutionary vitalism that Fanon shares with Léopold Senghor and Aimé Césaire.[107] In Fanon, this trace is liberated from the confines of an individual will. It appears in and through our human relations and in the interaction between subjects and objects. Fanon's negative dialectic precludes the idealism of hypostatized subjectivity. I have described this comportment, where revolutionary vitalism greets "the seriousness, the suffering, the patience, and the labor of the negative," in terms of a spontaneous receptivity to others and objects.[108] Spontaneous receptivity in Fanon turns on the primacy of politics and a politics of lived experience. (In this way, it is rather different from Adorno's negative dialectic, which turns on the primacy of critique and the critique of experience.) *Wretched* trades explicitly in the category of spontaneity, with the spontaneously revolutionary forces that become available during a process of decolonization and the political organization necessary to build these forces. Using examples from Kenya and the Congo, Fanon writes: "It is among these masses, in the people of the shanty towns and in the lumpenproletariat that the insurrection will find its urban spearhead. The lumpenproletariat, this cohort of starving men, divorced from tribe and clan, constitutes one of the most spontaneously and radically revolutionary forces of a colonized people."[109] Fanon's confidence in the *lumpenproletariat* registers a point of disagreement with Marx, who saw the "rabble" as unreliable and undisciplined, more often a conservative or counter-revolutionary class. In the shantytowns, among a peasantry dispossessed of land and an underclass with nothing to lose, Fanon sees the conditions for a spontaneously revolutionary force. Here he also sees the affective energies so vital to a revolutionary movement and organization. In a Gramscian vein, Fanon's political thinking revolves around the interaction between the organization and the people—how the party mobilizes popular passions, but also how it answers and directs the people's desires and discontents. But Fanon also avows the irreducible gap that separates theory from action. This much he shares with Adorno too: "The theoretical question . . . whether the bourgeois phase can be effectively skipped . . . must be resolved through revolutionary action and not reasoning."[110] Fanon parts company with Adorno, finally, in positing the primacy of practice and the real possibility of revolution. This move also constitutes his return to Marx, or a tradition of revolutionary Marxism.[111] Perhaps Fanon, too, bears Marx's concealed wounds—and announces the coming African Revolution so authoritatively because he knew he wasn't entirely sure about it.

Luce Irigaray has argued that the couple constitutes the starting point for the ethical relationship required by democracy. On the principle that "democracy begins between two," Irigaray demands substantive justice between a man and a woman as the foundation for a political definition of democracy.[112] Irigaray's ethical orientation to democracy also finds its basis in a politics of the ordinary: "A real democracy must take as its basis today, a just relationship between man and woman. A distorted relationship between them gives rise to so many forms of antidemocratic power. Unless we can transform this, *the most everyday element of our lives*, we will never bring about change across the world."[113]

Fanon depicts this movement in the other direction. In the parallel movements of a man and woman to change the world, the relationship between them changes as well. Irigaray follows a "private" ethical relationship into the public, into the politics of democracy. Fanon's thought moves from the politics of revolution to the militancy of everyday life. This politics is not always named democracy and is not always linked to the work of critique, but this chapter has sought to amplify the voice in Fanon that speaks on behalf of both. A passage from *Wretched* points to this potentially simpatico relationship between democracy and critique:

> Self-criticism has been much talked about of late, but few people realize that it is an African institution. Whether in the *djemaas* of North Africa or the palavers of West Africa, tradition has it that disputes which break out in a village are worked out in public. By this I mean collective self-criticism with a touch of humor, because everybody is relaxed, because in the end we all want the same thing.[114]

To the skeptic's question concerning New Humanism—"Are we still in politics or a dream?"—we have most certainly departed the dreamscape.[115] Dreams are fantasy, or compensatory mechanisms for what we are denied in our waking hours: "Hence the dreams of the colonized subject are muscular dreams, dreams of action, dreams of aggressive vitality."[116] By contrast, these democratic institutions offer a rare moment of relaxation in Fanon and a glimpse into the political shape of his New Humanism. Collective self-criticism, in which the people do not reach for their knives but work out their conflicts in public, is not a European tradition—or even a latent universalism preserved in the particular history of Europe. Fanon reminds us that democracy is an "African institution"—or precisely that which Europe's history demonstrates that it has been hell-bent to destroy.

Democracy means sharing in the space that forms when disputes break out, when divisions occur, when conflicts must be worked out in public. Democratic equality lets us laugh and lighten up. Democratic freedom lets us take risks and bear responsibility. A more democratic reality might permit us hope, against hope. But the ruthless critique of everything existing means learning to live with despair.

Concluding Postscript

No single thinker has done more to shape the idea of critical theory in the postwar period than Jürgen Habermas. As I see things, Habermas turns away from a potential project opened up by the thinkers considered in this study—not just Adorno, to whom his connection is obvious, but also Bataille, of whom he is substantially more critical, and Fanon, about whom he says nothing. In recent years, Habermas has turned his attention to questions pertaining to philosophy and religion, the relationship between reason and faith, and the connection between postmetaphysical thinking and theological endeavors. These inquiries are exciting, for they suggest a softening of the hard universalism in his earlier writings. As anxiety eases concerning the status of reason, hermeneutic and anthropological insights in his work finally come to the fore. On another level, however, Habermas's "postmetaphysical" reflections refine and rearticulate an argument that he has been making for decades: communicative reason may not save us, but it is our only hope.

Recall that, for Hegel, one of the main problems to which modern philosophy addresses itself is the opposition of knowledge and faith. The age of Enlightenment, culminating in the figures of Kant and Fichte, maintained this opposition by assuming it. Because of this, Hegel believed Enlightenment reason no less dogmatic than religious orthodoxy. In the attempt to repair the breach between reason and revelation, Hegelian philosophy demands rational reflection on religion's truth-content. Christianity, for Hegel, represented what philosophy was to comprehend: the unity in difference of the finite and the infinite, the particular and the universal, the human and the divine. While all historical religions prior to Christianity contain their own "truth" as different moments in the history of religion and culture, they remain caught in the bifurcation of Spirit in consciousness and self-consciousness. Christianity is both a moment within and the culmination of the history of religion, where the struggle for freedom and ethical life are joined. The gospel, says Hegel, gives expression to this truth-content, long buried or distorted by Church dogma. Secular tendencies in the age of Enlightenment put philosophy, finally, in the position to apprehend and seize upon that truth-content, to liberate faith from ideology, and to restore the relationship between religion and reason. Andrew Shanks calls it "a theological celebration of secularization, and the secular state, for the way it removes, at any rate, the grosser political motives for the distortion of the gospel."[1] I would qualify this account by saying that Hegel's theological perspectives, from his seminary years at Tübingen to the Berlin lectures on religion in the 1820s, are drawn from and directed at the concrete, historical life of human beings. Not life in an animal-biological sense or a spiritualized-sacred sense, but human life in its historical shapes— this is Hegel's consistent focus.

As is well known, his radical critics in the 1830s and 1840s took issue with Hegel's philosophy of religion, the modern state, and political history. They saw in it the deification of the Prussian state and the rationalization of Protestant Christianity.[2] These nineteenth-century Left Hegelians articulated and opposed the "political theology" they took the Prussian state to represent. And they criticized Hegel as an apologist and ideologue of the state. Habermas, for his part, draws upon this Left Hegelian critique of Hegel in his construction of the idea of communicative reason and the tasks of critical theory. The basic problem with Hegel's reconciliation of knowledge and faith, as Habermas sees it, is that his system presumes what it needs to demonstrate, namely, "that a kind of reason which is more than an absolutized understanding [*Verstand*] *can* convincingly reunify the antithesis that reason *has to* unfold discursively."[3] The argument recalls, at least formally, Marx's critique of political economy in the *1844 Manuscripts*, namely, that Hegel assumes as a fact what needs to be explained and demonstrated. Hegelian reason, says Habermas, assumes the historical achievement that it purports to reveal. It is thereby cut off from historical reality, temporal contingencies, and the procedures of critical reflection. And it is also severed from the historical processes through which these demonstrations might be given. Here is Habermas on the "force" Hegel brought into being— *historical consciousness*—that also meant ruin for the system:

> With historical consciousness Hegel brought a force into place whose subversive power also set his own construction teetering. A history that takes the self-formative processes of nature and spirit up into itself, and that has to follow the logical forms of the self-explication of this spirit, becomes sublimated into the opposite of history. To bring this to a simple point that has already irritated Hegel's contemporaries: a history with an established past, a predecided future, and a condemned present, is no longer history.[4]

Hegel's great philosophical innovation—to make modernity a philosophical problem by positing subjectivity as an irreducibly historical form—results in "a stoic retreat" from history, a point that both Marx and Kierkegaard would make in their respective claims for the primacy of praxis and existence.[5] For Habermas, the collapse of Hegel's construction announces the need for a reconstruction of a postmetaphysical critical theory, grounded not in the strong path to salvation, but in what he describes as the "weak and transitory unity of reason" that underwrites the history of modernity.

Communicative reason, for Habermas, "frees us from the dilemma of having to choose between Kant and Hegel" by reducing the transcendental antinomy between the objective world of appearances and the moral world of autonomous action to a "tension" within the lifeworld of communicative action: "a tension between the unconditional character of context-bursting transcendent validity claims on the one hand and, on the other hand, the factual character of context dependent 'yes' and 'no' positions that create social facts *in situ*."[6] I am not sure that the language of tension resolves so much as it obscures an enduring antinomian dilemma. More importantly, one wonders what becomes of that "force" in Hegel—historical consciousness—which seems to have receded into Habermas's formal concept of rationality, if not disappeared altogether.

At any rate, Habermas's investments in ordinary communicative practices and the "trivial suppositions of commonality" necessary for the multiple uses of language are supposed to ward off the dangers of strong theory.[7] His aim is to keep critique *of this world* and announce philosophy's respectful retreat from the ground better covered by world religion. He describes it as a "weak but not defeatist" response to the collapse of metaphysics: a postmetaphysical critical theory. It is a variety of critique that purports to escape the highway of despair.

The emphasis on the everyday practices of communicative actors is both theoretically rich and politically admirable. The political-theoretical stakes of these efforts become clear in the following claim:

> The transitory unity that is generated in the porous and refracted intersubjectivity of a linguistically mediated consensus not only supports but furthers and accelerates the pluralization of forms of life and the individualization of lifestyles. More discourse means more contradiction and difference. The more abstract the agreements become, the more diverse the disagreements with which we can *nonviolently* live.[8]

There are several things to note about this passage. First, the historico-political directionality of this "transitory unity" is toward pluralization, individualization, and the entanglement of individuals with diverse forms of life. It advances a project of life as style. Further, discourse is presented here as the *source* of contradiction and difference (which it may well be) but not as a *sign* (which it may also be). The result is a critical theory that cannot give silence, indirect communication, noise, laughter, or tears—also signs of contradiction—any real significance in political life. (Kierkegaard, Adorno, and Bataille have much more to say about these extra-discursive phenomena.) Finally and relatedly, nonviolence is presented as an abstract principle and a principle served by abstraction, the support system for communicative action, which is also supported by "more discourse." In other words, nonviolence has no history, no politics, and no powers behind *its* articulation. (Fanon offers a different view. I explore this in chapter 5, where I present his critique of nonviolence in terms of the effort to excavate the history, politics, and powers that reside in the doctrine of nonviolence.)

Intersubjective linguistic utterances, says Habermas, require certain presuppositions about understandability, the testability of validity-claims, and the possibility for consensus—presuppositions that point to the emancipatory core of communicative reason. What, one might wonder, are the ethico-political implications of these preliminary presuppositions in everyday communication? For Habermas, they are drawn from the illocutionary act of positing an "I"—the fragile site of intersubjective recognition and responsibility. Interestingly, he leans on Kierkegaard to elaborate on the ethical force of illocutionary individuality:

> Since Kierkegaard we have been in a position to know that individuality can only be read from the traces of an authentic life that has been existentially drawn together into some sort of an appropriated totality. The significance of individuality discloses itself from the autobiographical perspective, as it were, of the first-person—I alone can performatively lay claim to being recognized as an individual in my uniqueness. If we liberate this idea from the capsule of absolute inwardness . . . grafting it onto the medium of a language that crosses processes of socialization and individualization with each other, then we will find the key to the solution of this final and most difficult of the problems left behind by metaphysics.[9]

Habermas insists that the ethico-political meaning of this Kierkegaardian idea of individuality be wrested from Kierkegaardian interiority. Fair enough. But it is curious that Kierkegaard serves as the touchstone for autobiographical performance, for his thinking is animated by nothing if not the *difficulties* that communication poses for the disclosure of individuality. Kierkegaard's various pseudonyms take up the difficulties of discursive disclosure with ironic loquacity. (*Fear and Trembling* is exemplary in this respect: just as Abraham could not disclose his intentions to Sarah, Johannes de Silencio strives and fails to communicate the secret of Abraham's faith. An absolute silence accompanies every act of faith—and is preserved in every effort to communicate its significance.) In Habermas, the "appropriated totality" of autobiography banishes most of these difficulties. The result may be to diminish the importance of individuality rather than demonstrate or disclose it.

The imperative to speak—and not just to speak, but to speak with language that gives *reason* to one's ordinary experiences—distinguishes Habermas's "postmetaphysics" from any "negative metaphysics." This is how he puts it:

> The latter after all continues to offer an equivalent for the extramundane perspective of a God's-eye view: a perspective radically different from the lines of sight belonging to innerworldly participants and observers. That is, negative metaphysics uses the perspective of the radical outsider, in which one who is mad, existentially isolated, or aesthetically enraptured distances himself from the world, and indeed from the lifeworld as a whole. *These outsiders no longer have a language, at least no speech based on reasons, for spreading the message of that which they have seen.* Their speechlessness finds words only in the empty negation of everything that metaphysics once affirmed with the concept of the universal One.[10]

Negative metaphysics is an "empty negation" in that it abandons concrete determinations in language. It trades the transcendence of positive metaphysics for the rapture of abyssal immanence. Note that Habermas values "speech based on reasons" for its world-disclosing and rhetorical power, for "spreading the message." (Communicative reason, it turns out, also speaks in a proselytizing voice.) I remain unconvinced that mundane experience—experience drawn from "the lifeworld as a whole"—can really find full articulation in speech based on reasons. World-disclosure and rhetoric may require that speech press at the determinate limits of reason, in order to partake of paradox, absurdity, irony, exaggeration, nonsense, and silence. And the language of everyday life—as well as the language of extraordinary encounters—ought to express the passions through which our worlds in common are created, maintained, and destroyed.

Silence proves especially menacing for Habermas. In a somewhat different context (his own inability to remain silent in reply to his critics), he remarks: "The person who is addressed and remains silent, clothes himself or herself in an aura of indeterminate significance and imposes silence. For this, Heidegger is one example among many. Because of this authoritarian character, Sartre has rightly called silence 'reactionary.'"[11] But do the directive to speak and the prohibition on silence compromise the connection, so fundamental to Habermas's thought, between communication and freedom? Does the emancipatory content preserved in the formal presuppositions of communication not also require the "right to remain silent" (somewhat distinct from no-saying) as mute testimony to the right of speech?[12] And can any speech or silence escape this "authoritarian character," the imposition on another? The person who is addressed as a "significant other" and "reacts" with silence (the nonresponse that is also a response) refuses the particular determinations of that address. Whether this refusal is cowardly or noble has everything to do with the scene and structure of address. Moreover, the person who addresses the other presents himself with the conviction of determinate significance and imposes speech and extracts some response, even if that response is silence. This approach to communicative action—which seems oddly undisturbed by questions of power and communicability, unmoved by the poetics of critical discourse, and unconcerned with the creative, strategic, and political deployment of language and silence *against* ordinary speech—risks the stoic retreat from the world that Habermas criticizes in Hegel.

Here is Habermas again, on the role of religion in a world disclosed by communicative reason:

> Communicative reason cannot withdraw from the determinate negations in language, discursive as linguistic communication in fact is. *It must therefore refrain from the paradoxical statements of negative metaphysics*: that the whole is the false, that everything is contingent, that there is no consolation whatsoever. Communicative reason does not make its appearance in an aestheticized theory as the colorless negative of a religion that provides no consolation. It neither announces the absence of consolation in a world forsaken by God, nor does it take

it upon itself to provide any consolation. . . . *As long as no better words for what religion can say are found in the medium of rational discourse, it will even coexist abstemiously with the former, neither supporting it nor combating it.*[13]

Habermas betrays his deepest secular liberalism in these last remarks. His defense of religious speech is not quite half hearted, but neither is it full throated, and the ambivalence and aversion that Left critics have identified with the liberal discourse of tolerance are repeated here.[14] Contained in the "as long as" is both a sigh of regret that the Enlightenment project goes as yet unfulfilled and a cool confidence that comes when theory attaches itself to this project. Curiously, it is also the one place, in the face of religious language, where communicative ethics quite literally *falls silent*—"neither supporting it nor combating it."

Why the loss of words? Why now? Does it mean that critical theory, in relinquishing a strong concept of theory, must also abandon the part of its tradition that is concerned with ideology critique, with the attempt to discern how religion "speaks" to a community of believers? What does religion say? To what ends and to what effects? How does religion relate to other elements of culture and society? How do political and economic conditions shape religious life? Why must "rational discourse" abstain from speaking to such questions? What form of discourse may be permitted to say something?

Habermas's postmetaphysics tolerates religion, as one among many lifeworld practices, only so long as rational discourse maintains its monopoly on truth. Admittedly, religion is not just any lifeworld practice. Even in Habermas, religious discourse facilitates contact with precisely that which philosophy, in the ruins of metaphysics, must surrender: the extraordinary. This is confirmed by Habermas's emphasis on ordinary speech acts and everyday intersubjectivity. The reluctant toleration of religion, then, springs from a recollection of philosophy's lost origins in the extraordinary. Habermas makes room for faith by admitting to it a consolatory function that philosophy requires but cannot, in a "postmetaphysical" context, assume for itself. William Connolly has already identified and criticized what he calls the "Kantian effect" in postsecular liberalism—and Habermas would seem an exemplary case.[15] I am interested in the posture that post-metaphysical thinking assumes toward the extraordinary, an apparent humility that conceals a deeper hubris. Reason is humbled—and silenced—before that which remains beyond its epistemological (Kant) or discursive (Habermas) grasp. Communicative reason neither supports nor combats religion, because that which is expressed by religion is beyond the limits of what is knowable or sayable by reason alone.[16]

Adorno is a clear target in the critique of negative metaphysics, as Habermas cites the well-known formulation from *Minima Moralia* that "the whole is false"—itself an inversion of Hegel's pronouncement that only the whole is true.[17] *Minima Moralia* is filled with inversions of this sort, exaggerations and their defense, little absurdities drawn from the realm of subjective experience that, in the context of greater objective irrationality and the damage done to individuality by history's catastrophic dialectic, become sites for the articulation of something approximating truth or justice or morality. Paradox, to stand in opposition to or distinction from *doxa*, indicates neither an interiorized heroics nor an empty withdrawal into the "colorless negative" of religion that has forsaken us. Instead, as I argue in chapter 3, it suggests a fidelity to history—both to what once was but is no more and what was never permitted to be—and to whatever remains of philosophy's attempt to find knowledge in the historical life of human beings. Fragments, essays, aphorisms, and thought-images (*Denkbilder*)—each experiments in the forms of writing that may convey this fidelity.

Behind the admirable modesty of communicative reason lies conceit. Consider how Habermas retains and revises the idea of the Absolute:

> The moment of unconditionability that is preserved in the discursive concepts of a fallibilistic truth and morality is not an absolute, or it is as most *an absolute that has become fluid as a critical procedure.* Only with this residue of metaphysics can we do battle against the transfiguration of the world through metaphysical truths—the last trace of "*Nihil contra Deum nisi Deus ipse*" [nothing can stand against God but God himself]. *Communicative reason is of course a rocking hull—but it*

does not go under in the sea of contingencies, even if shuddering in high
seas is the only mode in which it "copes" with these contingencies.[18]

The trace of the Absolute preserved in critical procedures is what keeps reason afloat in a sea of contingencies. Shuddering before the contingencies of individual and collective life but battling against their transfiguration into metaphysical truths, communicative reason is a curious kind of *post*metaphysical thinking. Indeed, it appears to confirm that the prefix can hardly indicate the end of metaphysics or its complete overturning. What appears instead is a reworking of an ancient and familiar metaphor in the history of Western thought—a ship—on behalf of communicative reason. Is the image of a ship cast out to sea not one of existential isolation, of separation from the world? Further, and to give some precision here, we are dealing here with the main body and structure: the hull includes the deck, both sides, and the bottom of the vessel, but does not include its "superstructure"—masts, rigging and equipment, engines, etc. It is the *watertight* body of the ship. This image reflects Habermas's conviction about communicative reason: It may be flexible and fallible, but it is also foundational and impermeable. It has no leaks or cracks. It is not porous or penetrable. Nothing gets in, but everything stands on top of it. Furthermore, reason is figured as *separate from* the "sea of contingencies" and autonomous from the world upon which it floats—in this way, it is abstracted from history and context. What Habermas claims as a mere "residue" of the Absolute retains the deepest of metaphysical impulses: *Nothing can stand against God but God himself.* Nothing can do battle against metaphysics but metaphysics itself—or communicative rationality as our last remaining source of absolute refuge.

This is no antidote to despair. On the contrary, it is a metaphysical urge reiterated and reinstalled at the heart of critical theory. However, because this metaphysical urge is buried in a theoretical reconstruction of communicative rationality that cannot avow or assume the "performative contradiction" of its emphatic faith, it quite literally *does not will to be what it is.* For Kierkegaard, this is the formula of despair, symptomatized not only by border patrolling around "reason" (so that "religion" might not be permitted in) but also by the universality that this idea of communicative reason is alleged to formalize.

And what is the "shudder" to which Habermas refers if not an extrarational sensation that risks blurring the boundary between reason and its other, between philosophy and poetry? Adorno links the shudder to the aesthetic. In a passage from *Aesthetic Theory*, Adorno remarks:

> Ultimately, aesthetic comportment is to be defined as the capacity to shudder, as if goose bumps were the first aesthetic image. What later came to be called subjectivity, freeing itself from the blind anxiety of the shudder, is at the same time the shudder's own development; life in the subject is nothing but what shudders, the reaction to the total spell that transcends the spell. Consciousness without shudder is reified consciousness. That shudder which subjectivity stirs without yet being subjectivity is the act of being touched by the other.[19]

This aesthetic experience involves the transformation of the senses: refracted vision restored against "blind anxiety" and the touch of the other. The shudder is an aesthetic experience that opens up to ethics and politics, an effect of "the spell" that also escapes it, a quiver that enlivens subjectivity in an ecstatic encounter with difference. The shudder, says Adorno, "joins eros and knowledge"—passion and reason awaken subjectivity to nonidentity.

If, for Habermas, the fate of philosophy in general and critical theory in particular depends entirely on a watertight idea of communicative reason, this is insofar as a reconstructed rationality, lodged in intersubjective communication, suggests *a way out* of the paradoxes and contradictions that ensnared a previous generation of critical theorists. This idea of a way out is absolutely crucial to Habermas's philosophical project and precisely the program that the preceding pages have set out to challenge. Here is Habermas again, this time in the conclusion to his well-known critique of Horkheimer and Adorno from *The Philosophical Discourse of Modernity*: "Anyone who abides in a paradox on the very spot once occupied by philosophy with its ultimate groundings is not just taking up an uncomfortable position; one can only hold that place if one makes it at least minimally plausible that there is *no way out*. Even the retreat from an aporiatic situation has to be barred, for otherwise there is a way—the way back."[20] The paradox to which Habermas refers is the radical critique of Enlightenment, or the use of reason to demonstrate how reason itself becomes domination. Habermas sees this critique as "absolute" and, therefore, contradictory. And the prohibition on contradiction—performative and logical—is paramount in his work. That Horkheimer and Adorno proffer a critique that is not absolute but rather a determinate negation of reason's historical entanglement with domination is clear enough. That Habermas is overly reliant on the notion of performative contradiction—and its capacity to invalidate a philosophical argument—is also true. And I think Amy Allen is right to insist that it is precisely the contradictory impulses of Enlightenment that Horkheimer and Adorno intend to explicate.[21]

What is also striking in Habermas's position is the felt yearning for *a way out*, lest critical theory become mired in despair. Philosophical critique without at least a minimally plausible escape from the horrors of history becomes complicit with those horrors. And it is imperative, says Habermas, that critical theory furnish a way out—not just a way forward, for that risks the repetition of an aporetic situation. Thomas McCarthy details the rhetorical representation of communicative reason as our best hope for rescue from the dialectic of history, describing it as the "road indicated but not taken" by the Young Hegelians and the early Frankfurt School.[22] Underscoring the Hegelian legacy in the theory of communicative action, McCarthy presents it as the "determinate negation" of subject-centered reason. Hegelian themes don't end there, says McCarthy, for "Habermas follows Hegel also in viewing reason as a healing power of unification and reconciliation," if not in a strong concept of the Absolute, then in "the unforced intersubjectivity of rational agreement."[23] A reconciliatory project in Hegel is undeniable, but that is only one tendency in his thinking. I have suggested, *pace* Habermas, that the voice in Hegel that resounds today and calls out to critical theory is one that speaks to and of despair.

To those who say despair is a private feeling and take issue with a political and philosophical approach to the passions, I appeal to another towering figure in this intellectual tradition, Herbert Marcuse. He introduces the 1961 edition of *Eros and Civilization* with the assured declaration that his study "employs psychological categories because they have become political categories."[24] Here, Marcuse is saying that concepts in Freud, such as thanatos and repressive desublimation, though they would seem limited to the interior structure of the psyche, shed a certain light on the structure of society and assist in the analysis of political formations and events. Put another way, psychoanalytic categories have become indispensable to social science. (On this specific point, every thinker in the second part of this book is in agreement.) Marcuse is also saying, in an affirmative spirit, that concepts like drive and the pleasure principle may be usefully developed for the theory and practice of freedom. For Marcuse (and, again, this is also true of the thinkers treated in these pages), the boundary between psychology and politics—the psychic life of human beings and their political experience—has eroded: "private disorder reflects more directly than before the disorder of the whole, and the cure of the personal disorder depends more directly than before on the cure of the general disorder."[25] This collapse of psychic and social life is a historical process and occurs, says Marcuse, as a result of a crisis in traditional authority.[26] But this crisis also presents an opportunity, and in the later "Political Preface" of 1966, Marcuse concedes that his study of Freud reflected an "optimistic, euphemistic, even positive thought . . . to learn the gay science (*gaya sciencia*) of how to use the social wealth for shaping man's world in accordance with his Life Instincts, in the concerted struggle against the purveyors of Death."[27] The language of "concerted struggle"—life as the concerted struggle against death—betrays Marcuse's deepest (Left) Hegelianism. Adorno, Bataille, and Fanon share in this basic view, and speak in different ways to its political significance.

Though I have resisted an approach to despair as a psychological category per se, the preceding pages turn on the conviction that it has indeed become a political category. By this, I mean that a seemingly subjective passion cannot be considered apart from its objective conditions, and that radical political thinking today cannot be thought apart from the despair that both encourages and impedes it. What is more, I have hoped to complicate a conventional story that says that despair is corrosive of political vision and to consider the opportunities for theory and practice that open up in its depths.

What John Berger describes in his "Dispatches" from Occupied Palestine is helpful in this context. He describes an "undefeated despair" among those struggling *simply to exist* in the territories, where existence itself is a sign of struggle: "a despair without fear, without resignation, without a sense of defeat, makes for a stance towards the world here, such as I have never seen before."[28] There is no hope in his account; indeed, for Berger, despair is what fills the void left by abandoned hopes. If it risks a certain romanticism of the lost cause, it does not obfuscate the reality of its conditions.[29] Here is Berger: "The whole of the West Bank plus the Gaza Strip is smaller than Crete (the island from which Palestinians may have originally come in prehistory). Three and a half million people, six times as many as in Crete, live here. And systematically, each day, the area is being rendered smaller. The towns becoming more and more overcrowded, the countryside more fenced in and inaccessible."[30] Berger talks about despair as an emotion, while I think of it as a condition that can take on a whole range of "emotional" expressions. He says that "despair is the emotion which follows a sense of betrayal," while I take it to be the condition that follows from a crisis in direction or movement.[31] But where I am in perfect agreement with Berger is here: "Despair has nothing to do with nihilism. Nihilism is resignation before the contention that Price is all. It is the most current form of human cowardice."[32] In an almost Kantian vein, it might be said that *critique is the art of becoming a little less cowardly.*[33]

Critique has everything to do with despair, for ours is a world organized by the contention that Price is all—and even in revolt against this contention, critical theory cannot wholly escape it.

Further, and reiterating Marcuse's injunction, to learn the gay science remains a critical task. I have found resources for these efforts in some unlikely sources. Adorno calls his own aphoristic reflections a "melancholy science"—a formulation that, as I see it, invokes the project it rewrites. There is a gaiety at the heart of Adorno's aporetics that too few commentators have considered—and where there is despair, it is never permitted the last word. For Bataille, the idea of chance connects the art of critique to the gay science. More than an ontology of contingency, Bataille's aleatory dialectics suggests a radical rethinking of the politics of freedom. Somewhat against the grain, then, I aim to take Bataille seriously as a critical political thinker. And in Fanon, gaiety comes with armed struggle, political militancy, and the elective affinities born of exile. He persists in the ruthless critique of everything existing, while persevering in the impossible task of changing the world.

The challenge for contemporary critical theory is to inhabit this no-man's-land between the prevailing order of things and a more just and humane world. This position is drawn from the limits of reason and faith, from the aporias of knowledge, and from the forceful determination of our passions. What is needed is the cultivated misrelation to the present that comes with the work of the negative. That is to say, what lives in the gay science is nourished by our despair.

NOTES

INTRODUCTION

1. Gillian Rose, *The Broken Middle: Out of Our Ancient Society* (Oxford: Blackwell, 1992), xiv.
2. Georg Lukács, *The Theory of the Novel: A Historico-Philosophical Essay on the Forms of Great Epic Literature* (Cambridge, Mass.: MIT Press, 1971), 22.
3. V. I. Lenin, "Notes on Anarchism and Socialism," in *Marxism Versus Anarchism*, ed. Nick Soudakoff (Australia: Resistance Books, 2001), 202.
4. Slavoj Žižek, "Shoplifters of the World Unite!," *London Review of Books*, August, 19, 2011.
5. Here I am referring of the work of Brian Masumi, Lauren Berlant, Sarah Ahmed, Patricia Clough, and Teresa Brennan.
6. Diana Coole, *Negativity and Politics: Dionysus and Dialectics from Kant to Post-structuralism* (London: Routledge, 2000), 1.
7. Bernard Yack, *The Longing for Total Revolution: Philosophic Sources of Social Discontent from Rousseau to Marx and Nietzsche* (Berkeley: University of California Press, 1992).
8. Jürgen Habermas, *The Philosophical Discourse of Modernity: Twelve Lectures*, trans. Frederick G. Lawrence (Cambridge, Mass.: MIT Press, 1990), 129.
9. Ibid., 114.
10. Seyla Benhabib, *Critique, Norm, and Utopia* (New York: Columbia University Press, 1986), 166.
11. Nikolas Kompridis, *Critique and Disclosure: Critical Theory Between Past and Future* (Cambridge, Mass.: MIT Press, 2006), 245.
12. Jane Bennett, *The Enchantment of Modern Life: Attachments, Crossings, and Ethics* (Princeton: Princeton University Press, 2001), 161.

13. Frantz Fanon, *Black Skin, White Masks*, trans. Richard Philcox (New York: Grove, 2008), 206.

14. This distinction is somewhat overstated, complicated by those who combined the medical treatment of melancholia with theological reflections on despair. A pioneering work in this respect is Robert Burton's monumental *The Anatomy of Melancholy*, appearing in various folios from 1621 until 1638. It could be argued that Julia Kristeva is a contemporary heiress to this marriage of medical and theological discourses. In *New Maladies of the Soul*, she notes:

    > Doctors of antiquity returned to the metaphysical distinction between the body and the soul and came up with a viable analogy that prefigured modern psychiatry: they spoke of "maladies of the soul" that were comparable to maladies of the body. (3)

    Indeed, ancient philosophy overflows with efforts to draw parallels and analogies between structures of the body and of the soul. As is well known, Plato takes the argument further in *The Republic*: the healthy body, the healthy soul, and the healthy polis share the same hierarchical structure. That said, ancient medical discourses were perhaps less bound by the analogy than Kristeva suggests. Greek medicine conceived melancholy not as a "malady of the soul," but as caused by a particular distribution of the humors, fluids, and substances in the body. Highly disproportionate levels of black bile in the human body produced disorders internal and external. Nonetheless, I am in agreement with Kristeva's view that "several aspects of psychoanalysis cross the boundary between body and soul and explore various elements that transcend this dichotomy" (5). See Julia Kristeva, *New Maladies of the Soul*, trans. Ross Guberman (New York: Columbia University Press, 1995).

15. For an excellent treatment of despair in Medieval and Renaissance thought, see Susan Snyder, "The Left Hand of God: Despair In Medieval and Renaissance Tradition," *Studies in the Renaissance* 12 (1965): 18–59.

16. Martin Luther, "Theses for the Heidelberg Disputation," in *Martin Luther, Selections from His Writings*, ed. John Dillenberger (New York: Doubleday, 1962), 502. Søren Kierkegaard will develop this Lutheran position in his treatment of despair in *The Sickness Unto Death*. For a fuller treatment of Kierkegaardian despair, see chapter 3.

17. See Stephen K. White, *Sustaining Affirmation: The Strengths of Weak Ontology* (Princeton: Princeton University Press, 2000).

18. Jacques Derrida, *Specters of Marx: The State of Debt, the Work of Mourning, and the New International*, trans. Peggy Kamuf (London: Routledge. 1994).

19. See, for example, Fritz Stern, *The Politics of Cultural Despair: A Study in the Rise of the Germanic Ideology* (Berkeley: University of California Press, 1974).

20. G. W. F. Hegel, *Phenomenology of Spirit*, trans. A. V. Miller (Oxford: Oxford University Press, 1977), §10, hereafter cited by paragraph.

21. The opening lines from "Problems Connected with Thought, Intelligence, and Wisdom":

    Why is it that all men who have become outstanding in philosophy, statesmanship, poetry or the arts are melancholic, and some to such an extent that they are infected by the diseases arising from black bile?

    "Problems" provides one of the most influential discussions of the humoral theory of melancholy from an Aristotelian perspective. The authorship of this text remains a vexed question; some scholars believe the author to have been one of Aristotle's followers. Regardless, the text is patently *Aristotelian* and accords with Aristotle's writings on biology and medicine. Galen of Pergamum, a Greek physician of the Roman period writing some six hundred years after Hippocrates, further develops this medicine of the humors, devoting considerable attention to the disorder caused by black bile. For the original texts of the Greek physicians, see Jennifer Radden, ed., *The Nature of Melancholy* (Oxford: Oxford University Press, 2000).

22. Physicians of the Renaissance period drew an important distinction between melancholy as a normal part of the human experience and melancholia as a sickness. Even in Aristotle, a distinction appears between the normal presence of "spleen" and its pathological excesses.

23. Dana Luciano, "Passing Shadows: Melancholic Nationality and Black Critical Publicity in Pauline E. Hopkins's *Of One Blood*," in *Loss: The Politics of Mourning*, ed. David L. Eng and David Kazanjian (Berkeley: University of California Press, 2003), 156. With the expansion of genetics in the biological and neurological sciences, the question of predisposition resurfaces in the psychiatric diagnoses of depression. While the humoral arguments of the classical period hold no legitimacy in contemporary psychiatry, the view of depression as a genetic inheritance, written into the genetic code of the patient, could appear as a partial rehabilitation of a classical model. However, it is not clear that the earlier formulations of humoral melancholy advanced a strong claim for *pre*disposition (admittedly, the question is begged by the Aristotelian emphasis on the melancholic's creative and intellectual powers); a more striking point of intersection is the classical formulation of melancholy as a *disposition*, which reappears, though in different terms, in the modern theories of depression. For the physicians of antiquity, melancholy was the result of *imbalance* and, similarly, the biomedical diagnoses of depression focus on chemical deficit, surplus, or dysfunction in the brain. A genealogical account, well beyond my scope here, might explain how the language of melancholy has been absorbed by the psycho-scientific language of depression and how, even in psychoanalytic theory, the question of melancholy is abruptly reframed as a question concerning depression and depressive disposition.

24. Sigmund Freud, "Mourning and Melancholia," in *The Freud Reader*, ed. Peter Gay (New York: Norton, 1989), 586.

25. Though Wendy Brown does not develop the concept of melancholia for her specific account of "wounded attachments" and draws instead on Nietzsche's idea of resentment, her later writings on melancholia build upon this early idea in her work. See Wendy Brown, "Wounded Attachments," *Political Theory* 21, no. 3 (August 1993): 390–410; and Brown, "Resisting Left Melancholy," *boundary* 2, 26, no. 3 (1999): 19–27. On the politics of mourning, see, for instance, Alessia Ricciardi, *The Ends of Mourning: Psychoanalysis, Literature, Film* (Stanford: Stanford University Press, 2003) and the essays contained in Eng and Kazanjian, *Loss*. For a psychoanalytic interpretation of the racial identification as a melancholic drama of loss and compensation, see Anne Anlin Cheng, *The Melancholy of Race: Psychoanalysis, Assimilation, and Hidden Grief* (Oxford: Oxford University Press, 2000). From a postcolonial perspective and transnational perspective, see Paul Gilroy, *Postcolonial Melancholy* (New York: Columbia University Press, 2005). On the melancholy of gender attachments, see Judith Butler, *The Psychic Life of Power: Theories in Subjection* (Stanford: Stanford University Press, 1997), esp. chaps. 5 and 6.

26. Gillian Rose, *Mourning Becomes the Law: Philosophy and Representation* (Cambridge: Cambridge University Press, 1996), chap. 3.

27. Brown, "Resisting Left Melancholy," 19–27.

28. See Lauren Berlant, *Cruel Optimism* (Durham: Duke University Press, 2011).

29. Sara Ahmed, *The Promise of Happiness* (Durham: Duke University Press, 2010).

30. Ibid., 169.

31. Ibid.

32. Dominick LaCapra, "Trauma Studies: Its Critics and Vicissitudes," in *History in Transit: Experience, Identity, Critical Theory* (Ithaca: Cornell University Press, 2004), 117.

33. Joshua Dienstag, *Pessimism: Philosophy, Ethic, Spirit* (Princeton: Princeton University Press, 2006).

34. Gillian Rose, *The Melancholy Science: An Introduction to the Thought of Theodor W. Adorno* (New York: Columbia University Press, 1978), ix.

35. Dienstag, *Pessimism*, 19.

36. As Raymond Williams puts it in *Marxism and Literature*: "not feeling against thought, but thought as felt and feeling as thought: practical consciousness of a present kind, in a living and inter-relating continuity." Williams, *Marxism and Literature* (Oxford: Oxford University Press, 1978), 132.

37. Adorno, *Negative Dialectics*, trans. E. B. Ashton (New York: Continuum, 1973), 377–78.

38. Lucien Goldman, *The Hidden God: A Study of Tragic Vision in the "Pensées" of Pascal and the Tragedies of Racine*, trans. Philip Thody (New York: Routledge, 1964), 17.

39. Simone de Beauvoir, *The Ethics of Ambiguity*, trans. Bernard Frechtman (New York: Citadel Press, 1976).

40. Ibid., 15.

41. Theodor W. Adorno, "Progress," in *Critical Models: Interventions and Catch-words*, trans. Henry W. Pickford (New York: Columbia University Press, 1998), 155.

1. Under the influence of Friedrich Schelling, a youthful Hegel adopted the term, but for the most part he took distance from *Kritik*.
2. "The true shape in which truth exists can only be the scientific system of such truth. To help bring philosophy closer to the form of science, to the goal where it can lay aside the title 'love of knowing' and be *actual* knowing—this is what I have set myself to do." G. W. F. Hegel, *Phenomenology of Spirit*, trans. A. V. Miller (Oxford: Oxford University Press, 1977), §5, hereafter cited by paragraph.
3. It is important to keep in mind the more expansive meaning of *Wissenschaft* in German.
4. Stargazing is a complicated metaphor. Susan Buck-Morss is right to remind us that "those who endured the Atlantic Crossing" understood that "the stars were survival itself." She continues:

    > Before the invention of the marine chronometer to measure longitude, Atlantic sailors were at the mercy of the starry heavens, guided by the southern constellation known as the Hydra, the ancient sign of mariners. The origin of slaves sold in the Americas was ascertained through their recollections of the positions of the stars during their land journeys to the African coast.

    Buck-Morss reads Hegel's "indifferent"—and even dismissive—attitude toward the stars as a mark of "hubris" and the reflection of a rather impoverished idea of freedom. She contrasts a grumpy and surly Hegel with the reverential and awe-struck Kant, and takes the sublimity of the starry skies as an opening for the idea of a "common humanity." I am, in many ways, very sympathetic to this critique, as well as the larger project, which is among the most powerful of recent efforts at decolonizing critical theory. That said, I think Buck-Morss is too severe with Hegel—or, better, neglects the side of Hegel that looks with awe not to the distant stars above, but to the scene unfolding right before our eyes. This side of Hegel is, in my view, indispensable for any contemporary revaluation of the idea of universal history. See Susan Buck-Morss, *Hegel, Haiti, and Universal History* (Pittsburgh: University of Pittsburgh Press, 2009), 119. For his retrieval of a "negative" concept universal history that takes its explicit bearings from Adorno and Benjamin, but is also compatible with the reading of Hegel I propose here, see Antonio Y. Vázquez-Arroyo, "Universal History Disavowed: On Critical Theory and Postcolonialism," *Postcolonial Studies* 11, no. 4 (2008): 451–73.
5. Robert B. Pippin, *Hegel's Idealism: The Satisfactions of Consciousness* (Cambridge: Cambridge University Press, 1989).

6. Of course, for Hegel, "philosophy must beware the wish to be edifying" and it is often against this impulse explicitly that critical theorists have invoked the power of the negative.

7. Robert B. Pippin, "Nietzsche and the Melancholy of Modernity," *Social Research* 66 (1999).

8. Hegel, *Phenomenology*, §78.

9. Ibid., §77.

10. Jean-Luc Nancy, *Hegel: The Restlessness of the Negative*, trans. Jason Smith and Steven Miller (Minneapolis: University of Minnesota Press, 2002), 3. Judith Butler has further developed this "ecstatic" interpretation of subject-formation in the *Phenomenology*, arguing that "the 'I' repeatedly finds itself outside itself and that nothing can put an end to the repeated upsurge of this exteriority that is, paradoxically, my own." Against those who see in the struggle for recognition an assimilationist or even an imperialist project, Butler offers this account of the Hegelian subject:

    > I am, as it were, always other to myself, and there is no final moment in which my return to myself takes place. In fact, if we are to follow *The Phenomenology of Spirit*, I am invariably transformed by the encounters I undergo; recognition becomes the process by which I become other than what I was and so cease to be able to return to what I was. There is, then, a *constitutive loss* in the process of recognition, since the "I" is transformed through the act of recognition.

    Despair, as I see it, names this persistent inability of the "I" to find rest in itself, and so there is agony in this ecstasy. Though I employ the language of despair instead of mourning and melancholy, for reasons indicated in the introduction, much of my analysis is consistent with this line of interpretation. See Judith Butler, *Giving an Account of Oneself* (New York: Fordham University Press, 2005), 27–28 (italics mine).

11. This is not to suggest that contemporary critical theory has nothing to learn from this mature philosophy of the state. My focus remains on the problem of the negative in the *Phenomenology*, not a terribly surprising place to begin. A true innovation in the interpretation of Hegel would demonstrate the persistence of the negative in later writings on politics and world history. This is far beyond my present capacities.

12. Patchen Markell, *Bound by Recognition* (Princeton: Princeton University Press, 2003), 93.

13. Ibid.

14. Ibid., 95 (italics in original).

15. Hegel, *Phenomenology*, §§7, 78.

16. Michael Theunissen makes a similar point in connection with Kierkegaard's *Sickness Unto Death*, which I discuss in the next chapter. See Michael Theunissen, *Kierkegaard's Concept of Despair*, trans. Barbara Harshav and Helmut Illbruck

(Princeton: Princeton University Press, 2005), esp. 118. Theunissen has also developed a critical reading of Hegel's *Logic*.

17. Hegel, *Phenomenology*, §32.

18. Ibid., §26.

19. Ibid., §78.

20. Ibid., §1.

21. Ibid., §3.

22. Ibid.

23. Judith Butler makes a similar point about critique and the delay or suspension of judgment in an essay on Foucault. See Judith Butler, "What Is Critique: An Essay on Foucault's Virtue," in *The Political: Readings in Continental Philosophy*, ed. David Ingram (London: Basil Blackwell, 2002).

24. Hegel, *Phenomenology*, §3.

25. Ibid., §3.

26. Even serious and rigorous readers have registered their frustration with the preface. Robert Solomon calls it "horrendous" and notes its "unwarranted sarcasm" and "arrogant" tone. See Robert C. Solomon, *In the Spirit of Hegel* (Oxford: Oxford University Press, 1983), 250, 291.

27. Hegel, *Phenomenology*, §70.

28. Ibid., §67.

29. Ibid.

30. Jacques Rancière, *The Philosopher and His Poor*, trans. John Drury, Corinne Oster, and Andrew Parker (Durham: Duke University Press, 2003).

31. Ibid. It is Kojève who christens Hegel a sage.

32. Hegel, *Phenomenology*, §70.

33. Ibid., §71. See also Jean Hyppolite, *The Genesis and Structure of Hegel's Phenomenology of Spirit*, trans. Samuel Cherniak and John Heckman (Evanston, Ill.: Northwestern University Press, 1974), 3.

34. Cited in Bruno Bosteels, "Hegel in America," in *Hegel and the Infinite: Religion, Politics, and Dialectic*, ed. Slavoj Žižek, Clayton Crockett, and Creston Davis (New York: Columbia University Press, 2011), 69.

35. Hegel, *Phenomenology*, §76.

36. The preface contains, for example, a lengthy discussion of mathematics and the limits of mathematical reasoning (see §§42–46), not precisely irrelevant to the project of the *Phenomenology*, but extraneous to it.

37. Hyppolite, *Genesis and Structure*, 4.

38. Solomon, *In the Spirit of Hegel*, 291.

39. Solomon reads the *Phenomenology* as a polemic against epistemological method as such, against "the very idea of a method which would be antecedent to and independent of the knowledge it sought to establish." Instead, Solomon argues, the real lesson of the *Phenomenology* is that learning comes with doing, that "one learns what knowledge is, not by developing a *method* with which to prove it, but by assuming, from the outset, that we do know something—quite a lot,

in fact—that we are in contact with the Absolute, the things of the world, and do not need a method to prove this." This is why, for Solomon, "the Preface is not only unnecessary but an actual obstacle to understanding the book," for he takes it to offer a preliminary outline of phenomenology as method. I read it differently. Or, more precisely, I interpret Hegel's ambivalence about prefaces, his included, as an extension of this lesson. Further, I think this meta-argument—that learning comes with doing—is precisely what the preface performs and enacts, so there is a partial truth to the view that it is a discourse on method. It is an instrument of initiation into a distinctive philosophical practice. Ibid., 293.

40. Hegel, *Phenomenology*, §78.
41. Solomon, *In the Spirit of Hegel*, 304.
42. Hegel, *Phenomenology*, §78.
43. Ibid.
44. I am grateful to Lisa Ellis for reminding me that despair (des-*pair*), too, preserves this doubling on its surface. However, the etymology of the term does not quite support this move. I discuss the etymology of "despair" in the introduction. For now, suffice it to say that the term comes from the Latin *de-sperare*, or the absence of hope.
45. Hyppolite, *Genesis and Structure*, 7.
46. Hegel, *Phenomenology*, §31.
47. Ibid., §77.
48. Ibid., §69.
49. Ibid., §68.
50. Ibid., §69.
51. For a more complex and detailed treatment of "animal life" in Hegel, which emphasizes its Aristotelian foundations and draws not only from Hegel's philosophy of nature but also from his aesthetics, see Terry Pinkard, *Hegel's Naturalism: Mind, Nature, and the Final Ends of Life* (Oxford: Oxford University Press, 2011), esp. chap. 1.
52. Hegel, *Phenomenology*, §77.
53. Ibid., §80.
54. Nancy, *Hegel: The Restlessness of the Negative*, 4–5.
55. Hegel, *Phenomenology*, §33.
56. Ibid., §32.
57. Ibid., §33.
58. Judith Shklar, *Freedom and Independence: A Study of the Political Ideas of Hegel's Phenomenology of Mind* (Cambridge: Cambridge University Press, 1976), 208.
59. Ibid., 72.
60. Hegel, *Phenomenology*, §26.
61. Ibid., §27.
62. Ibid., §38.
63. Ibid., §80.

64. Katrin Paul, "The Way of Despair," in Žižek, Crockett, and Davis, *Hegel and the Infinite*.

65. Kimberly Hutchings, *Hegel and Feminist Philosophy* (Cambridge: Polity, 2003), 30.

66. See Gillian Rose, *Love's Work: A Reckoning with Life* (New York: Schocken, 1997).

67. Gillian Rose, *The Broken Middle: Out of Our Ancient Society* (Oxford: Blackwell Publishers, 1992), 5.

68. Gillian Rose, *Mourning Becomes the Law: Philosophy and Representation* (Cambridge: Cambridge University Press, 1996), 72.

69. Ibid., 63–64.

70. Ibid., 75.

71. See Vincent Lloyd, "The Secular Faith of Gillian Rose," *Journal of Religious Ethics* 36, no. 4 (2008).

72. Rose, *Mourning Becomes the Law*, 75.

73. Ibid., 7, 64 (italics in original).

74. Ibid., 75.

75. The strand of post-Hegelian critical theory of particular interest to me is the one that contests the supremacy of "work" in Hegel and in the hegemonic part of the Hegelian-Marxist tradition, to say nothing of bourgeoisie society. Adorno and Bataille speak to this question at length in the context of the critique of philosophy and bourgeois society. Though Fanon retains the Hegelian esteem for work, he develops this view in the context of a critique of Hegel and refashions the idea of work according to a politics of militancy. In this context, one is also reminded of the critique of work implicit in Walter Benjamin's idea of "dialectics at a standstill."

76. Timothy Bahti, "The Indifferent Reader: The Performance of Hegel's Introduction to the *Phenomenology*," *Diacritics* 11, no. 2 (Summer 1981): 75.

77. Following Adorno's discussion of spectatorship in "Meditations on Metaphysics," it might be said that such a reading practice, the expression of bourgeois coldness that wants to rise above devastation, is also the most human way of reading Hegel.

78. A full discussion of the Christian character of Hegel's philosophy, a question that dates back to the debates between Right and Left Hegelians in the immediate aftermath of Hegel's death in 1831, is well beyond the scope of this study. Christology, in particular, is just one of the many concerns within this larger interpretive debate. For a general survey of more recent discussions, see Paul Lakeland, "A New Pietism: Hegel and Recent Christology," *Journal of Religion* 68, no. 1 (January 1988). See also Andrew Shanks, *Hegel's Political Theology* (Cambridge: Cambridge University Press, 1991); C. O'Regan, "Hegel's Philosophy of Religion and Eckhartian Mysticism," in *New Perspectives in Hegel's Philosophy of Religion*, ed. D. Kolb (Albany: State University of New York Press, 1992); Quentin Lauer, *Hegel's Concept of God* (Albany: State University of New York Press, 1982); James Yerkes, *The Christology of Hegel* (Albany: State University of New

York Press, 1983); Hans Küng, *The Incarnation of God: An Introduction to Hegel's Theological Thought as Prolegomena to a Future Christology*, trans. J. R. Stephenson (New York: Crossroad, 1987); Harold Schöndorf, SJ, "The Othering (Becoming Other) and Reconciliation of God in Hegel's *Phenomenology of Spirit*," and Martin J. De Nys, "Mediation and Negativity in Hegel's Phenomenology of Christian Consciousness," in *The Phenomenology of Spirit Reader: Critical and Interpretive Essays*, ed. Jon Stewart (Albany: State University of New York, 1998).

79. See chapter 4 for a fuller discussion of Georges Bataille's interpretation of a-theistic sacrifice in the *Phenomenology*.

80. Jean Hyppolite, *Genesis and Structure*, 190.

81. Judith Butler, "Stubborn Attachment, Bodily Subjection: Rereading Hegel on the Unhappy Consciousness," in *The Psychic Life of Power: Theories in Subjection* (Stanford: Stanford University Press, 1997), 31.

82. Ibid.

83. Solomon, *In the Spirit of Hegel*, 457.

84. Hegel, *Phenomenology*, §199.

85. Ibid.

86. Charles Taylor, *Hegel* (Cambridge: Cambridge University Press, 1977), 159.

87. Hegel, *Phenomenology*, §205.

88. Hegel quoted in Hyppolite, *Genesis and Structure*, 205.

89. Butler, "Stubborn Attachment, Bodily Subjection," 50.

90. Taylor, *Hegel*.

91. Rebecca Comay, *Mourning Sickness: Hegel and the French Revolution* (Stanford: Stanford University Press, 2010).

92. Hegel, *Phenomenology*, §47.

2. KIERKEGAARD'S DIAGNOSTICS

1. Bernstein continues: "Kierkegaard would agree with Marx that the philosophers have interpreted the world only, but he would add, the point is for each of us as unique individuals to change *ourselves*." This voluntarist gloss is complicated somewhat by Kierkegaard's reflection on his present age, which announces the sociohistorical dimension of despair, as well as his anxiety about the influence of crowds, which he believed conspired against any such change. Richard J. Bernstein, *Praxis and Action: Contemporary Philosophies of Human Activity* (Philadelphia: University of Pennsylvania Press, 1971), 123.

2. Paul Ricoeur, "Philosophy After Kierkegaard," in *Kierkegaard: A Critical Reader*, ed. Jonathan Ree and Jane Chamberlain (Oxford: Blackwell, 1988), 9.

3. Ibid., 10.

4. Søren Kierkegaard, *The Sickness Unto Death*, ed. and trans. Howard V. Hong and Edna Hong (Princeton: Princeton University Press, 1985), 70.

5. Michael Theunissen's work is exemplary in its efforts to develop the philosophical relation between Kierkegaard's philosophy of interiority and Marx's dialectical materialism and mobilize both for contemporary critical theory.

6. Alastair Hannay, "Kierkegaard and the Variety of Despair," in *The Cambridge Companion to Kierkegaard*, ed. Alastair Hannay and Gordon D. Marino (Cambridge: Cambridge University Press, 1998), 339.

7. Søren Kierkegaard, *Concluding Unscientific Postscript*, trans. David F. Swenson and Walter Lowrie (Princeton: Princeton University Press, 1941), 102.

8. Ibid., 98.

9. Ibid., 107.

10. Ibid., 109.

11. Ibid., 332.

12. Ibid., 112–13.

13. Ibid., 205.

14. Søren Kierkegaard, *Fear and Trembling/Repetition*, trans. Howard V. Hong and Edna H. Hong (Princeton: Princeton University Press, 1983), 53.

15. Quoted from Kierkegaard, "Historical Introduction," in *The Sickness Unto Death*, xxii.

16. Kierkegaard, *Sickness Unto Death*, 24.

17. Ibid., 23. Anti-Climacus distinguishes his own work from the physicians of the soul, even if only indirectly by his insistence upon their mutual consensus. "The physician of the soul will certainly agree with me that, on the whole, most men live without ever being conscious of being destined as spirit—hence, all the so-called security, contentment with life, etc., which is simply despair." Ibid., 26.

18. Ibid., 25. Adorno further develops this point in aphorism 36 from *Minima Moralia*, where damaged life transposes health and sickness.

19. Even social and political criticism today finds inspiration in medical discourses, as if it speaks at the bedside of a sick society. See, for instance, Axel Honneth, *Pathologies of Reason: On the Legacy of Critical Theory* (New York: Columbia University Press, 2009).

20. Reinhart Koselleck, *Critique and Crisis: Enlightenment and the Pathogenesis of Modern Society* (Cambridge, Mass.: MIT Press, 1988). See also Jürgen Habermas, "Between Philosophy and Science: Marxism as Critique," in *Theory and Practice*, trans. John Viertel (Boston: Beacon, 1973), 195–252; Seyla Benhabib, *Critique, Norm, and Utopia: A Study of the Foundations of Critical Theory* (New York: Columbia University Press, 1986), 19–21; and Beatrice Hanssen, *Critique of Violence: Between Poststructuralism and Critical Theory* (London: Routledge, 2000), 3–11.

21. For a fuller discussion of critique in ancient forms, including the Socratic critique of Athenian *krinein*, see Wendy Brown, "Untimeliness and Punctuality: Critical Theory in Dark Times," in *Edgework: Critical Essays on Knowledge and Politics* (Princeton: Princeton University Press, 2005).

22. Kierkegaard, *Sickness Unto Death*, 5.

23. Ibid., 18.

24. Ibid., 8.

25. On the theme of courage in particular, see Nicholas Tampio, *Kantian Courage: Advancing the Enlightenment in Contemporary Political Theory* (New York: Fordham University Press, 2012).

26. Judith Butler, "Kierkegaard's Speculative Despair," in *The Age of German Idealism*, ed. Robert C. Solomon and Kathleen M. Higgins (London: Routledge, 1993), 366.

27. Kevin Newmark, "Secret Agents: After Kierkegaard's Subject," *MLN* 112, no. 5 (December 1997), 722.

28. Kierkegaard, *Sickness Unto Death*, 31.

29. Ibid., 33.

30. Ibid., 34.

31. Ibid., 36.

32. Ibid., 39–40.

33. Ibid., 41.

34. Ibid., 49.

35. The author underscores women's tendency toward so-called weak despair, problematic enough, but then limits his treatment to the men who suffer it. Beauvoir's *Second Sex* would seem to represent a decisive intervention into the philosophical problematic set by Hegel and Kierkegaard insofar as it considers the pathway of despair as lived by woman. Beauvoir carries the philosophical analysis of despair to the place that Kierkegaard suggests it might be lurking, to the devotional posture assumed by woman. In so doing, she never relinquishes the Hegelian or Kierkegaardian search for self-identity and self-restoration, but insists that salvation can be had only in this world and, for women, only through collective praxis. See Simone de Beauvoir, *The Second Sex*, trans. Constance Borde and Sheila Malovany-Chevallier (New York: Vintage, 2001).

36. Kierkegaard, *Sickness Unto Death*, 60.

37. Ibid.

38. E. M. Cioran, *On the Heights of Despair*, trans. Ilinca Zarifopol-Johnston (Chicago: University of Chicago Press, 1996).

39. Ibid., 69.

40. Ibid., 70.

41. Michael Theunissen, *Kierkegaard's Concept of Despair*, trans. Barbara Harshav and Helmut Illbruck (Princeton: Princeton University Press, 2005), 118.

42. Ibid.

43. Kierkegaard, *The Sickness Unto Death*.

44. Merold E. Westphal, *Kierkegaard's Critique of Reason and Society* (University Park: Pennsylvania State University Press, 1992), 33.

45. Søren Kierkegaard, *Training in Christianity*, trans. Walter Lowrie (Princeton: Princeton University Press, 1944), 89.

46. Judith Butler, *Precarious Life: The Power of Mourning and Violence* (London: Verso, 2006).

47. Michael Theunissen, *Kierkegaard's Concept of Despair*, trans. Barbara Harshav and Helmut Illbruck (Princeton: Princeton University Press, 2005), 11.

48. Vigilius Haufniensis, the pseudonymous author of *The Concept of Anxiety*, does mention "objective anxiety," but the relationship between anxiety and despair in

Kierkegaard's writings is a complicated question beyond the scope of this chapter. Suffice it to say here that Haufniensis's brief discussion of objective anxiety at least raises the possibility that the sickness unto death might be interpreted as a social, historical, and political condition. See Kierkegaard, *The Concept of Anxiety*, trans. Reidar Thomte (Princeton: Princeton University Press, 1981).

3. THEODOR W. ADORNO: APORETICS

1.   Martin Jay, *Adorno* (Cambridge, Mass.: Harvard University Press, 1984), 24.
2.   Ibid.
3.   Robert Hullot-Kentor, *Things Beyond Resemblance: Collected Essays on Theodor W. Adorno* (New York: Columbia University Press, 2006), 155.
4.   Ibid., 156.
5.   Ibid.
6.   Ibid., 159.
7.   Evan Watkins, "On Doing the Adorno Two-Step," in *Rethinking the Frankfurt School: Alternative Legacies of Cultural Critique*, ed. Jeffrey T. Nealon and Caren Irr (Albany: State University of New York Press, 2002).
8.   Jürgen Habermas, "The Entwinement of Myth and Enlightenment: Horkheimer and Adorno," in *The Philosophical Discourse of Modernity: Twelve Lectures*, trans. Frederick Lawrence (Cambridge, Mass.: MIT Press, 1990), 121.
9.   Ibid., 118.
10. Ibid., 119.
11. Hullot-Kentor, *Things Beyond Resmblance*, 167.
12. The celebrated passage from the final aphorism of *Minima Moralia* reads: "The only philosophy which can be responsibly practiced in face of despair is the attempt to contemplate all things as they would present themselves from the standpoint of redemption." Theodor Adorno, *Minima Moralia: Reflections from Damaged Life*, trans. E. F. N. Jephcott (New York: Verso, 1974), 247.
13. Commentaries from Drucilla Cornell, Peter Dews, and Judith Butler seize upon the ethical and moral resonance in Adorno's writings, but probably the most systematic interpretation of Adornian ethics comes from J. M. Bernstein, *Adorno: Disenchantment and Ethics* (Cambridge: Cambridge University Press, 2001). In my view, Bernstein's ambitious efforts are troubled by the antinaturalism and defense of the fragmentary that course through Adorno's work: his reading risks attributing to Adorno a generalized nostalgia for enchanted and holistic nature. That said, Bernstein is especially insightful when clarifying Adorno's critique of nihilism: "nihilistic despair is not final, and it cannot be without being self-contradictory" (38). That is, nihilism has no need for despair. To despair is also to conjure its constitutive other—hope—and to dwell in the region where these forces overlap. Adorno speaks of the unthinkability of absolute despair not to advance a modernist ethics in the face of nihilism and disenchantment, but precisely to think despair as a determinate

and worldly form. See also Drucilla Cornell, *The Philosophy of the Limit* (New York: Routledge, 1992); Peter Dews, *The Idea of Evil* (West Sussex, UK: Blackwell, 2008); and Judith Butler, *Giving an Account of Oneself* (New York: Fordham University Press, 2005).

14. Gianni Vattimo claims Adorno on behalf of a weak metaphysics, taking inspiration from the "paradoxical recuperation of metaphysics" that comes with its critique. Ultimately, though, Vattimo rejects the attachment to Hegel and the dialectic, and finds a preferable position in Heidegger and Nietzsche (at least Heidegger's Nietzsche) and an ethical supplement in Levinas. See Vattimo, "Metaphysics, Violence, and Secularization," in *Recoding Metaphysics: The New Italian Philosophy*, ed. Giovanna Borradori (Evanston, Ill.: Northwestern University Press, 1988).

15. See Hent deVries, *Minimal Theologies: Critiques of Secular Reason in Adorno and Levinas* (Baltimore: Johns Hopkins University Press, 2006).

16. Ibid., 534.

17. Though he pursues different ends—democratic pluralism, not *minima theologica*—William Connolly has a similar tendency to see everything that is not philosophical rationalism as "religion" and also allows real religiosity to fall strangely out of view. See William E. Connolly, *Why I Am Not a Secularist* (Minneapolis: University of Minnesota Press, 2000).

18. Seyla Benhabib, *Critique, Norm, and Utopia: A Study of the Foundations of Critical Theory* (New York: Columbia University Press, 1986), 166.

19. Arendt's attraction to Kierkegaard and Christian theology dates back to her early teenage years. On this peculiar fascination, she recalls: "I had some misgiving only as to how one deals with this if one is Jewish." See Hannah Arendt, "What Remains? The Language Remains," in *Essays in Understanding, 1930–1954*, ed. Jerome Kohn (New York: Harcourt Brace, 1994), 9. Arendt was hardly the only German-Jewish philosopher of her generation cultivating a comfortable fluency in the Christian thinker.

20. Adorno, *Kierkegaard: Construction of the Aesthetic*, trans. Robert Hullot-Kentor (Minneapolis: University of Minnesota Press, 1989), 4.

21. Ibid., 3.

22. Ibid., 5.

23. As Susan Buck-Morss points out, Adorno's attack on Kierkegaard was at least tempered by an appreciation of his work as "an unintended expression of social truth." See Susan Buck-Morss, *The Origin of Negative Dialectics* (New York: Free Press, 1977), 121. The same cannot be said for Heidegger's ontology of Being. For Adorno, Heidegger's ahistoricist ontology of Being squanders any critical purchase in Kierkegaard. In this early work, Adorno is sometimes attentive to the differences between Kierkegaard and Heidegger, but too often the critique is overburdened by his quarrels with German existentialism. For Adorno's critique of Heidegger, see Theodor Adorno, "The Actuality of Philosophy," trans.

Benjamin Stone, *Telos* 31 (Spring 1977); 120–133; and Adorno, *Jargon of Authenticity*, trans. Knut Tarnowski and Frederic Will (London: Routledge, 1973); and Adorno, *Negative Dialectics*, part 1, *Relation to Ontology*, trans. E. B. Ashton (New York: Continuum, 1973). On the dynamism of existence and Heidegger's misinterpretation of Kierkegaard's intention, see Adorno, *Kierkegaard: Construction of the Aesthetic*, 69.

24. Adorno, *Kierkegaard: Construction of the Aesthetic*, 82.

25. Ibid., 112.

26. Ibid., 84.

27. Ibid., 29.

28. Ibid., 42. For a discussion of the *intérieur* in Adorno's reading of Kierkegaard, see Buck-Morss, *The Origins of Negative Dialectics*, 114–21.

29. Adorno, *Kierkegaard: Construction of the Aesthetic*, 126.

30. Ibid., 208.

31. Theodor W. Adorno, "Progress," in *Critical Models: Interventions and Catchwords*, trans. Henry W. Pickford (New York: Columbia University Press, 1998), 155.

32. Adorno, *Kierkegaard: Construction of the Aesthetic*, 131 (italics mine).

33. Bernard Yack, *The Longing for Total Revolution: Philosophic Sources of Social Discontent from Rousseau to Marx and Nietzsche* (Berkeley: University of California Press, 1992). Adorno's own observations on the residues of an "unresolved" Left Hegelianism in his critical models come in part 2 of *Negative Dialectics*. There he focuses his attention on questions concerning the relationship between theory and practice. Gillian Rose has pointed out that negative dialectics resolutely opposes any kind of abstract humanism, which would seem to be a necessary feature of conventional Left Hegelianism. She does suggest, though, that Adorno's elevation of theoretical activity over praxis risks reproducing a Left Hegelian antinomy already undone by Marx in his famous eleventh thesis on Feuerbach. I suggest a somewhat different way of glossing Adorno's position on Marx's thesis. See Gillian Rose, *The Melancholy Science: An Introduction to the Thought of Theodor W. Adorno* (New York: Columbia University Press, 1978).

34. Yack, *The Longing for Total Revolution*, 130.

35. Adorno, *Kierkegaard: Construction of the Aesthetic*, 140.

36. An example of Adorno's critical attitude toward dreams comes in aphorism 72 of *Minima Moralia*. In it, he notes how dreams leave one feeling "disappointed, cheated of the best in life." Adorno, *Minima Moralia*, 111.

37. Adorno, *Kierkegaard: Construction of the Aesthetic*, 140.

38. Theodor W. Adorno, "Resignation," in *Critical Models*, 289.

39. Waite discusses the aporia in connection with Bataille, but it is apropos to my reading of Adorno. Geoff Waite, *Nietzsche's Corps/e: Aesthetics, Politics, Prophecy, or the Spectacular Technoculture of Everyday Life* (Durham: Duke University Press, 1996), 188.

40. Michel Foucault presses this point in his celebrated essay on critique. See Michel Foucault, "What Is Critique?," in *The Politics of Truth*, ed. Sylvère Lotringer and Lysa Hochroth (New York: Semiotext[e], 1997).
41. Theodor W. Adorno, "Cultural Criticism and Society," in *Prisms* (Cambridge, Mass.: MIT Press, 1984), 31.
42. Ibid.
43. Ibid.
44. Ibid., 32.
45. Ibid.
46. Ibid.
47. Max Horkheimer, "Traditional and Critical Theory," in *Critical Theory: Selected Essays*, trans. Matthew J. O'Connell (New York: Continuum, 1995), 211.
48. Steven Helmling, "Constellation and Critique: Adorno's Constellation, Benjamin's Dialectical Image," *Postmodern Culture* 14, no. 1 (September 2003).
49. Adorno, "Cultural Criticism and Society," 33.
50. Adorno, *Minima Moralia*, 74.
51. Adorno argues that Kierkegaard misunderstood this crucial point in Hegel: "mediation is never a middle element between extremes, as, since Kierkegaard, a deadly misunderstanding has depicted it as being; instead, mediation takes place in and through the extremes, in the extremes themselves. This is the radical aspect of Hegel, which is incompatible with any advocacy of moderation." Theodor W. Adorno, "Aspects of Hegel's Philosophy," in *Hegel: Three Studies*, trans. Shierry Weber Nicholsen (Cambridge, Mass.: MIT Press, 1993), 8–9.
52. Alain Badiou, "On the Connection Between Negative Dialectics and a Particular Assessment of Wagner," *Lacanian Ink* 33 (2009): 95.
53. Adorno, *Negative Dialectics*, 385.
54. Ibid., 403–4.
55. Walter Benjamin, *The Origin of German Tragic Drama*, trans. John Osborne (New York: Verso, 1998).
56. Jürgen Habermas, "Consciousness-Raising or Redemptive Criticism: The Contemporaneity of Walter Benjamin," *New German Critique* 17 (Spring 1979): 30–59.
57. Adorno, *Negative Dialectics*, 388.
58. Ibid.
59. Ibid.
60. Adorno, "Aspects of Hegel's Philosophy," 7.
61. Ibid., 9–10.
62. Theodor W. Adorno, *Metaphysics: Concepts and Problems*, trans. Edmund Jephcott (Stanford: Stanford University Press, 2000), 144.
63. Theodor W. Adorno, "Skonteinos, or How to Read Hegel," in *Hegel*, 146.
64. G. W. F. Hegel, *Philosophy of Right*, trans. T. M. Knox (Oxford: Oxford University Press, 1967), 13.
65. Adorno, *Negative Dialectics*, 377–78.

66. Adorno, *Minima Moralia*, 200.

67. Ibid.

68. Walter Benjamin, "Goethe's *Elective Affinities*," in *Selected Writings*, vol. 1, *1913–1926*, ed. Marcus Bullock and Michael W. Jennings (Cambridge, Mass.: Belknap Press of Harvard University Press, 1996), 356. Also cited by Adorno, *Negative Dialectics*, 378. Benjamin's Goethe essay is one of his most significant, where he also introduces a concept of fate that finds its way into Adorno's critical theory.

69. David Jenemann, *Adorno in America* (Minneapolis: University of Minnesota Press, 2007).

70. Max Horkheimer and Theodor W. Adorno, *Dialectic of Enlightenment: Philosophical Fragments*, trans. Edmund Jephcott (Stanford: Stanford University Press, 2002), 110.

71. Ibid., 111.

72. Theodor W. Adorno, *Aesthetic Theory*, trans. Robert Hullot-Kentor (Minneapolis: University of Minnesota Press, 1997), 40.

73. Isobel Armstrong underscores this point in Adorno. See Isobel Armstrong, *The Radical Aesthetic* (Oxford: Blackwell, 2000).

74. See Adorno's contributions to Fredric Jameson, ed., *Aesthetics and Politics* (London: Verso, 1980), esp. 177–95.

75. Adorno, *Aesthetic Theory*, 40.

76. Ibid.

77. Ibid.

78. See the aphorisms of *Minima Moralia* for Adorno's reflections on pleasure, especially 37.

79. Theodor W. Adorno, "The Essay as Form," in *Notes to Literature*, trans. Shierry Weber Nicholsen (New York: Columbia University Press, 1991), 17. Of the essay, he notes: "Its form complies with the critical idea that the human being is not a creator and that nothing human is a creation. The essay, which is always directed toward something created, does not present itself as creation, nor does it covet something all-encompassing whose totality would resemble that of a creation." *Endgame* is a bit different. It is not directed toward something created, but something destroyed—the drama revolves around the theme of destruction. Further, though it does not present itself as creation as much as the tragic comedy of destruction, there persists an aspiration to totality—a shattered and ruined totality—in *Endgame* that sets it apart from the essay.

80. Theodor W. Adorno, "Trying to Understand *Endgame*," in *Notes to Literature*, trans. Shierry Weber Nicholsen (New York: Columbia University Press, 1991), 243.

81. Ibid., 244.

82. Ibid., 248.

83. Ibid., 259.

84. Ibid.

85. Ibid., 257.

86. Ibid., 263.
87. Adorno, *Minima Moralia*, 72–73.
88. Adorno, "Trying to Understand *Endgame*," 241.
89. Ibid. (italics mine). In very different ways, both Axel Honneth and Amy Allen advance the project of a philosophical anthropology for contemporary critical theory. Honneth's pursuit of a philosophical anthropology extends from early collaborations to his more recent work on reification, which he describes it as an "anthropology of social action." Allen reconstructs a philosophical anthropology through an interpretation of Kant's anthropology and Foucault's critical theory. See Axel Honneth and Hans Jonas, *Social Action and Human Nature* (Cambridge: Cambridge University Press, 1988); Axel Honneth, *Reification: A New Look at an Old Idea* (Oxford: Oxford University Press, 2008); Amy Allen, *The Politics of Our Selves* (New York: Columbia University Press, 2008).
90. Adorno, "Trying to Understand *Endgame*," 266–67.
91. Ibid., 252.
92. Ibid., 266.
93. Adorno, *Minima Moralia*, 151.
94. And the importance of waste—garbage, refuse, things thrown away—links both of them to Jane Bennett's contributions to a "new materialism." Though *Vibrant Matter* rejects a dialectic approach and takes its bearings from Bergson and a vitalist philosophical tradition, there are opportunities here for the further development of a "philosophical anthropology." Jane Bennett, *Vibrant Matter: A Political Ecology of Things* (Durham: Duke University Press, 2010).
95. Adorno, "Resignation," 289.
96. Ibid.
97. Ibid.
98. Ibid.
99. Ibid., 290.
100. Ibid.
101. Ibid.
102. Ibid., 291.
103. Ibid., 292.
104. Morton Schoolman pursues a similar claim in Schoolman, *Reason and Horror: Critical Theory, Democracy, and Aesthetic Individuality* (New York: Routledge, 1991). Schoolman interprets Adorno in terms of a critique of subjectivity and a defense of individuality, and a corresponding preference for aesthetics over philosophical abstractions. Schoolman sees aesthetic individuality as Adorno's enduring contribution to democratic theory.
105. Adorno, "Resignation," 292.
106. Ibid., 293.
107. The dedication, with its expression of friendship, comes before the book's contents as well. Adorno dedicates the melancholy science to his friend and fellow traveler Max Horkheimer. Their jointly authored *Dialectic of Enlightenment*

models one type of experimentation with philosophical form. Subjective reflections from damaged life that begin in announcement of camaraderie and collaboration offer another.

108. Haider and Mohandesi focus on Louis Althusser's late writings, which resonate in some surprising ways with Adorno's thought. Asad Haider and Salar
Mohandesi, "Underground Currents: Louis Althusser's 'On Marxist Thought,'"
Viewpoint Magazine: Investigations in Contemporary Politics 2 (September
2012), www.viewpointmag.com.

109. Vladimir Ilyich Lenin, "What Is to Be Done?," in *Essential Works of Lenin: "What
Is to Be Done?," and Other Writings* (New York: Dover, 1987), 69.

110. Theodor W. Adorno, "Ernst Bloch's *Spuren*: On the Revised Edition of 1959," in
Notes to Literature, 202.

111. Adorno, "The Essay as Form," 11.

4. GEORGES BATAILLE: ALEATORY DIALECTICS

1. Bruno Gullì charges Bataille with conflating the "useful" with the "servile" and I
do not dispute this claim. I am less convinced that a "radical ontology of labor"
of the sort Gullì defends is the only way to rescue "labor . . . or all doing for that
matter" from servility. Writing, play, and ritual all suggest practices that refuse
servility. See Bruno Gullì, *Earthly Plentitudes: A Study on Sovereignty and Labor*
(Philadelphia: Temple University Press, 2009).

2. Michel Foucault's "A Preface to Transgression" offers a sustained engagement
with Bataille and an early statement of his views on sex, power, and subjectivity.
See Michel Foucault, *Language, Counter-Memory, Practice: Selected Essays and
Interviews* (Ithaca: Cornell University Press, 1974). Jean Baudrillard uses Bataille
as a touchstone for a critique of Marxism's productivist bent. See Jean Baudrillard, *The Mirror of Production*, trans. Mark Poster (St. Louis: Telos Press, 1975).
Derrida's well-known essay on Bataille, "From Restricted to General Economy:
A Hegelianism Without Reserve," deals to some extent with the importance of
chance in Bataille, especially for his critique of Hegel. See Jacques Derrida, *Writing and Difference*, trans. Alan Bass (Chicago: University of Chicago Press, 1978).
Jean-Luc Nancy draws from Bataille to sketch an idea of community apart from
communitarian nostalgia and the Hegelian-Marxist emphasis on work. See
Jean-Luc Nancy, *The Inoperative Community*, trans. Peter Conner et al. (Minneapolis: University of Minnesota Press, 1991).

3. Noteworthy exceptions include Jesse Goldhammer, who deals with Bataille in
the final chapter of Goldhammer, *The Headless Republic: Sacrificial Violence in
Modern French Thought* (Ithaca: Cornell University Press, 2007); and also in
Goldhammer, "Dare to Know/Dare to Sacrifice: Georges Bataille and the Cri-
sis of the Left," in *Reading Bataille Now*, ed. Shannon Winnbust (Bloomington:
Indiana University Press, 2007). In *Horrorism*, Adriana Cavarero draws from
Bataille for an account of horror and reflects also on Hannah Arendt's passing

critique of Bataille in *The Origins of Totalitarianism*. See Adriana Caverero, *Horrorism*, trans. William McCuaig (New York: Columbia University Press, 2009). And like Caverero, Talal Asad in his lectures on suicide bombing deals with Bataille in connection with the concept of horror and the experience of corporeal vulnerability. See Talal Asad, *On Suicide Bombing* (New York: Columbia University Press, 2007).

4. See Jacques Rancière, *Disagreement: Politics and Philosophy*, trans. Julie Rose (Minneapolis: University of Minnesota Press, 1999).

5. In his reflections on this essay, Jürgen Habermas glosses the relationship between Bataille and his Frankfurt School predecessors as follows:

> [Bataille's] analysis can be still translated into the concepts of Critical Theory: Fascism ultimately only serves to render inner nature's revolts against instrumental reason adaptable to the imperatives of the latter. The decisive difference between the two approaches, however, lies in the way they specify the suppressed or excluded and outlawed parts of subjective nature. For Horkheimer and Adorno, the mimetic impulse carries with it the promise of a "happiness without power," whereas for Bataille happiness and power are indissolubly fused in the heterogeneous: In the erotic and in the sacred, Bataille celebrates an "elemental violence." With the help of the same idea, he also justifies in fascism that element (so characteristic of Carl Schmitt) of groundless of "pure" leadership.

For Habermas, the absence of a "violence-transcending point of reference" in Bataille renders unstable and improbable any distinction between socialist revolution and fascist reaction. See Jürgen Habermas, "Between Eroticism and General Economics: Georges Bataille," in *The Philosophical Discourse of Modernity: Twelve Lectures*, trans. Frederick G. Lawrence (Cambridge, Mass.: MIT Press, 1987), 219–20. Richard Wolin goes still further in the argument concerning Bataille's alleged "Left fascism" and argues that this essay in particular "contains a barely veiled admiration for the vitality and energy of the existing fascist states" and "a critique of parliamentarianism that is as zealous as anything one finds in the work of Carl Schmitt." See Richard Wolin, "Left Fascism: Georges Bataille and the German Ideology," *Constellations* 2, no. 3 (1996): 413.

6. See Sara Ahmed, "Affective Economies," *Social Text* 79, vol. 22, no. 2 (Summer 2004).

7. Whereas the Islamic Khalifat had no "recourse to an established nation, much less a constituted state," Bataille argues that fascism takes the existing state as, first, a thing to conquer and control and, then, an instrument and framework for the consolidation of domination. Georges Bataille, "The Psychological Structure of Fascism," in *Visions of Excess: Selected Writings, 1927–1939*, ed. and trans. Allan Stoekl (Minneapolis: University of Minnesota Press, 1985), 153.

8. Jane Bennett, for example, has argued for a "vital materialism" that dwells in debris, garbage, and waste, suggesting a certain affinity with Bataille's base mate-

rialism. See Jane Bennett, *Vibrant Matter: A Political Ecology of Things* (Durham: Duke University Press, 2010). See also Diana Coole and Samantha Frost, eds., *New Materialisms: Ontology, Agency, and Politics* (Durham: Duke University Press, 2010).

9. These representations come together in Richard Wolin's treatment of Bataille. Using "telling circumstantial evidence" and minimal textual analysis, Wolin alleges that Bataille harbored "national socialist" yearnings and that his open excitement for fascism in the 1930s gave way to an "inner emigration" in the 1940s. See Wolin, "Left Fascism."

10. Sylvère Lotringer, from the introduction, "Furiously Nietzschean," in Georges Bataille, *On Nietzsche*, trans. Bruce Boone (St. Paul, Minn.: Paragon House, 1994), viii. Bataille's critique of "actionism" anticipates the position Theodor Adorno stakes out in his essay on resignation from 1969.

11. This critique may be productively considered in relation to the critique of pseudo-action that Adorno develops in his essay on resignation. See Theodor W. Adorno, "Resignation," in *Critical Models*, trans. Henry W. Pickford (New York: Columbia University Press, 1999), and my discussion of the essay in chapter 3.

12. Bataille, *On Nietzsche*, xxiv.

13. Quoted in Simonetta Falasca-Zamponi, "A Left Sacred or a Sacred Left?: The Collège de Sociologie, Fascism, and Political Culture in Interwar France," *South Central Review* 23, no. 1 (Spring 2006): 46.

14. Bataille, "Games of Chance," in *Guilty*, in *The Bataille Reader*, ed. Fred Botting and Scott Wilson (Oxford: Blackwell, 1997), 51.

15. Jean-Michel Besnier, "Georges Bataille in the 1930s: A Politics of the Impossible," trans. Amy Reid, *Yale French Studies* 78 (1990): 169–80.

16. Habermas, "Between Eroticism and General Economics," 211.

17. Ibid., 221.

18. Ibid., 220.

19. Geoff Waite, *Nietzsche's Corps/e: Aesthetics, Politics, Prophecy, or The Spectacular Technoculture of Everyday Life* (Durham: Duke University Press, 1996), 187.

20. For Allan Stoekl, the paradoxical quality of Bataille's thought turns on his idiosyncratic use of allegory to reflect on the collapse of allegory and its traditional hierarchies. See Allan Stoekl's introduction to Bataille, *Visions of Excess*, xiii–xvi. In this respect, Bataille's critical theory bears some affinity with Walter Benjamin's, though not only for the treatment of allegory in *The Origins of German Tragic Drama* or their mutual concern with mystical experience, the sacred, and myth. On the reading I develop here, Bataille and Benjamin share an investment in the allegorical image of the gambler and converge on the primacy of chance in modern life. To be sure, Benjamin is substantially more critical in his handling of this image.

21. Bataille, *Guilty*, 53.

22. Alain Badiou is arguably the leading contemporary thinker in this tradition, both for the centrality of mathematical theory for his philosophical project and for idea of the "communist wager" in political reasoning.

23. Georges Bataille, "The Critique of the Foundations of the Hegelian Dialectic," in *Visions of Excess*, 111. Though its title suggests otherwise, this is an essay about Engels; Hegel makes only occasional appearances.

24. Alain Badiou pursues this project—the revaluation of mathematics for radical philosophy—more aggressively than even Bataille could have anticipated.

25. "The very elements that suddenly become, for Marx and Engels, the method's foundations are precisely those that offer the most resistance to the application of this method, and not only by definition, but above all in practice." Bataille, "The Critique of the Foundations of the Hegelian Dialectic," 107. Bataille is talking here about nature and the natural sciences. Mathematics is resistant too, aligned with *Verstand* and not *Vernünft* (definition) and marked by abstraction rather than concretization (practice).

26. Ibid.

27. Ibid., 113.

28. Ibid.

29. Ibid.

30. Ibid., 107.

31. John Lechte, "Bataille and Caillois: Chance and Communication," *Thesis Eleven*, 83 (November 2005): 100. Lechte provides a deft reading of both thinkers—and is right to consider them in relation. Recall that Roger Caillois was a founding member, with Bataille and others, of the secret society and journal *Acéphale* and, immediately thereafter, the Collège de Sociologie. Despite temperamental and intellectual differences, Caillois and Bataille were steady collaborators—and they shared a mutual investment in chance as a social, political, and cultural force. Here I disagree with Lechte, who argues that "chance doesn't have any real status as a category in Caillois' thinking" (97). Chance is one of the dominant categories in Caillois's anthropology of play; *Man, Play, and Games* contains substantial and studied reflections on what he termed *alea*, from the Latin for dice games. For Caillois's recollections of his friendship with Bataille, see the interview with Gilles Lapoouge in June 1970, reprinted in Caillois, *The Edge of Surrealism: A Roger Caillois Reader*, ed. Claudine Frank (Durham: Duke University Press, 2003), 141–46. Michel Surya's intellectual biography, notwithstanding its superb and extensive treatment of Bataille as a *political* thinker, deals more with his well-documented contempt for André Breton than with his collaborations with Caillois, Michel Leiris, and others. See Michel Surya, *Georges Bataille: An Intellectual Biography*, trans. Krzysztof Fijakkowski and Michael Richardson (London: Verso, 2002). Richard Wolin's review of the biography, which predictably reads as a summary verdict on Bataille's life and legacy, further glosses the legendary animosity between Bataille and Breton. See Richard Wolin, "Story of I: Unearthing Georges Bataille," *Bookforum*, Spring 2004. For a very careful treatment of Bataille and Caillois for their contributions to political sociology and ambiguous political legacies, see Falasca-Zamponi, "A Left Sacred or a Sacred Left?," 40–54.

32. Bataille, *On Nietzsche*, 70. Another key term in this family of words is "decadence," also from the Latin *cadere*, "to fall."

33. G. W. F. Hegel, *The Phenomenology of Spirit*, trans. A. V. Miller (Oxford: Oxford University Press, 1977), §32.

34. G. W. F. Hegel, *The Philosophy of History*, trans. J. Sibree (New York: Dover, 1956), 9.

35. Ibid., 12.

36. Ibid., 10 (italics mine).

37. Ibid., 33.

38. Ibid., 13–14.

39. Quoted in Mark Lilla, *The Reckless Mind: Intellectuals in Politics* (New York: Random House, 2003), 122.

40. Georges Bataille, "Hegel, Death, and Sacrifice," trans. Jonathan Strauss, *Yale French Studies* 78 (1990): 2–28, reprinted in *The Bataille Reader*.

41. Ibid.

42. Ibid.

43. Jacques Derrida, "From Restricted to General Economy: A Hegelianism Without Reserve," in *Writing and Difference*.

44. Bataille, "The Sorcerer's Apprentice," in *Visions of Excess*, 229–30. This essay appeared in the influential *Nouvelle Revue Francaise* in 1938 alongside articles by Michel Leiris and Roger Caillois. It introduced to a broad intellectual community in France some of the questions, themes, and methods of the Collège de Sociologie.

45. Ibid., 230.

46. Ibid.

47. For a superb treatment of Bataille's atheology, see Amy Hollywood, *Sensible Ecstasy: Mysticism, Sexual Difference, and the Demands of History* (Chicago: University of Chicago Press, 2002).

48. Stuart Kendall offers the provocative suggestion that *On Nietzsche* "can be read as an act of war" but that writing on Nietzsche in wartime is "also yet another way of pleading guilty" to a certain complicity with fascist power. See the editor's introduction to George Bataille, *The Unfinished System of Nonknowledge* (Minneapolis: University of Minnesota Press, 2001), xxii.

49. See Martin Jay, *Downcast Eyes: The Denigration of Vision in Twentieth-Century French Thought* (Berkeley: University of California Press, 1993).

50. Bataille, *On Nietzsche*, xxvi.

51. I have said nothing of Bataille's infamous quarrel with Sartre, but here we can see just how radically Bataille opposes the existentialist fixation on transcendence.

52. He cites Nietzsche from *Ecce Homo* on behalf of failure: "Failure should be honored *because* it is failure." Bataille, *On Nietzsche*, 87.

53. Ibid., 109.

54. Ibid., xxvii.

55. Bataille, "The 'Old Mole' and the Prefix *Sur* in Words *Surhomme* and *Surrealist*," in *Visions of Excess*, 37.
56. Ibid., 38.
57. Ibid., 37.
58. Bataille, *On Nietzsche*, xxv–xxvi.
59. Ibid., xxxi.
60. Ibid.
61. Ibid., xxxiii. See also ibid., 139–40.
62. Ibid., 120.
63. Ibid., xxvi.
64. Ibid., 111.
65. Georges Bataille, *The Accursed Share*, trans. Robert Hurley (New York: Zone Books, 1991), 3:283.
66. Ibid., 459–60.
67. Ibid., 206.
68. Ibid.
69. Ibid., 369 (italics in original).
70. Gilles Deleuze, *Difference and Repetition*, trans. Paul Patton (New York: Columbia University Press, 1994), 198.
71. Ibid.
72. Ibid., 199.
73. Bataille, *The Accursed Share*, 3:373.

5. FRANTZ FANON: CRITIQUE, WITH KNIVES

1. "The principle of the modern world-thought and the universal . . . has given courage a higher form, because its display now seems to be more mechanical, the act not of this particular person, but of a member of a whole. Moreover, it seems to be turned not against single persons, but against a hostile group, and hence personal bravery appears impersonal. It is for this reason that thought has invented the gun, and the invention of this weapon, which has changed the purely personal form of bravery into a more abstract one, is no accident." G. W. F. Hegel, *Philosophy of Right*, trans. T. M. Knox (Oxford: Oxford University Press, 1967), 212.
2. Frantz Fanon, *The Wretched of the Earth*, trans. Richard Philcox (New York: Grove, 2004), 232.
3. See especially the discussion of Fanon in Hannah Arendt, "On Violence," in *Crisis of the Republic* (San Diego: Harcourt, 1969). Arendt concedes that Fanon's attitudes toward violence are more nuanced than his admirers think; still she misrepresents these attitudes in entirely subjectivist terms. Arendt treats Fanon only in terms of whether he is for or against violence. This approach entirely misses the critical point Fanon is making. Colonialism as a structure permits *nothing* to stand against violence. Even the doctrine of nonviolence is immanent

to the history of violence in the colony. Fanon's first chapter from *Wretched* is not an ethical demand for redemptive violence as much as it is a political interpretation of how violence works—and fails to work—on behalf of colonial power.

4. Françoise Vergès, "Creole Skin, Black Mask: Fanon and Disavowal," *Critical Inquiry* 23, no. 3 (Spring 1997): 580.

5. Ibid., 593.

6. Ibid., 594.

7. The best readers of Fanon and the French philosophical tradition complicate the conventional narratives of influence. George Ciccariello-Maher, for example, reads Fanon as the decisive influence on Sartre's formulation of the concept of situation, not the other way around. See George Ciccariello-Maher, "The Internal Limits of the European Gaze: Intellectuals and the Colonial Difference," *Radical Philosophy Review* 9, no. 2 (2006): 139–66.

8. Albert Memmi, "The Impossible Life of Frantz Fanon," trans. Thomas Cassirer and G. Michael Twomey, *Massachusetts Review* 14, no. 1 (Winter 1973): 22.

9. Ibid., 11.

10. Ibid., 33.

11. Henry Louis Gates, "Critical Fanonism," *Critical Inquiry* 17, no. 3 (Spring 1991): 470. The problem with this insistence is that Gates concedes at the start that he will *not* be pursuing a reading of Fanon, and is more interested in the ways more recent scholars have taken up the legacy of Fanon. With its focus on Critical Fanonisms and not Fanonian critique, the article seems to do with Fanon exactly what Gates argues we should not do.

12. Fanon, *The Wretched of the Earth*, 44.

13. Neil Lazarus, *Resistance of Postcolonial African Fiction* (New Haven: Yale University Press, 1990), 30.

14. Ibid., 32.

15. On this point, Lazarus is at least more generous than Christopher Miller. "What matters most, what is most impressive in reading Fanon," Miller writes, "is the sheer power of a theoretical truth to dictate who shall live and who shall be liquidated." See Christopher Miller, *Theories of Africans: Francophone Literature and Anthropology in Africa* (Chicago: University of Chicago Press, 1990), 50–51.

16. Ato Sekyi-Otu's work on Fanon remains the most accomplished in this respect (and many others). Sekyi-Otu examines Fanon's rhetorical strategies and narrative techniques in their diversity and detail, arguing for an intersubjective and dialogical approach to Fanon. See Ato Sekyi-Otu, *Fanon's Dialectic of Experience* (Cambridge, Mass.: Harvard University Press, 1996). For a critical review of Sekyi-Otu that underscores its unacknowledged debt to J. L. Austin, see K. Martial Frindéthié, "Tracing a Theoretical Gesture: Patrick Taylor and Ato Sekyi-Otu Reading Fanon," *Research in African Literatures* 29, no. 3 (Autumn 1998): 162–70.

17. Frantz Fanon, *Black Skin, White Masks*, trans. Richard Philcox (New York: Grove, 2008), xi.

18. Sekyi-Otu, *Fanon's Dialectic of Experience*, 16.
19. Drucilla Cornell, *Moral Images of Freedom: A Future for Critical Theory* (Lanham, Md.: Rowman and Littlefield, 2008).
20. Sekyi-Otu, *Fanon's Dialectic of Experience*, 55. Still, it is striking that Hegel goes unmentioned—and that he should disappear just as Marx finally appears. Just as we can expect that Fanon's years in France featured conversations about Marx to complement the buzz around Hegel, we can assume that his later work with militant intellectuals and revolutionary strategists involved some considerations of Hegel.
21. Nigel C. Gibson, *Fanon: The Postcolonial Imagination* (Cambridge: Polity, 2003).
22. Sekyi-Otu, *Fanon's Dialectic of Experience*, 34.
23. Shamoon Zamir, for example, reads W. E. B. Du Bois in relation to Hegel, and argues that the logic of the first chapter of *The Souls of Black Folk* mirrors the dialectic of consciousness in the *Phenomenology of Spirit*. See Shamoon Zamir, *Dark Voices: W. E. B. Du Bois and American Thought, 1888–1903* (Chicago: University of Chicago Press, 1995). Susan Buck-Morss has also argued for Hegel's significance in the development of the idea of Black Liberation, as well as for the significance of Black Liberation, specifically, the Haitian Revolution, in the development of Hegel's philosophy. See Buck-Morss, *Hegel, Haiti, and Universal History* (Pittsburgh: University of Pittsburgh Press, 2009). An Afro-Trini Marxist, C. L. R James is a crucially important figure in this genealogy, both for the Hegel-Haiti connection and for his magnum opus, *Notes on the Dialectic*. Fanon differs from James in many respects, the most important for my purposes being Fanon's restlessly "negative" dialectic.
24. Homi Bhabha, *The Location of Culture* (New York: Routledge, 1994), 58.
25. Ibid., 59.
26. Ibid., 88.
27. Fanon, *Wretched of the Earth*, 4.
28. Ibid., 5.
29. Ibid., 51.
30. For a different reading, see Nelson Maldonado-Torres, "Frantz Fanon and C. L. R. James on Intellectualism and Enlightened Rationality," *Caribbean Studies* 33, no. 2 (July–December 2005): 149–94.
31. Fanon, *Black Skin, White Masks*, 43.
32. Sekyi-Otu, *Fanon's Dialectic of Experience*, 59.
33. Fanon, *Black Skin, White Masks*, 194.
34. Ibid., 112.
35. G. W. F. Hegel, *Phenomenology of Spirit*, trans. A. V. Miller (Oxford: Oxford University Press, 1977), §32.
36. Fanon, *Black Skin, White Masks*, 191. Of course, the very idea of the Black Man in his unity and singularity is a fiction and ideology: "the black experience is ambiguous, for there is not *one* Negro—there are *many* black men" (115).
37. Hegel, *Phenomenology*, §182.

38. Fanon, *Black Skin, White Masks*, 195.
39. Ibid., 187 (italics mine).
40. Ibid., 196–97.
41. Ibid., 196.
42. Ibid., 191.
43. Ibid., 197.
44. Ibid., 113–114 (italics in the original).
45. Fanon, *Wretched of the Earth*, 91 (italics mine). Interestingly, the same line appears in the preface to *A Dying Colonialism*: "Nevertheless, there is no end in sight, and we know that the French Army is preparing a series of offenses for the coming months. The war goes on." Decolonization begins to appear as a permanently unfinished project. Frantz Fanon, *A Dying Colonialism*, trans. Haakon Chevalier (New York: Grove, 1965), 27.
46. Hegel, *Phenomenology*, §178.
47. Fanon, *Black Skin, White Masks*, 195.
48. Ibid.
49. Fanon, *Wretched of the Earth*, 133.
50. Fanon, *Black Skin, White Masks*, 195.
51. Donna V. Jones, *The Racial Discourses of Life Philosophy* (New York: Columbia University Press, 2010), 167.
52. Ross Posnock, "How It Feels to Be a Problem: Du Bois, Fanon, and the 'Impossible Life' of the Black Intellectual," *Critical Inquiry* 23, no. 2 (Winter 1997): 329.
53. Fanon, *Wretched of the Earth*, 44 (italics mine).
54. Ibid.
55. Ibid., 50.
56. Ibid. (italics mine).
57. Ibid., 220.
58. This is the element of force in the General Strike, what Walter Benjamin identifies as a residue of an extortionist violence preserved in the cessation of work that "takes place in the context of a conscious readiness to resume the suspended action under certain circumstances." See Walter Benjamin, "Critique of Violence," in *Selected Writings*, vol. 1, *1913–1926*, ed. Marcus Bullock and Michael W. Jennings (Cambridge, Mass.: Belknap Press of Harvard University Press, 1996), 239.
59. Richard C. Keller, "Clinician and Revolutionary: Frantz Fanon, Biography, and the History of Colonial Medicine," *Bulletin of the History of Medicine* 81, no. 4 (Winter 2007): 838.
60. Ibid., 840.
61. As Macey shows, the closest Fanon gets to a psychoanalytic concept is in the hotly contested third chapter, on the Black man who desires white women, where he refers to Germaine Geux's idea of the *abandonnique,* or the abandonment syndrome. What attracts him to Geux is the search for a pre-Oedipal complex that may explain affective disorder, on the conviction that Black men

do not pass through the Oedipal stage. See David Macey, "The Recall of the Real: Frantz Fanon and *Psychoanalysis*," *Constellations* 6, no. 1 (1999): 104. Fanon insists that "whether you like it or not the Oedipus complex is far from being a black complex." Fanon, *Black Skin, White Masks*, 130. Here Fanon is also quarreling with Lacan and claiming Hegel for support. Readers ought to pay close attention to Fanon's endlessly fascinating footnotes.

62. Fanon, *Black Skin, White Masks*, xiv.

63. David Macey, "'I Am My Own Foundation': Frantz Fanon as a Source of Continued Political Embarrassment," *Theory, Culture, and Society* 27, no. 7–8 (2010): 35.

64. Memmi places even more emphasis on Fanon's professional ambitions, and speculates as to the disappointment he might have felt upon learning of his less lucrative Algerian assignment.

65. Judith Butler, *The Psychic Life of Power: Theories in Subjection* (Stanford: Stanford University Press, 1997). Fanon goes untreated in this text, though Butler has considered Fanon elsewhere. See especially Judith Butler, "Violence, Nonviolence: Sartre on Fanon," in *Race After Sartre: Antiracism, Africana Existentialism, Post-Colonialism*, ed. Jonathan Judaken (Albany: State University of New York Press, 2008).

66. Fanon, *Black Skin, White Masks*, 129.

67. Frantz Fanon, "Racism and Culture," in *Toward the African Revolution*, trans. Haakon Chevalier (New York: Grove, 1967), 32.

68. See Frantz Fanon, "The 'North African Syndrome,'" in *Toward the African Revolution*, 3–16.

69. Quoted in Vergès, "Creole Skin, Black Mask," 582.

70. Henri Lefebvre, *The Critique of Everyday Life*, trans. Gregory Elliott and John Moore (London: Verso, 2008); Michel de Certeau, *The Practice of Everyday Life* (Berkeley: University of California Press, 1984); and Thomas L. Dumm, *The Politics of the Ordinary* (New York: New York University Press, 1999).

71. Fanon, *Black Skin, White Masks*, 98.

72. Cedric Robinson, "The Appropriation of Fanon," *Race and Class* 35, no. 79 (1993): 89.

73. Fanon, *Black Skin, White Masks*, 102.

74. I borrow this formulation from Davide Panagia, *The Poetics of Political Thinking* (Durham: Duke University Press, 2006).

75. Frantz Fanon, "Letter to the Resident Minister," in *Toward the African Revolution*, 53.

76. Robinson, "The Appropriation of Fanon," 82.

77. Fanon, *Wretched of the Earth*, 8.

78. Ibid., 29.

79. Ibid., 17.

80. Svetlana Boym, *The Future of Nostalgia* (New York: Basic Books, 2001).

81. Fanon, *Wretched of the Earth*, 20.

82. Ibid., 51.

83. Patrick Taylor, *The Narrative of Liberation: Perspectives on Afro-Caribbean Literature, Popular Culture, and Politics* (Ithaca: Cornell University Press, 1989), 85.

84. Ibid.

85. Fanon, *Wretched of the Earth*, 30. For a superb treatment of the politics of listening, see Ian Baucom, "Frantz Fanon's Radio: Solidarity, Diaspora, and the Tactics of Listening," *Contemporary Literature* 42, no. 1 (Spring 2001): 15–49.

86. Fanon, *Wretched of the Earth*, 23.

87. Ibid., 34.

88. Frantz Fanon, "Toward the Liberation of Africa," in *Toward the African Revolution*, 105.

89. Fanon, *Black Skin, White Masks*, 204.

90. See Memmi, "The Impossible Life," 13; Vergès, "Creole Skin, Black Mask: Fanon and Disavowal," note 8.

91. Thomas Dumm, "Resignation," *Critical Inquiry* 25, no. 1 (Autumn 1998): 71.

92. Ibid., 57.

93. As Simon Critchley puts it, "Philosophy begins . . . in an experience of disappointment, that is both religious and political." Simon Critchley, *Very Little . . . Almost Nothing: Death, Philosophy, Literature* (London: Routledge, 1997), 2.

94. Ibid.

95. Fanon, *Wretched of the Earth*, 198.

96. Maldonado-Torres, "Frantz Fanon and C. L. R. James on Intellectualism and Enlightened Rationality."

97. Recall Benjamin's twelfth thesis on the concept of history, which laments "the indoctrination [that] made the working class forget both its hatred and its spirit of sacrifice." At least on the surface of things (which is where Fanon will insist that our drama unfolds) this position seems closer to Fanon than a restorative philosophy of love. See Walter Benjamin, "On the Concept of History," in *Selected Writings*, vol. 4, *1938–1940*, trans. Edmund Jephcott (Cambridge, Mass.: Harvard University Press, 2003), 394.

98. Dumm, "Resignation," 70.

99. Frantz Fanon, "Letter to the Resident Minister," in *Toward the African Revolution*, 53.

100. Ibid.

101. Simone de Beauvoir captures the complexity of resignation in her considerations on "women's situation and character" in *The Second Sex*. Of a woman's tendency toward passivity and the blind acceptance of her fate, Beauvoir writes: "Most often, she is not resigned to being resigned; she knows what she is going through, she goes through it in spite of herself; she is a woman without being asked, she does not dare revolt; she submits against her will; her attitude is constant recrimination." Simone de Beauvoir, *The Second Sex*, trans. Constance Borde and Sheila Malovany-Chevallier (New York: Vintage, 2010), 646. Here, not resigning oneself to resignation, though demonstrative of a certain will to power, is also capitulation and surrender. A Fanon-Beauvoir connection is

suggested in the secondary literature but still undeveloped as a site of historio-biographical or theoretical investigation. In her book on Beauvoir, Toril Moi posits a correspondence between *The Second Sex* and *Black Skin, White Masks.* "The parallels between the two texts are striking," Moi remarks, and speculates that Fanon was aware of and influenced by Beauvoir's account of woman's construction as other. Vergès endorses this suggestion, noting that Fanon was a faithful reader of *Les Temps Modernes*, the journal that had been publishing selections from Beauvoir's text. See Toril Moi, *Simone de Beauvoir: The Making of an Intellectual Woman* (New York: Blackwell, 1994).

102. Fanon, "Letter to the Resident Minister," 54.

103. Ibid.

104. Frantz Fanon, "Letter to the Youth of Africa," in *Toward the African Revolution*, 118.

105. In addition to Vergès, "Creole Skin, Black Mask," see also Diana Fuss, "Interior Colonies: Frantz Fanon and the Politics of Identification," *Diacritics* 24, no. 2–3 (Summer–Autumn 1994): 19–42; Gwen Bergner, "Who Is That Masked Woman? Or, the Role of Gender in Fanon's *Black Skin, White Masks*," *PMLA* 110, no. 1 (January 1995): 75–88; Jeffrey Louis Decker, "Terrorism (Un)veiled: Frantz Fanon and the Women of Algiers," *Cultural Critique* (Winter 1990–1991): 177–95.

106. On themes of corporeality and embodiment, scholars have emphasized Fanon's link to Merleau-Ponty much more than Sartre. And of course, feminist scholars have shown that Merleau-Ponty's thinking about the body and somatic life was shaped by the philosophy of Simone de Beauvoir.

107. Donna Jones offers a compelling interpretation of the Bergsonian vitalism in Négritude in *The Racial Discourses of Life Philosophy.*

108. Hegel, *Phenomenology*, §19.

109. Fanon, *Wretched of the Earth*, 81.

110. Ibid., 119.

111. Fanon's relationship to Marx is complex and I have not done justice to it here. His disagreements with Marx and with orthodox Marxism are many. He challenges Marx's views on the nature of precapitalist societies, the significance of the peasantry, the revolutionary potential in agrarian society, the forms of class stratification in the colonies, and the meaning of development in the postcolonial world. But Fanon agrees with the more general picture of "primitive accumulation" as described by Marx and sees colonialism—"violence in its natural state"—as a function of capitalist expansion.

112. Allow me to sidestep the heteronormativity in Irigaray's portrait (and Fanon's), as I am more interested in the idea of the couple, and of democracy beginning with two.

113. Luce Irigaray, *Democracy Begins Between Two*, trans. Kirsteen Anderson (New York: Routledge, 2000), 118 (italics mine).

114. Fanon, *Wretched of the Earth*, 12.

115. Memmi, "The Impossible Life," 35–36.
116. Fanon, *Wretched of the Earth*, 15.

CONCLUDING POSTSCRIPT

1. Andrew Shanks, *God and Modernity: A New and Better Way to Do Theology* (London: Routledge, 2000).
2. For a thorough treatment of the religious and political themes in Hegelian thought of the 1830s and 1840s, see Warren Breckman, *Marx, the Young Hegelians, and the Origins of Radical Social Theory* (Cambridge: Cambridge University Press, 1999).
3. Jurgen Habermas, "Hegel's Concept of Modernity," in *The Philosophical Discourse of Modernity*, trans. Frederick G. Lawrence (Cambridge, Mass.: MIT Press, 1990), 24.
4. Jürgen Habermas, "The Unity of Reason in the Diversity of Its Voices," in *Postmetaphysical Thinking: Philosophic Essays*, trans. William Mark Hohengarten (Cambridge, Mass.: MIT Press, 1992), 130.
5. Habermas, "Hegel's Concept of Modernity," 43.
6. Habermas, "The Unity of Reason," 142.
7. Ibid.
8. Ibid., 140 (italics in original).
9. Ibid., 144.
10. Ibid., 140.
11. Jürgen Habermas, "Transcendence from Within/Transcendence in This World," in *Religion and Rationality: Essays on Reason, God, and Modernity* (Cambridge, Mass.: MIT Press, 2002), 67.
12. Stephen White and Evan Farr make an intriguing case for the importance of "no-saying" in Habermas's communicative paradigm, suggesting that it is not "the great consensus machine" that its critics allege, but instead that it is premised on an "onto-ethical" commitment to the possibility of civil disobedience. I am raising a somewhat different point about silence. See Stephen K. White and Evan Robert Farr, "'No-Saying' in Habermas," *Political Theory* 40, no. 1 (February 2012): 32–57.
13. Habermas, "The Unity of Reason," 145 (italics mine).
14. Wendy Brown, *Regulating Aversion: Tolerance in the Age of Identity and Empire* (Princeton: Princeton University Press, 2008).
15. William Connolly, *Why I Am Not a Secularist* (Minneapolis: University of Minnesota Press, 2000).
16. Habermas wants to jettison Kantian metaphysics and, with it, the entire apparatus that fastens the link between human reason and what is called religion. One wonders if this is a kind of "cafeteria Kantianism" in which we get to have elements of the practical philosophy while leaving behind the metaphysics. It is beyond far beyond my scope to assess the viability of this approach to Kant, but

for an intriguing attempt to retrieve Kantian metaphysics for critical theory, see Peter Dews, *The Idea of Evil* (Oxford: Blackwell, 2008), chap. 1.

17. Habermas's critique of negative metaphysics finds some surprising parallels in Jean-François Lyotard's well-known attack on Adorno. Lyotard focuses on Adorno's theory of music and aesthetics, and reads it as a diabolical exercise in "negative theology." See Jean-François Lyotard, "Adorno as the Devil," *Telos* 19 (1974). Further, Adorno's "negative" endeavors—whether metaphysical or theological—are not quite the same as those found in Horkheimer's late works, despite their steady collaboration and mutual influence. In his reflections on Horkheimer's mature writings, Habermas marks a distinction between Horkheimer and Adorno on the question of metaphysics, resulting from their somewhat different responses to the dialectic of Enlightenment. He argues that "Horkheimer's thought is influenced even more than Adorno's by the harrowing historical fact that the ideals of freedom, solidarity, and justice deriving from practical reason, which inspired the French Revolution and were reappropriated in Marx's critique of society, led not to socialism but to barbarism under the guise of socialism." In accounting for this fact and discerning the value of philosophy in the context of historical barbarism, Horkheimer never quite abandons a positive metaphysics. Instead, he finds in Schopenhauer a negative-metaphysical justification for morality but, says Habermas, remains "aware of the shadow of performative self-contradiction that has haunted all negative metaphysics since Nietzsche and Schopenhauer." The result, in Horkheimer's later philosophy, is a frustrated vacillation between negative metaphysics "and a return to the faith of his forefathers." See Jürgen Habermas, "To Seek to Salvage an Unconditional Meaning Without God Is a Futile Undertaking: Reflections on a Remark of Max Horkheimer," in *Religion and Rationality*, 100–101. The admittedly minor place accorded to Horkheimer in this study ought not to be mistaken for a verdict on his legacy for critical theory. That said, I read Horkheimer's late philosophy as substantially more pessimistic than anything found in Adorno.

18. Habermas, "The Unity of Reason," 144 (italics mine).

19. Theodor W. Adorno, *Aesthetic Theory*, trans. Robert Hullot-Kentor (Minneapolis: University of Minnesota Press, 1997), 331.

20. Habermas, *The Philosophical Discourse of Modernity*, 128.

21. See Amy Allen, "Reason, Power, and History: Rereading the Dialectic of Enlightenment," *Thesis Eleven* 120, no. 1 (February 2014): 10–25.

22. Habermas, *The Philosophical Discourse of Modernity*, vii.

23. Ibid., xvi.

24. Herbert Marcuse, *Eros and Civilization: A Philosophical Inquiry Into Freud* (Boston: Beacon, 1966), xvii.

25. Ibid.

26. On the collapse of traditional authority, see Herbert Marcuse, "The Obsolescence of the Freudian Concept of Man," in *Five Lectures* (Boston: Beacon, 1970).

27. Marcuse, *Eros and Civilization*, xi.

28. John Berger, "Dispatches: Undefeated Despair," *Race and Class* 48, no. 23 (2006): 25.

29. Edward Said, "On Lost Causes," in *Reflections on Exile, and Other Essays* (Cambridge, Mass.: Harvard University Press, 2000).

30. Berger, "Dispatches," 24.

31. Ibid., 31.

32. Ibid.

33. Immanuel Kant, "An Answer to the Question: What Is Enlightenment," in *Practical Philosophy*, trans. Mary J. Gregor (Cambridge: Cambridge University Press, 1996), 11–22.

INDEX